THE NORTH SEA

A

THE NORTH SEA

George Morey

FREDERICK MULLER

First published in Great Britain 1968
by Frederick Muller Ltd., Fleet Street, London, E.C.4.

Copyright © 1968 George Morey

Printed in Great Britain by Ebenezer Baylis and Son, Ltd.
The Trinity Press, Worcester, and London
and bound by Leighton Straker Bookbinding Co., Ltd.

Contents

Contents

Illustrations

Introduction

IT IS A truism that the North Sea has counted for a great deal in the economic life of some of the prosperous, highly developed countries of Western Europe that border upon it. For some of them it is the only seaboard, providing access to sources of raw materials and to important overseas markets. Yet, oddly enough, it is only in the case of Britain, with its long coastline and so many ports, harbours and navigable waters, that the importance of the North Sea has been practically demonstrated. For a few months, in the early stages of the Second World War, with a view to safeguarding shipping, the Government banned the movement of cargoes by water along the East Coast. The transport system of the country—and with it, the whole economy—was quickly brought to the verge of collapse. Before any serious harm was done the Government decided that it was better to risk a few ships, and rescinded the instruction. The blockade of enemy ports in the two World Wars, and before that, Napoleon's blockade in reverse, when he closed the ports of Europe to English ships, undoubtedly inflicted great hardship. But, in those cases, it is a little more difficult to isolate what was happening in the North Sea area from what was happening elsewhere.

Since well before the days of recorded history the North Sea has played its part in the history of the peoples who lived round its margins. And, long before the Viking sea-rovers went in search of plunder and lands upon which to settle, merchants were already risking its hazards in search of distant markets.

Since then, the rise and decline of more than one commercial empire has been linked with its ability to acquire access to the North Sea, and to benefit from the trade which such a position gave.

Our own associations with the North Sea, and with our European neighbours, have been particularly strong since the time when the invasions of Teutonic and Nordic peoples implanted in these islands a form of civilization vigorous enough to withstand even the pressure and persuasiveness of Norman-French culture.

The discovery of natural gas, and with it more than a remote chance of finding oil, has been among the more exciting of recent events in the commercial history of both Britain and the Netherlands. It ought not, however, to obscure the significance, for example, of the place of the North Sea herring in the rivalry of the English and the Dutch; or the fortunate chance that made it possible to transport Newcastle coal by water. Without the cheap water transport that the coasters provided, the early history of the coal-trade, and of industrial development in Britain have been rather different.

Before the days of steam propulsion, and the rise of Germany, the naval commands in the North Sea were of secondary importance. Battles were fought there, particularly against the Dutch, but it was our position in the English Channel that gave us the advantage. The situation had changed radically by 1914, by which time the major units of the British Navy had been transferred to the Shetlands and the East Coast of Scotland.

In spite of this, the North Sea has been as much neglected by writers as have the other seas around the coasts of Britain. There are, of course, the specialist studies on hydrography and navigation, on oil prospecting and geology, on aspects of fishery research or the diplomatic and military history of the Scheldt, but, so far as I am aware no one has so far made the North Sea the subject for a book. Yet, at a time when Britain is becoming increasingly aware of its common ties with Western

Europe, there is much to be said for looking at the social, political and economic affairs of Britain and Europe, not as though they were separate and unrelated, but as matters in which our fortunes have been closely interwoven.

I am very conscious, in writing such a book upon so big a theme, of my obligation to the many authorities to whom I have to go for my facts. In the absence of footnotes, I hope that the bibliography will sufficiently indicate the authors to whom I am most indebted, and that readers interested in pursuing a particular topic will find this a sufficient direction to the best available book on the matter.

I should, in particular, like to acknowledge my indebtedness to the London Library. This is so common an acknowledgement that one might assume it an empty civility. I am only too well aware that without the Library and its staff it would have been impossible to write this book.

1

THE EVOLUTION OF THE NORTH SEA

A CLOUD OF BUBBLES, breaking to the surface of a dead-calm sea in mid-September 1965, was the first certain indication that gas had been struck under the North Sea. The strike was made by British Petroleum's rig, *Sea Gem*, 42 miles east of the Humber.

The company was quick to scotch the jubilation of the workers and exaggerated press comment, since a wave of wild speculation might have been started. And, indeed, there was no certain proof at the time that the gas found was in sufficient quantity to be of commercial value. But confidence everywhere ran high, particularly as there had been rumours, which were denied, that Amosea's *Mr. Cap*, which had been drilling since Christmas Day, 1964, had already struck methane. Exploration since then has more than fulfilled the hopes of the greatest optimist.

On a longer view, this valuable find is only the latest instance of the way in which the North Sea has affected the fortunes of the peoples who live around its margins, while the existence of gas is the clearest proof of the vast changes that have taken place in this part of the globe in the long eras that make up geological time.

Most of the great gas and oil deposits of the world lie within the Tropics, and the association of oil-production and tropical conditions is close. This applies to the North Sea, too. Ten thousand feet below the surface are the coal measures, which are the product of the lush tropical forests that flourished in the area 300 million years ago, when the Northern Hemisphere was a great deal warmer than it is now. Wherever, in

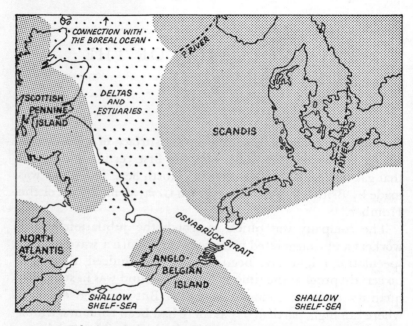

The North Sea Area about 150 million years ago

An outline of the probable land areas has been superimposed upon the map as it exists today. By this date, the deserts of an earlier age had become restricted and much of the land consisted of forested or swampy plains with lakes and meandering rivers. The climate was moist and temperate: there is no evidence of an ice-cap

[Based on *Palæogeographical Atlas of the British Isles*, by L. J. Wills (1952)]

these conditions, there was fauna and marine life in abundance there existed the raw materials of petroleum and of the gases associated with it.

The geology of the North Sea area shows that within a few

million years—roughly 230–270 million years ago—the luxuriant tropical forest had given way to arid desert conditions, and the sands in due course became the sandstone of the so-called Permian stratum in which the North Sea gas became trapped.

The development of the area in the millions of years that followed is still known only in the barest detail, and could be more easily depicted on a map than described in words. But even after passing in this way over long periods of time, it is still possible to describe the northern part of the North Sea as a very ancient sea, with a continuous history extending over many millions of years. But it was only much nearer still to our own time that the great geological movements occurred that brought into being a sea that more nearly resembles the North Sea as it is today. For while the great upheaval of the Miocene period, about 12–25 million years ago (which had so important a part in the formation of the Alps) had lost much of its force before it reached southern England, it did have the effect of confining the North Sea in the centre of its basin, and more nearly within its familiar limits. It is more than likely, too, that the resultant folding of the Downs and the deepening and broadening of the London Basin may, for a time, have brought the North Sea into direct connection with the warmer waters of the western ocean. At least, fossil remains suggest it. But such a change in the North Sea, if it occurred, was of short duration. The broaching of the Caledonian mountain ridge, which extends north-eastwards from Scotland to Scandinavia, permitted the mingling of the colder waters of the northern ocean with the North Sea at the same time as the sea was retreating northwards from the London Basin, Belgium and Germany. This retreat was followed by the development of a river system, which drained the Weald, and may have linked the Thames with the Rhine. Fossil remains of the elephant, hippopotamus and rhinoceros, dating from this period, have been found in England, and are the clearest confirmation of the land-link with the Continent existing at that time.

It is likely that climatic conditions over the southern part of the North Sea were not markedly different from those of the present time, although the climate of England may have been more nearly Continental, with rather colder winters and warmer summers. But the evidence of rocks of Scandinavian origin found scattered around the coast of East Anglia suggests the early formation of an ice-cap in Scandinavia, which gave rise to icebergs that carried the rock debris southwards.

During the Pliocene period, which lasted 11 million years, and ended roughly a million years ago, the weather over the North Sea area was becoming steadily colder, and augured the onset of the Ice Age.[1]

The glacial period in Northern Europe was spread over more than three-quarters of a million years, although the successive cold spells were separated by long periods during which the climate was warmer, and the ice-fronts were in retreat.[2]

There seems little doubt that the First British Glaciation had its beginnings in the high mountains of Scandinavia, and that, in time, a vast floating ice-mass extended southwards and westwards over the North Sea. Except perhaps in Durham and Yorkshire the ice-sheet did not encroach upon the shores of Britain. The Second British Glaciation (360,000–235,000 B.C.) was more severe. Much of the North Sea area, as far south as the present Thames estuary, was filled with dense ice that had its origin in Scandinavia. It was, however, held at a distance from the coast of England by the Great Eastern Glacier that flowed from the Pennines and the Highlands of the North; and gouged deeply into the bed of the North Sea before sweeping southwards across East Anglia. This ice-field reached the outskirts of London. And it was at this period that

---

[1] The Great Ice Age presents the experts with many problems, resulting in part from the tendency of one glaciation to obliterate the evidence of an earlier one. The relationship of the Scandinavian to the Alpine is not clearly established, nor, indeed, whether England was directly affected by the ice-sheet during more than two of the four glaciations.

[2] I have followed the dating in Holmes' *Principles of Physical Geology* (1964).

the great ice-front lake, receiving not only the melt-water **of**
the ice, but the diverted streams of the Thames and the
Rhine, probably grew to the point where it was able to break

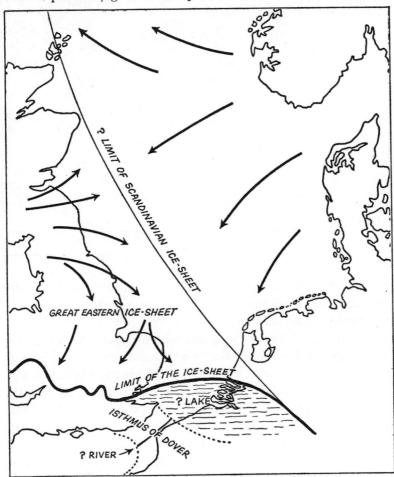

The North Sea Area in the Great Ice Age

Details of the maximum glaciation are superimposed on a map of
the present North Sea. The Strait of Dover was at that time closed
by an isthmus behind which a huge lake of melt-water probably
formed

[Based on *Palæogeographical Atlas of
the British Isles*, by L. J. Wills (1952)]

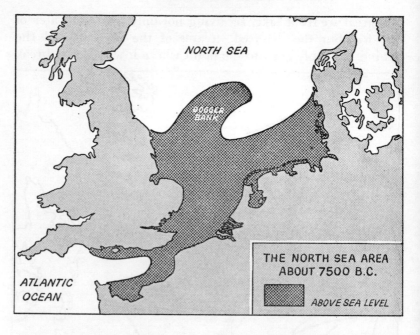

ATLANTIC
OCEAN

NORTH SEA

DOGGER BANK

THE NORTH SEA AREA
ABOUT 7500 B.C.

ABOVE SEA LEVEL

out towards the Atlantic. It is likely that the way was thus
prepared for final breaching of the Strait of Dover, which
occurred very much later.

During the Third Glaciation, which began about 125,000
years ago, the ice-field of Scandinavia did not extend far out
into the North Sea, but the whole of Denmark, the Baltic and
much of northern Germany was in the grip of ice. As a result,
some of the great rivers of central Europe were forced to find
a new outlet to the North Sea. Along the East Coast of England
the Little Eastern Glacier (so called to distinguish it from its
predecessor) extended many miles out to sea. It stopped short
in Norfolk, where the Cromer Ridge is its terminal moraine.

The retreat of the Scandinavian ice-sheet had a number
of important consequences. The Dogger Bank, and the area
to the south of it, emerged temporarily as dry land. But, at the
beginning of the period, all of Southern Sweden, which had
been depressed beneath the weight of the ice, was still under

the sea, so that the North Sea was probably connected directly with the icy waters of the White Sea. In the course of time, the removal of the weight of ice allowed the emergence of the area that corresponds to Denmark and Southern Sweden, and for a time the North Sea was cut off even from the embryonic Baltic.

During the period from 7500–5500 B.C., the melting of the ice led to a steady rise in the level of the sea over the whole globe, and, save where local forces were at work to raise the level of the land, there were incursions of the sea.

It is generally agreed that a sudden climatic change occurred about 5500 B.C. The climate remained warm, but it became wetter. This was the point at which the final retreat of the Scandinavian ice-cap began. At that time, the sea was some 30 to 40 ft. above its present level, and wide areas of the Fens, the Lincolnshire coast as far inland as the Wolds and many other low-lying areas on both sides of the North Sea were inundated. This was the period that saw the invasion of the Baltic by the waters of the North Sea as a result of the creation of channels between Denmark and Sweden, and this was the point at which the Strait of Dover was cut.

The problem of how the southern North Sea came to be inundated and the Strait of Dover broached is full of complexities about which experts differ.

There is, however, general agreement about the approximate date of the final breakthrough. That this is so is partly due to the development of a very interesting branch of botanical science. The application of pollen analysis to the solution of prehistorical problems had its origin in Scandinavia, but it has been applied with remarkable results to the British flora. Briefly, it starts from the fact that peat preserves intact the seeds and pollen of plants trapped within it. And so, by borrowing the methods of the archaeologist, and by examining in minute detail the contents of borings, layer by layer, it is possible to discover which plants flourished at the time when the peat in which their seeds and pollen have

[19]

survived was laid down. In this way it has been possible—particularly for the English Fenland—to draw up a table of the periods at which different flora flourished in the area, and from this to deduce the climatic changes which caused one plant species to supersede another. Some of the material that has been subjected to pollen analysis has come from the sea-bed of the Dogger Bank and of an area to the east and north-east of it. This has been shown to contain the pollen of plants which grew in the area before, or soon after, 7500 B.C., when peat was forming on land that is now the floor of the North Sea.

Two major factors in the drowning of land masses, or their emergence from the sea, have been the absolute rise or fall in the level of the sea all over the globe, coinciding with the expansion or retraction of the polar ice caps; and, sometimes quite independent of that, the rise or fall in the height of the land above sea level. These are generally slow processes, and they are continuing at the present time. Nor is the process everywhere uniform.[1]

One factor that has had a bearing upon the gradual elevation of the land in North-western Europe has been the retreat of the Ice Age glaciers, which for hundreds of thousands of years depressed the soil beneath their weight.

It is impossible now to trace the steps by which the Southern North Sea was drowned. It was probably the results of steady encroachment, although the end may have come with a sudden catastrophic breakthrough of the waters to link up with the Atlantic. Nor is it certain that the broaching of the Channel 7,500 years ago was anything but the most recent of a number of occasions when the area was lost beneath the sea. Indeed, the contrary is very probable. The Great Ice Age was not uniformly cold. Over long periods of time warm spell succeeded cold spell, and was in turn succeeded by another cold spell. The sea level rose and fell in unison. During the Arctic spells when

---

[1] There is some evidence to suggest that even at the present time the whole of Britain is tilting—rising a few millimetres a year in the north-west, and sinking by a similar amount in the south-east.

much of Europe and the surrounding sea lay beneath a deep mantle of ice, the sea-level was perhaps 200 ft. lower than its present level. In the warmer spells some of the ice melted and the sea level rose. It is likely, therefore, that the shallow southern North Sea was dry land, or water, two or three times over.

In the years before the invasion of the sea, the area south of the Dogger Bank and stretching from the present East coast of England to the shores of Denmark and Germany was a vast low-lying plain across which meandered the Rhine and its tributaries. Among them, perhaps, was the Thames. The retreat of the ice had left a tundra-like plain which became the home of the hairy elephant and the mammoth. Forests of birch, lime, hazel and some broad-leaved trees flourished later in parts of the region, while the Dogger Bank appears to have been fen over which peat accumulated. Further south, the chalk ridge of the North Downs continued eastwards in line with a similar formation in France, and it is possible that the line of the South Downs continued in the direction of France. The rivers of the area flowed either northwards to find an outlet in the North Sea, or south-westwards to the English Channel, which, at that time, was a gulf extending about as far as Beachy Head. The steps by which this isthmus was breached provide much scope for speculation, since little is known for certain about the topography of this isthmus at that time.

The effect of all this was to bring into being a sea with marked characteristics of its own. From the Strait of Dover, which is so shallow that St. Paul's Cathedral would rise above the waters if it were sunk in the deepest part, the sea increases in depth. But it is not until a point well beyond the Shetland Islands that depths of 100 fathoms are found. Some areas of the southern North Sea, and notably the broad shoal of the Dogger Bank, are particularly shallow. No less important to the geography of the region, the North Sea was exposed to new and complex currents and tides that were to have a considerable influence upon the coastlines.

Taken in conjunction with the tides and the stormy nature of the North Sea, the very shape of the sea has produced the major disasters that have occurred throughout its history. At any time, when a severe gale has been blowing from the Atlantic for days on end—and particularly if this coincides with the spring tides—there is need for caution round the North Sea coasts. A map explains the reason. A rectangle with the Orkneys and the coast of Norway to the north, and a point on the Norfolk coast and Heligoland to the south, encloses an area of some 120,000 square miles. The triangle formed by continuing the lines from Heligoland and the Norfolk coast down to the Strait of Dover encloses an area which is only one-twentieth of the size. And so the great masses of water which the Atlantic piles into the North Sea through the gap between the Orkneys and the Norwegian coast can only escape through the narrow funnel-opening of the Strait. Such times are always occasions for watchfulness. When, as in January 1953, after winds of hurricane force and spring tides have built up the volume of water in the North Sea, the water is prevented from escaping, the results are disastrous.

By comparison with what had gone before, the changes that have taken place in historic times have been relatively insignificant, and have owed as much to the works of man as to the natural process of erosion and accumulation and to the changes of land- and sea-level. No part of the coast has wholly escaped the action of the sea, but the effect has been most marked where the nature of the shore, or the set of the tides, has been most favourable. Between Flamborough Head and Spurn Head, for example, the erosion has been continuous, and often serious. A reconstructed map of the Roman coastline suggests that on average a strip of 2½ miles wide has disappeared beneath the waves, and with it has gone some thirty small towns and villages which are known to have existed. Most important of them was undoubtedly Ravenser, the port at the mouth of the Humber which was important enough in the fourteenth century to return two Members to Parliament. Leland's reference to it in 1535 is the last known.

At different times it is likely that the waters of the North Sea extended inland to cover much of what is now the Fenland, and that the inhabitants of the patches which rose above the inundation lived a life that was not markedly different from that of the Frisians who lived across the North Sea on what is now the Dutch coast. In Romano-British times the areas of silt deposit, and the islands that rose above the water, were cultivated, but subsequently the area reverted once more to its original state, perhaps because the newcomers lacked the necessary skills in drainage and reclamation, or perhaps because of natural causes, such as the silting of the drains or the lowering of the Fens. It would, however, be a mistake to regard the area in the Middle Ages as one of waste and desolation. By the standards of the times, it was comparatively wealthy and made an important contribution to the economy of the region. As Hugh Candidus said in the twelfth century. "This marsh is very useful to men; for in it are found wood and twigs for fires, hay for the fodder of cattle, thatch for covering houses and many other useful things. It is, moreover, productive of birds and fish. For there are various rivers, and very many waters and ponds abounding in fish. In all these things the district is most productive."

Throughout the Middle Ages, the preservation of what had been won from the water was entirely a local effort, reinforced when necessary by the appointment of Commissioners of Sewers who surveyed the watercourses and compelled landowners to do what was necessary. It was not until the reign of Elizabeth I that serious thought was given to the possibility of a large-scale scheme for the whole area. But it was only in the following century that the principal local landlords, under the leadership of the fourth Duke of Bedford, commissioned the Dutchman Vermuyden to devise the first scheme for the drainage of the Fens, which has since made this one of the richest agricultural areas of England.

The coastline of East Anglia has greatly changed since the Roman period. Along the north coast a wide belt of salt marsh has been formed by constant accretion. This can be seen most strikingly at Brancaster, where the Roman fort, which appears to have guarded one of the approaches to a passage over the Wash, now stands a mile inland. The small neighbouring ports, too, were once thriving. A muster taken in 1570 showed that while Lynn found twenty-four ships, Holme produced two, Wells ten, and Blakeney, Wiveton and Cley eleven, eight and thirteen respectively. Even after overseas trade declined, the coastal trade thrived. And so it continued until the middle of the nineteenth century, when lines of wagons waiting to unload corn on the quay at Cley were a common sight. Finally the railways completed the work that silting and sanding had begun, leaving only Wells with a semblance of trade.

The changes along the East coast have been no less considerable, and probably more economically important. Here, in different places the forces of erosion and deposition have been at work. The sea which swallowed Shipden (the predecessor of modern Cromer) and Dunwich and has deeply eroded the North-east coast, built a long sand-spit which obstructed the harbour at Yarmouth. At one time it stretched to Corton, with the result that the trade of the port was greatly handicapped and the town was obliged during the Middle Ages to make many appeals for relief. To the south of Aldeburgh, too, the tides have formed a spit nearly eleven miles long, and in so doing have diverted the river, which at one point runs within a few yards of the open sea.

The story of the formation of the Norfolk Broads, however, is very different, and has presented a problem that has only recently been solved.

The visitor, sailing perhaps with an easterly breeze as a constant reminder of the nearness of the sea, will probably, if he gives a thought to the matter, imagine the Broads to be the relics of a time when the North Sea was free to sweep far up the river valleys, before silting and marsh vegetation, and later embanking and drainage, put an end to it. That was certainly an accepted view until comparatively recently.

But there have always been a number of factors which proved difficult to reconcile with the theory of a natural origin of the lakes. There were, for example, the sudden, and often rectilinear, boundaries to these natural features. There were the steep-cut banks, and the loose muds at the bottom of the lakes, which did not correspond with samples from borings made into the untouched strips of land between the Broads and the rivers. There were the narrow baulks of peat which continued in straight lines at, or near, the surface across some of the Broads. And there were the many Broads, closely associated with a river valley, which were never part of the river's course. Even the Ant, which now flows through Barton Broad, at one time flowed to one side of it. As J. W. Gregory observed, "Instead of the river passing through the Broads, it kept sullenly aloof from them; as we sailed down the river there was Broad to the left of us, Broad to the right of us, Broad in front of us, but by a series of ingenious twists and turns, it managed to wind through the whole lot of them, either eluding any direct contact with them, or communicating only through a few narrow and overgrown passages."

Possibly one difficulty in the way of believing that the Broads were man-made has been the difficulty of imagining that men in times past could have excavated the 900 million cub. ft. of soil which covered the Broads at their greatest extent. But, in fact, over a period of three centuries or more this is what happened.

In prehistoric times, the low-lying country east and north-east of Norwich, in the valleys of the Waveney, Yare, Bure, Ant and Thurne, and particularly the districts of Flegg and Lothingland, were almost uninhabited, and much of it was under water. By 879, when the Danish leader, Guthrum, was seeking land upon which to colonize his troops, the water had receded from much of the area as a result of the rising of the land above sea-level, and the area was ripe for colonization. It lacked wood for fuel, but there was an abundance of peat. Throughout the early medieval period records make constant reference to the turbaries, from which peat was dug, and which made an important contribution to the profits of the manors and estates. A comparison with old estate maps shows that surviving baulks, which run across a Broad, correspond exactly with divisions between holdings. In some cases the peat was cut to depths of 10 or 12 ft., and depths of 6 ft. were common. This was below the level of neighbouring rivers, but peat-cutting went on unhindered for centuries because the clay deposited on the river beds formed an impermeable barrier, and other surface water was easily removed. Then suddenly, about the beginning of the fourteenth century, the records show the profitable industry to have stopped. Where it continued, a system of dredging and moulding of peat blocks had been substituted for the former method of cutting. The catastrophe which destroyed the industry is nowhere described, but archaeological evidence shows that the great North Sea storm of 1287 flooded the river valleys and the workings, and began the slow process by which the Broads were formed.

The European coastline, as it exists today, and particularly the stretch from Calais to the Frisian Islands, has been much modified within the period of recorded history. The coastline of Holland is, in fact, more completely artificial than any comparable area in Europe. One of the notable changes—the draining of part of the Zuider Zee—was begun only at the end of World War I, and another important piece of work—the building of flood barriers that will seal all save one of the many mouths of the Rhine—has only just been begun. As the Dutch have said, "God made the world, and the Dutch made Holland."

Breaching the Strait of Dover introduced new and complex tides and currents into the North Sea, and, in time, this had an effect upon the contour of the European coast. One result was the gradual formation of a great off-shore sand-bar that ran from Sangatte (near Calais) to the Scheldt-Maas-Rhine estuaries, and then, resuming at the Hook, continued to Den

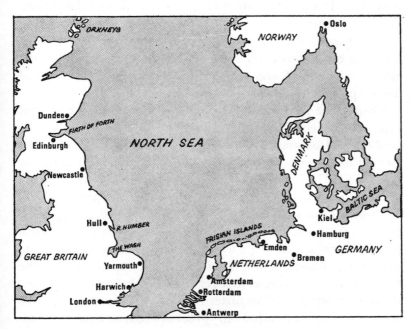

The North Sea coastline as it exists today

Helder and the Frisian Islands. The immediate effect of this sand-bar along the coast of the Netherlands was to create a chain of salt-water lagoons. Then, with the broadening of the bar, and the appearance of sand-dunes, the bar became strong enough to hold out the sea almost completely for a time. The salt-water lagoons gave place (as in the Fenlands of East Anglia) to fresh-water peats. It is not difficult to imagine this desolate, featureless coastal fringe as it existed nineteen hundred years ago. The Elder Pliny said of it that he did not know whether it belonged to the land or the sea. There were many differences of detail from the map as we know it. At that time Holland's best-known feature, the Zuider Zee, existed only as a huge lake whose waters found their way into the North Sea along a number of small channels. The Rhine reached the sea a little to the north of Katwijk where now the Oude Rijn meanders. It was only much later, as a result of tidal action, that the Rhine took its present more southerly course. The same deep-scouring of the southern estuaries had an even more immediate and profound economic effect when it opened the present estuary of the Scheldt, and permitted the rise of Antwerp as a great international seaport.

Some of the physical changes that have taken place are not easily explained. Sometime before A.D. 1000 the line of the sand-bar shifted, southwards of Texel, and a new line of dunes formed to seaward of the old dunes. It was not all gain. By late Roman times the dunes had been unequal to the violence of the North Sea, and large areas in Zeeland, to the south, and in Friesland and Groningen, to the north, had disappeared beneath the waves. It was not until the seventh and eighth centuries that any attempt was made to erect artificial dykes to contain the waters. Then barriers were set up to contain the Zuider Zee. They were at first very feeble constructions, placed above high-water level in order to escape the destructive force of the waves, and intended only to act as a barrier against exceptional flooding. Elsewhere in Friesland and Groningen the dykes erected were in the nature of low embankments enclosing areas of alluvial flat exposed at low tide, similar to those built by the monks of Canterbury when they were reclaiming the Romney Marsh.

As a generalization, the North Sea gained at the expense of the land down until about 1300 when, had the Dutch not begun to take urgent steps, the whole of Zeeland, South Holland as far inland as Utrecht and Gorinchem, and all North Holland (in addition to the Zuider Zee) would gradually have disappeared beneath the waves. Even so, the sea continued to make some important gains, and much reclaimed land was subsequently lost, either temporarily or for all time.

In 1300, Zeeland-Flanders, the southern part of South Holland, and North-west Brabant formed an area that was very different from what it is today. It formed an archipelago of over sixty small islands. The change is particularly noticeable in the islands of South Holland. Voorne was very much smaller, and the large island of Goeree-Overflakkee hardly existed as dry land at all. This was an area of active reclamation. To begin with, the inhabitants threw dykes round the higher ground, which was flooded only in exceptional circumstances, and then joined these into bigger units by building dams across the smaller inlets and watercourses before beginning the reclamation of the surrounding mud-flats. In the early days the old dykes were levelled as each fresh advance was made. But this practice was later forbidden as a result of disasters that occurred when the sea broke through. In spite of what was won by hard toil, and the lessons gained by experience, the Dutch can never have felt that they were masters of the sea. Their efforts are better documented after 1300, and in a short period of less than fifty years, between 1374 and 1421, there were no fewer than eight major disasters in South Holland and Zeeland.

Some time before 1400, a change of far-reaching significance not only for Antwerp, but for the course of European relations, took place. It is possible that at one time the Scheldt joined the Maas near its mouth, and that the two rivers flowed together into the North Sea. Later, the river discharged principally into what is now known as the East Scheldt. It was of little commercial significance, and the stream that is now the West Scheldt was a shallow strait, which did not form a continuous waterway. Quite suddenly the position was changed. The action of the tides gave the West Scheldt a deep-water channel which provided Antwerp with easy access to the sea, while the East Scheldt sank into insignificance.

A little to the North, another familiar feature of the Dutch coastline was created at about this time. On the seaward side of Dordrecht, considerable progress had been made since the thirteenth century in reclaiming land exposed at low tide. But the situation was always precarious, and, by the fifteenth century, the North Sea had recaptured much. The big catastrophe, which had long threatened, occurred in November 1421, when a westerly storm and a high tide carved out the great arm of the sea that is known today as the Hollandsch Diep.

Along many stretches of the Dutch North Sea coast reclamation has been impossible, and between the Hook and Scheveningen, and again in the extreme north, the authorities have fought an unequal battle against the steady advance of the sea. At one point, in spite of the protective works, the sea advanced 700 yds during the seventeenth and eighteenth centuries, and later, when more modern defences were constructed, the foot of the dunes was still forced back 16 yds in half a century. The Frisian Islands (with the exception of Texel), consisting mainly of dunes and sandy flats and poldered fields, have undergone many changes. Elsewhere gains have balanced losses. In Zeeland, South Holland and Brabant the steady reclamation of mud flats, aided by natural silting has radically altered the map by consolidating many small islands into a few bigger ones. But, economically, this was less important than the work done in the area between the Maas, the North Sea and the Zuider Zee, which has turned an area much broken up by inland water into the economic and political heart of the country.

2

THE INVADERS

IN THE CENTURIES following the withdrawal from Britain of the Roman garrisons Britain was subjected to a series of invasions by peoples from across the North Sea who radically changed the existing pattern of British culture. This is an unusually difficult period of British history because, for the first time in five centuries, Britain was out of touch with Europe, and literate men on the Continent, who might have said something of events in Britain had problems of their own. As a result, there are many obscure stretches of Anglo-Saxon history and many leading characters that are names without substance. And even when events are better documented the great movements of population are not always easy to explain. Speaking of the Viking raids which began at the end of the eighth century, Sir Thomas Kendrick, author of the fullest survey in English, has written: "It is impossible to explain in final and satisfactory terms the huge outpouring of the northern peoples that is known as the Viking expansion." Yet the invasion of Britain and other countries bordering the North Sea, which took place between the departure of the Roman garrisons from Britain and the Norman Conquest, were of the first importance in the history of Britain. They brought about the establishment of Teutonic and Nordic peoples in this island in place of the Celts; the establishment of English as the language of the people, and one which was sufficiently deeply implanted to survive the rivalry of Norman-French; the establishment of a unified kingdom in England, and the establishment of a Christian church.

The ancestors of the first of these invaders had been among the peoples who had bothered the Romans while they still garrisoned this island. And it was to deal with them that the Count of the Saxon Shore was appointed and a chain of defence posts established. To the Roman writers of the third and fourth centuries these raiders who crossed the North Sea to harry the east and south-east coast were simply Saxons without differentiation. According to Gildas, the first of the Saxons came to Britain by invitation of one of the British rulers to help in repelling invaders from the North, and were given land upon which to settle. The first three shiploads of settlers were followed by others. All went well for a time, and their numbers must already have been considerable when a dispute with the British over provisions led to a wide-scale revolt in which the settlers did a great deal of damage throughout the country.

It is likely that the raiders came from a variety of different tribes, although it is probable that in the process of migration and occupation some of these distinctions became blurred. Bede, who wrote a long time after the first invasions took place, was nonetheless interested to discover what he could about the early history of these people. According to him, the invaders came from three tribes, the Saxons, the Angles and the Jutes. The one certain fact is that the invaders came from somewhere along the coastal area stretching from the Low Countries to the Jutland Peninsula. But beyond that there is a great deal of uncertainty. Tacitus, who mentions the Anglii, speaks of them as one of a group of seven tribes who worshipped a goddess, Nerthus, in an island sanctuary. The evidence which King Alfred collected from two sea-captains who were well acquainted with Scandinavian waters supports the belief that they lived originally in the southern part of the Jutland peninsula. According to Bede, their northern neighbours, in the

Above, seventeenth-century packets putting out of Harwich. From a contemporary engraving; *below*, a North Sea revenue cutter chasing a lugger, *c.* 1830

Above, British fishing vessels in the Shetlands; *below,* a contemporary engraving of the Northern whale fishery

Jutland peninsula, were the Jutes, but scholars have found great difficulties in accepting this.[1] Tacitus does not mention the Saxons, and the area from which they are supposed to have come—between the Elbe and the Weser—was occupied in his day by the Chaucii. But, in the centuries after he wrote, it appears that the Saxons moved in large numbers into part of

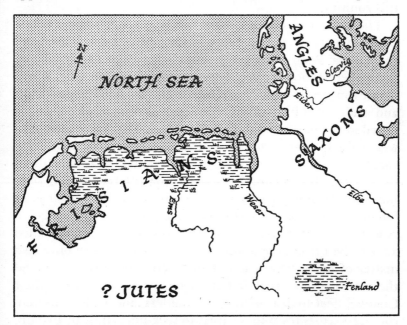

The Continental homelands of the Germanic invaders

the coastal area, where they quickly established a reputation as bold sea-raiders.

One other author, although he was writing far away in Byzantium, has something of importance to say, and in the words of Sir Frank Stenton, contributes "the first certain fact in English history". He was Procopius, whose *History of the Wars* is nearly two centuries earlier than Bede's writings. He learned from visiting Englishmen that the peoples living in Britain

[1] There is reason for thinking that they had relations with the Rhineland.

were the English and the Frisians. Although he believed that Britain was the abode of the souls of the dead who were ferried across the sea, and that only serpents could live north of the Roman Wall, nonetheless there is sound linguistic evidence to support the belief that Frisian, rather than Germanic or Nordic influences, were dominant in forming the language of this country.

The lands from which some of the Anglo-Saxon settlers came (and particularly those coastal lands between the Weser and the Zuider Zee), must have provided a difficult livelihood. Somewhere about 500 B.C.—well before the time with which we are concerned—the North Sea had invaded the coastal lands and made them uninhabitable. Then, as time went on, silting raised some small areas above water-level. These *terpen,* as they were called, were occupied by local communities, who cultivated them and, with incredible labour, enlarged and fertilized them to the point where they could support large farming communities. In time, whether as a result of outside pressures or for other reasons, the coastlands became heavily populated. And there is evidence to show that the Saxons had intruded among the Frisian populations of the *terpen.* It can only be a matter of conjecture whether these circumstances prompted the acts of piracy that led the Romans to strengthen their Channel fleet to deal with Saxon raiders, and which later encouraged tribes from these areas to seek new lands in Britain.

Even without the evidence of the early chronicles, and place-names and archaeological finds, it would be possible to guess roughly where the invaders would choose to settle, for they looked at the land not only as warriors but as farmers. The heavy clay soils—particularly as these were often thickly wooded in Saxon times—had little attraction, nor indeed did the areas of sand and gravel, such as the Bagshot country, the Norfolk Breckland or the Suffolk Sandlings. Nor did they find anything to attract them in the Downland chalk country, where cultivation had flourished under their predecessors. The newcomer wanted soil that was not sterile or acid, and water that was near the surface. Not that the settlers disdained areas of sand and gravel at lower elevation, where there was often an admixture of clay and loam.

This essential interest in the soil has led historians to suppose that the invaders deliberately avoided the settlements and lines of communication which the Romans had established, and preferred to settle where rivers provided a convenient means of communication. It would be easy to over-emphasize both facts. The essential interests of the Romans and the newcomers were entirely different. The Romans had been administrators and soldiers, and the roads they built were primarily for strategic purposes; their successors were farmers for whom such strategic questions had no significance. Nor is it certain that the rivers along which the early settlements are to be found were easily navigable over much of their length, even by the boats of the period. The valley bottoms did, however, often offer the immigrant something more important: spring water from the gravel terraces, level ground for dwellings and trackways, and, sometimes, good arable soil.

The nature of the conquest has been long disputed. Historians who have rejected the Chroniclers' stories of incursions by small, separate bands, have found it equally difficult to accept the idea of a large concerted operation. There is probably a measure of truth in both theories. The idea of some preconceived plan for the carving-up of Britain by Angles, Saxons and Jutes must be abandoned, too. At most we are left with the idea of large-scale invasions across the North Sea in each of which one tribe predominated. Nor is there any evidence that, in the early stages, the invaders staked out any recognizable territorial domain. The coastal kingdoms of Anglo-Saxon England were the first to come into being. According to the Anglo-Saxon Chronicle, they existed by the end of the fifth century. But even there, the authority of their rulers may not, at first, have extended very far, and their boundaries may not have been defined much before the days of the Heptarchy.

The period falls into three unequal parts. During the first, the invaders struggled for a foothold against British resistance, which was much stronger than is sometimes supposed. Then the great British victory of Mons Badonicus, about the year A.D. 500, gave the victors a respite which lasted for half a century or more, and resulted, as Precopius relates, in bands of hard-pressed Anglo-Saxons crossing the North Sea to re-gain for themselves, a new footing in their old homelands. The third and final stage of the Anglo-Saxon conquest began prob-ably about A.D. 570, and was followed by a succession of vic-tories, as a result of which the invaders extended their authority over much of southern England. By the year A.D. 600 the exis-tence of ten independent States south of the Humber can be recognized.

Britain north of the Humber remained undisturbed by outside interference. This is the more surprising in view of the trouble that the Romans had experienced in safeguarding their northern frontier. With the departure of the Roman garrisons, however, it appears that the region between the Humber and the Forth passed into the control of British rulers who were strong enough to resist attack from whatever quarter it came. And so it was not until the sixth century that the Eng-lish invaders were able to overcome opposition, and gradually to extend their authority northwards. The English, however, did not possess more than half the mainland of Britain when the Viking raids on Britain reached the point of full-scale invasion.

The Viking incursions are no less difficult to explain than the raids of the Anglo-Saxons. This sudden outburst of activity was marked by almost simultaneous raids upon the coasts of England and France, and by disturbances along the Eider boundary between Denmark and the Kingdom of the Franks. It was not, of course, the first contact between the Norsemen and other peoples of the West, but it is the best documented because the churches of the West were deeply involved, and their records of what happened have long prejudiced the inter-pretation of the period. Indeed, from time immemorial, the

Vikings had roamed far and wide in their open boats over the North Sea and the Atlantic. These early voyages have left few records. It is clear, however, that contact with the Roman world existed by the reign of Augustus, by which time the furs and amber of the North were being exchanged for articles of gold, silver and glass—for such things as the coins and necklaces, the goblets, platters and brooches that are to be found in the Scandinavian graves of the period. The finds among the treasure of Sutton Hoo in Suffolk show, too, that the Norsemen had made contacts with England long before the Norse raids of the eighth century began. It is possible that the "pirates" who attacked the island of Eigg in the Hebrides, and Tory Island off Donegal in the seventh century were these same Norsemen. In that century, too, it was the arrival of Scandinavian settlers that compelled the Irish anchorites, who dwelled there, to move on to the remoter Faroes. The sculptured stones of Gothland, dating from this period, clearly show the influence of Celtic art.

The first of a long succession of Viking raids across the North Sea began towards the end of the eighth century. The very earliest raids may have occurred in 793, when the monastery of Lindisfarne, off the coast of Northumbria, was plundered. It was followed in succeeding years by the looting of the monasteries of Jarrow and Iona. By 795 the Norsemen were busy around the coast of Ireland and, in 799, reached the shores of Aquitaine. The early raids, in which the Norwegians rather than the Danes were prominent, gradually increased in intensity, and mark the beginning of two centuries of upheaval and aggrandizement.

The early raids both horrified and shocked the monks who recorded them. These raiders came primarily for plunder and, being heathens, had no regard for the sanctity of the religious houses, which they regarded as easy prey. Alcuin, who came from Northumbria, although he spent many years on the Continent, wrote: "It is nearly 350 years that we and our fathers have inhabited this lovely land, and never before has such a terror appeared in Britain as we have now suffered from a pagan race, nor was it thought that such an inroad from the sea could be made". The Annals of St. Bertin, telling of the sacking of Rouen in 841, records the scene of terror: "Carrying everywhere a fury of rapine, fire and sword, they gave up the city, the monks and the rest of the people to carnage and captivity. Some of the monasteries and other places near the Seine they devastated, the rest they left filled with terror, having received much money." Year by year the invasions grew in intensity, more and more abbeys and towns on both sides of the North Sea were sacked, and large tracts of land, particularly in the Netherlands and North-western France, were laid waste.

In the circumstances, it is inevitable that the chroniclers should have emphasized the violence to which fellow monks and church property were exposed. It has had the effect, however, of obscuring the positive contributions of Nordic culture. It may, too, by its exaggeration of the intensity and violence of the raids, make it unnecessarily difficult to accept simpler explanations of this long-drawn-out movement.

It has been suggested that concentration of royal power in the hands of Harold Fairhair after the middle of the ninth century resulted in many leaders preferring to find a means of livelihood and a home elsewhere, rather than accept even his limited overlordship. Something of the sort, too, may have happened in the time of the lesser Norwegian kings who preceded Harold.

It is possible, too, that the decline of Frisian naval and commercial power, which culminated in the final defeat of the Frisians by Charlemagne in 785, played its part. The argument has been put forward. But it has yet to be proved that the Frisians, at the height of their power were able to restrain their neighbours. Certainly the Frankish kingdom of Charlemagne and his successors was never able to control the North Sea. In consequence, the Danish sea rovers had complete independence of action, and the coasts of Britain and the Frankish

Empire were at their mercy. It was, in fact, only because Charlemagne and his son, Louis the Pious, appreciated the power of the Danish rulers, and succeeded by diplomacy and intrigue in playing one member of the Danish household off against another, that danger was held off for as long as it was. When the sons of Louis fell out among themselves, the coasts on both sides of the North Sea were laid open to invasion.

After the earliest attacks, the coastlands of England and the Continent were spared for a number of years. But the Norsemen continued to cross the North Sea to raid Ireland and neighbouring areas, almost without intermission, to the point where they were no longer content with isolated raids, but came with large fleets and established settlements along the coast. "The sea spewed a flood of strangers over Erin," reports the Annals of Ulster, "and there was no harbour, no landing-place, no fortification, no fortress, no bulwark without fleets of Vikings and pirates."

On the European mainland the shores of Frisia were a special objective when attacks were resumed, and the once-famous trading town of Dorstadt was ravaged four times. Further south, Danish fleets entered the Scheldt and Maas to burn and plunder Antwerp and the island of Walcheren. Attacks upon the coast of France were closely linked with attacks upon the coasts of southern England. A couple of years later, Arab chroniclers were writing of the Norseman's ships poised over the coasts of Spain "like dark red sea-birds".

Down until 865 the Norse attacks upon Britain were isolated incidents. The raiders crossed the North Sea in the spring, and returned home with their loot before the onset of the autumn gales. Such settlements as they made were both small and scattered, and did not provide the core from which a kingdom could grow. There were, moreover, two distinct streams. The one led from Norway to Shetland and Orkney and thence on to the Western Isles and Ireland: the other from Jutland ran down the Channel to the shores of England and France, and then on again, by way of Land's End, to Southern Ireland.

Only thirty years separate the first of a series of concerted attacks upon the coasts of England from the landing of the Danish army of invasion in 865. The speed with which the Norsemen had achieved this position indicates the extent to which the Germanic peoples had abandoned the use of arms and had become peace-loving farmers. Indeed, the earliest Viking invaders were astonished that so much wealth should have belonged to people who carried no arms to protect it.

The invasion of 865 began in the autumn with incursion into East Anglia by a powerful Danish force that had been bribed by Charles the Bald to leave the Seine. Unlike earlier raiders they were prepared to spend several years in occupation to secure what they wanted. They did not, however, follow any regular plan of campaign. Their general practice, in the early stages, was to seize a strong position, preferably by a navigable river, fortify it, and ravage the surrounding country until the local population sued for peace. Their use of horses for transport, in particular, gave them considerable tactical advantages over their opponents. It was not until the later years of the ninth century, when Alfred, King of Wessex, established a firm alliance with Mercia and began his heroic struggle that the Danish menace was contained. It culminated in the agreement, known as the Peace of Wedmore, whereby Guthrum the Dane became a Christian and the country was divided. An area south-west of a line following Watling Street (together with London) remained to Alfred. Guthrum's kingdom included Norfolk, Suffolk, Essex and Cambridgeshire as well as parts of Bedfordshire and Hertfordshire. It is not certain how far his authority extended northwards. The position in the North was further confused in the years which followed by the invasion of the northern counties by Norsemen from Dublin. They came originally from Norway, and although kinsmen of the Danes were scarcely better disposed towards them than towards the English.

By the end of the tenth century a new and formidable menace had appeared. This was the formation in Denmark of brotherhoods of highly trained soldiers, who lived only to fight and pillage, subjected themselves to the strictest rules of military discipline and admitted to their membership only warriors of tried valour. Today the island upon which Copenhagen stands is much changed from what it was a thousand

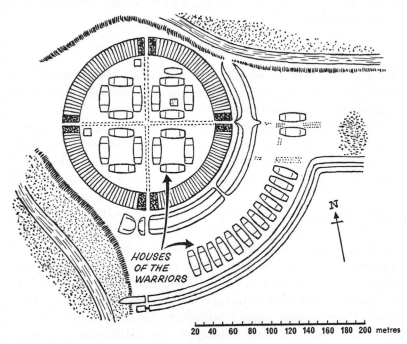

Ground plan of the Viking fortress at Trelleborg, Denmark

years ago, and even the Trelleborg promontory juts out over a great plain once filled by a lake, but its solitude and the massive earthworks of the Viking fortress still provide some hold upon the imagination, and give support to the saga of the Jómsvikings. This community, we are told, lived in the fortress of Jómsborg, near the mouth of the Oder. It consisted of a fortified harbour, large enough for three hundred ships to shelter in it, and a land fortress with catapults mounted on its walls. Jómsborg has never been found, but four similar fortresses have been excavated.

The wages of the soldiers were paid from the tribute that their leaders levied, and terror was the first sanction.

"The sword bit, blood fell on spear,
The flow of warm blood gladdened the raven and waxed greatly,
Fire played mightly among the houses,
The wolf reddened his tooth,
To the west of the salt seas sword rang on brow."

In 991, the raiders who came to England were bought off with 22,000 lbs. of gold and silver: in later years the amount of Danegeld demanded steadily rose.

Of the Jómsvikings who came to England the most famous was Swein Forkbeard, the reputed founder of Jómsborg, and a man of far-reaching ambitions, who had driven his father from the throne of Denmark before making himself King of England as well. He reigned only a few months, and was succeeded on his death by his son, Cnut. Thereafter, for twenty-five years, England was ruled by Danish kings. They were years of comparative peace and harmony in which Cnut assured himself of the loyalty of his English subjects and the good-will of the Church. And his subjects, for their part, found in the presence of one of Scandinavia's greatest warriors a guarantee against outside attack. Moreover, his very preoccupation with Scandinavian affairs entailed the delegation of purely English administrative affairs, which was entirely to the liking of his most powerful English subjects.

3

EARLY TRADING LINKS
ACROSS THE NORTH SEA

VERY LITTLE HAS survived about the earliest forms of trade
around the North Sea. The barter of goods is probably as old
as mankind, but organized trade was dependent upon the
existence of stabilized communities which only became established with the development of agriculture in western Europe
in later neolithic times. Flint implements of all kinds formed
one of the earliest articles of trade, but except where the flints
had a distinctive colour it is impossible to tell their place of
origin. It is likely that the celebrated flints of Brandon in
Suffolk formed an important part of Britain's overseas trade,
but it is impossible to tell.

Later, an active trade in Irish gold and copper grew up. The
communities around the North Sea had no share in it at first,
for it found its way to the Mediterranean and Aegean by way
of the Cornish peninsular. But later a branch of this enterprise
was developed by way of the Clyde-Forth isthmus to Scandinavia. Then, somewhere about 1000 B.C. (corresponding
roughly with the end of the middle Bronze Period), an important change in the old trade routes occurred, and articles of Irish
gold began to find their way to Europe across the lowlands of
central England, and so across the North Sea to the Continent.
It seems likely that this change was linked with the development of the amber trade.

[43]

Jewellery and luxury articles of Italian manufacture, which incorporated Scandinavian amber, prove conclusively the existence of a trade route that ran down the North Sea coast of Jutland, and then by way of the valleys of the Elbe and Moldau, the Danube and Inn and across the Alpine passes, to the plain of Lombardy. From then, until at least the fourth century B.C., a lively trade continued in the amber of Jutland and the Baltic, which was prized above the Sicilian product for its appearance and the ease with which it could be worked.

Before the coming of the Romans the rising power of the Belgic peoples, who occupied the borders of the Rhineland and parts of northern Gaul, and their conquest of a part of Britain including northern Kent as well as Essex and Hertfordshire, developed the links across the Narrow Seas and added to the importance of the route from the Thames to the Rhine. This was particularly so after Caesar had destroyed the important trading-post of Corbilo at the mouth of the Loire, and in so doing disrupted the trade which had previously flowed south via the Cornish peninsula.

The invasions of Britain by the Romans, Anglo-Saxons, Danes and Normans all served to add links to our connection with the Continent. But little is known about our trading relations at that time. It is usually only when something out of the ordinary happened that the records afford a glimpse of the normal state of things. So, about 790, after the Emperor Charlemagne and Offa, King of Mercia had disagreed about the proposed marriages of their children, the Frankish ports were closed to English merchants, and it can be inferred that in normal times there was a regular trade across the North Sea. This is confirmed by a letter in which the Emperor complains that English cloths sent to Germany are not of the accustomed length, and asks the King to ensure that this does not occur again. And by a further letter, in which the Emperor states that English merchants were going to Europe in the guise of pilgrims to avoid paying tolls, and that those who came openly would be given the protection of the law. In 796, when friendly relations had been re-established, the two rulers entered into the first commercial treaty in English history, guaranteeing protection to each other's merchants, and the right of access to the king when in trouble. The material is scanty, but various grants of freedom from tolls to monasteries owning sea-going ships, brief mention of trade and traders, and the discovery of early English coins on the Continent serve to reinforce the impression of an established system of trade.

How big a share the English merchants were able to take for themselves will never be known. But it is clear that for two centuries, until towards the close of the eighth century, the Frisian seamen of the Low Countries dominated the North Sea. In 679, Bede refers to a merchant from the Low Countries who was prepared to buy an English prisoner from his captors, and by the end of the eighth century there was an important Frisian colony in York. And thus it remained, until the forces of the Emperor put an end to Frisian independence.

The Frisians' part in the trade of Western Europe is a remarkable one. Their homeland stretched along the shores of the North Sea from the estuary of the Weser to the Zwin (on the banks of which Bruges later grew). It was not particularly fertile, but it was admirably situated as a centre of trade. Its principal town, Dorstadt, stood on the old estuary of the Rhine, and when that declined, partly as a result of armed raids and partly as a result of changes in the river bed, its place was taken by Tiel on the River Waal. With its network of navigable rivers, its sea connections and the many well-sheltered channels between the islands along the coast, it was natural that the Frisians should turn to fishing and water-borne trade. Along the trade routes of the West—to England, Scandinavia and the Baltic, to Gaul and West Francia—and in the chief trading centres, they were busy and successful intermediaries. A good deal of their business flowed down the Rhine, along which they carried cloth, fish and other goods to pay for the Alsatian corn and wine which they shipped back. From the North Sea ports their trade route to Francia ran through the Channel to Etaples, from whence they made their way to Rouen, Amiens and other parts of Western France. In the early part of the eighth century they were active, too, at the fair of St. Denis, the most important fair in France at that time.

It says a great deal for their tenacity that they succeeded in penetrating into the age-old trading centres of the Scandinavians, and maintained a hold even at a time when Viking sea-rovers were burning down their "capital", Dorstadt. The reason why the Scandinavians, too, were so active seems in part to be that they, like the Frisians, were unable to support themselves upon their barren lands. Some of them turned to the sea as robbers, adventurers and colonizers, or simply as fishermen. But others, whose activities began long before the Viking raids started and continued long after they were over, took to the sea as traders.

The important thing about the history of Scandinavian commerce is not its length—though it was still developing when that of Frisia collapsed—but the nature of its connections. The Norsemen in their travels had penetrated westward to Iceland, to Greenland and even to the shores of North America. Eastwards, they were at home in the farthest reaches of the Baltic: they established a settlement in Novgorod, and penetrated Russia to the Crimea. Some found their way to Constantinople, where they enlisted as mercenaries, or traded as merchants. The trading links which were thus forged were of prime importance to the countries of Western Europe which depended upon the Baltic for supplies of timber, furs, pitch and hemp, but had not themselves built trade links with the area. Traders from Scandinavia were still to be found in the East Coast ports of England in the thirteenth century but already the trade of western Europe was passing into other hands.

It is unlikely that, even in the period of greatest disruption in Britain, the trading links between this country and the Continent were broken. A passing reference by Bishop Aelfric shows that English merchants were carrying their goods directly

[46]

to Rome along the established Italian trade routes.[1] And, at about this time, too, the Baltic route to Russia, of which Haithaby, near Schleswig, was the entrepôt, was opened up. The document that gives the clearest impression of trade with the Continent, however, is the treaty between King Aethelred and the King of Norway in 991. By it, any merchant ship of any country brought into an English estuary was to be immune from attack, and if any ship had been wrecked, and therefore a lawful object of plunder, the crew, together with any cargo they might have been able to carry away, were to come within the King's protection. Another clause provided that if the ships of the King of Norway should come upon any subject of Aethelred's in any country outside the scope of the treaty, he should be accorded peace for himself, his ship and his cargo, whether his ship was afloat or beached: but if he had entrusted his goods to another man he should have nothing but security for his life. Yet another document of around A.D. 1000 shows that German merchants and the men of Huy, Liège and Nivelles, who traded to London, enjoyed extensive privileges, while the men of Rouen were obliged to expose their goods and pay toll on the wharf or on shipboard. There is no reference to merchants from Scandinavia in this record, but it is clear that at that time merchants from every region from Norway to France were crossing the sea to trade in London. A City record, referring to this pre-Conquest period, says not only that Danes and Norwegians were free to dwell in the City for a whole year at a time, but that the Danes were at liberty to visit fairs and markets all over the country, while the Norwegians were restricted to London. Nor had London a monopoly of the trade that flowed across the North Sea. By the tenth century, the Danes had established a thriving colony in York, just as the Frisians had done two centuries earlier.

---

[1] In the days of Cnut, a record of concessions won for English and Danish traders from the Emperor and the Duke of Burgundy makes it clear that his subjects were accustomed to travel to Rome for purposes of trade as well as pilgrimage.

A number of fortunate circumstances combined at an early date to bring industrial and commercial prosperity to the Lower Scheldt, and from there it rapidly spread. There was probably a cloth industry in Flanders by the late eighth century, and it is likely that the "Frisian" cloths sent by the Emperor Charlemagne to Haroun el Raschid were in fact manufactured in Flanders, and merely carried in Frisian boats. It is at least certain that the sheep on the lush meadowlands of the Scheldt estuary produced coarse wool in plenty. Its soil produced fullers' earth, and was suitable for growing dye-plants. An extraordinary rise in population, which is not to be explained, also made the region incapable of supporting itself by agriculture, and so compelled it to support itself by manufactures. The wealth piled up by industry had important sociological consequences. Unlike most of Western Europe, where society was predominantly agrarian, the Flemish towns dominated the countryside, and within the towns themselves a vast gap yawned between the wealthy masters who dominated the Gilds and the "blue nails", as the great mass of workers were contemptuously called. The real expansion began in the eleventh century, by which time Flanders had recovered from the depredations of the Norsemen, and it went ahead by great strides in the twelfth and thirteenth centuries. To begin with, the cloth industry was centred in the towns of Artois and Walloon Flanders, and especially in Arras, St. Omer and Douai, but these were later surpassed by the Flemish towns of Ypres, Ghent and Bruges. At a still later date Leyden began to assume an ever-increasing importance. The Flemings, too, acquired the technique of producing a luxury cloth, which equalled any of the woollens that the Italians could produce. This side of the industry, however, demanded finer wools than could be produced locally, and for these the Netherlanders had to go to England, Spain and Burgundy.

Here, again, Flanders was wonderfully favoured by its geographical situation. Its road and river systems gave it easy connections with the food-growing areas of Germany and

Northern France, and with markets further afield where manufactures could be traded against raw materials and foodstuffs.
The sea-routes through the North Sea to Britain, and down
the Channel to the Bay of Biscay and the Spanish Peninsula
were also of the first importance.

By the thirteenth century Flanders and the surrounding
areas had become the principal market and manufacturing
area of North-western Europe. Walloon merchants carried a
good deal of the trade. And the cloth-producing towns, having
achieved a position of independence for themselves and
dominance over the populations of the surrounding countryside, became pockets of capitalism in a pre-capitalist world.
Nowhere, save in Northern Italy, were the towns so large and
numerous. Ghent is said to have had 4,500 weavers in the
middle of the fourteenth century, and to this number must
be added the fullers, shearers, dyers and many others engaged
in keeping the weavers busy. Its total population may have
been 50,000, and, according to some estimates, Ypres was as
big, while Bruges probably had twice as many inhabitants.

Although Flanders had a variety of other industries, none
of them compared with the cloth-making in importance, at
least until the end of the fourteenth century. And this, in turn,
made Flanders the great commercial centre of Western Europe.
The pre-eminence of Bruges at the beginning of the thirteenth
century was probably due to the fact that it was the port of
entry for English wool, and it was at the time, open to sea-
borne trade from every quarter.

It was not long before Italian merchants were coming there
in large numbers. The earliest of them came overland, bringing from Venice and Genoa the luxuries of the Levant, which
they exchanged in the Low Countries for the fine wool that
their own factories needed. But before long the first voyages
through the Strait of Gibraltar further extended the trade.

The first to make the then dangerous voyage were the
Genoese, who, in 1277—a full quarter of a century before the
Venetians—had begun to brave the storms of the Bay of Biscay

and the North Sea. That they did so at that time was probably the result of two distinct factors: the development of the galley, which was capable of surviving the conditions to be encountered, and the heavy dues that had to be paid at many places along the overland route. By the mid-thirteenth century the galleys were being organized into State fleets under the command of a captain appointed by the senate of Genoa. The Genoese were joined within a few decades by the Venetians. The galleys of Florence only made an appearance in the early fifteenth century. The city was a late-starter because the State lacked good sea-ports, and until Florence was able to run a fleet of her own, her merchants had to use the ships of Genoa and Venice to carry her costly manufactures to exchange for wool, unfinished cloth and hides.

Throughout the fourteenth century the rival fleets of Venice and Genoa made their annual voyages to Flanders, but in the mid-fifteenth century, when the Italian position in the markets of Western Europe seemed most secure, dissension at home upset the commerce. Florence was the first to suffer, and, after the annual voyage had been cancelled on a number of occasions, it was finally abandoned in 1480. For the moment, the Genoese and Venetians benefited by the difficulties of a competitor, but by the end of the century wars at home and the rivalry of English traders weakened the Genoese. The Venetians maintained their positions rather longer, but when Portuguese penetration of the Indian Ocean cut the Venetian spice trade at its roots, Venetian commerce lost some of its attraction, and thereafter rapidly decayed.

No less important in the trade of Flanders were the Germans who established themselves as the biggest exporters of Flemish cloth. They also bought a good deal of Italian ware on sale there, and traded in the foodstuffs and raw materials from Eastern Europe, for which the German towns had become an important source of supply. It was not long before Bruges became a commercial centre of outstanding international importance.

By the thirteenth century, the rise of German commercial power, which was to dominate the economy of the whole North Sea and Baltic areas for a long time, began to make itself felt. It had its beginning much earlier, and its foundations were laid in the successful penetration of the lands to the east of the Elbe. German control of the raw materials and the foodstuffs of Eastern Europe, as well as their access to those markets, made them rich and powerful, and the commodities which they offered for sale earned them a welcome and trading privileges wherever they settled.[1]

Many factors, geographical, political and economic, contributed to the rise of Antwerp in the sixteenth century. It had long enjoyed excellent water connections which enabled it, with Middelburg, to play its part in the economic life of the Scheldt delta. It also possessed excellent river communications with Brabant, Hainault and Liège, and beyond that, with the plains of Northern France and the valleys of the Meuse and the Rhine. Before the great days of Antwerp's economic expansion, therefore, the city lay between a broad, rich hinterland and the great Scheldt-Maas-Rhine delta. It was also of inestimable value that Antwerp stood at the lowest part of the Scheldt secure from serious flood during the two centuries of inundations between 1370 and 1570. The town was thus making headway in competition with Bruges even before changes in the river estuary gave Antwerp direct communication with the sea.

No less important in promoting the early rise of Antwerp were the favourable conditions to be found there for trading, including freedom in the employment of capital, and exemption for outsiders from tolls. This was in marked contrast to the reactionary exclusiveness which foreign merchants found in Bruges. As a result, even before the silting of the Zwin made the ultimate decline of Bruges inevitable, foreign merchant communities had been attracted there.

[1] See below, Chapter Six.

The position turned further in Antwerp's favour during the course of the fifteenth century when flood and tidal action enlarged the channel of the Scheldt so that ships could sail directly to the city. It was thus able to add the role of a sea-port to that of river-port. "Antwerp," it was gratefully said, "owes the Scheldt to God, and everything else to the Scheldt." The city was fortunate, too, in escaping the worse effects of civil disorder, and in maintaining good relations with its overlords, the Dukes of Burgundy.

The half-century preceding the Revolt of the Netherlands was the golden age of Antwerp, and in that time it achieved pre-eminence in finance and commerce. Guicciardini, who lived in the city, has left an account of the trade of Antwerp at that time. The largest single item, amounting to nearly a third by value, was English cloth. This was followed by Italian luxury goods, and after that, in descending order, came Northern foodstuffs, German and French wines, Portuguese spices, Spanish wines and wool, German cloth, French dyes and salt and English wool. The Portuguese, Spaniards, southern Germans and Italians all had communities there and in 1564, the merchants of the all-powerful Hanseatic League established their headquarters there. It was these foreigners, rather than the native merchants who conducted the bulk of the business and raised the city to greatness. The shipping which thronged the waterway at that time was the wonder and envy of the outside world, for much of the trade on which Antwerp thrived was water-borne. It was, indeed, a remarkable stroke of fortune that the seaway should have been opened at the very time when international trade had grown to a point where it could support the market.

Conditions in Antwerp were very much to the advantage of the established foreign merchants. Trade in English cloth, South German fustians and Hungarian copper and alum was in the hands of their national syndicates, and it became the established practice for the King of Portugal to sell whole cargoes of East Indian spices to similar groups—an arrangement that led a contemporary to write: "The Portingall, like a good simple man, he sailed every yeere full hungerly about 3 parts of the earth almost for spices; when he had brought them home, the great rich purses of the Antwarpians . . . ingrossed them all into their own hands."

Trade in commodities led automatically to dealings in bills of exchange and to a rapid growth of speculation. In 1460 the first truly international bourse was opened there, and by 1530 the city had become established as the financial centre of Europe to which Governments as well as traders were prepared to resort.

The golden days of Antwerp were short. In 1572 the capture of Flushing by the Water Beggars, following the revolt of the Netherlands, was followed by the seizure of a Portuguese spice-fleet bound for Antwerp, and worth half a million gulden. Antwerp became at the mercy of whoever commanded the Scheldt estuary, and sea-borne trade stopped until 1576. For a brief time after that Antwerp became the centre of resistance to Spain, and as late as 1582 large merchant fleets were to be seen again on the Scheldt. But the end was near. In the spring of 1584 Bruges fell to the Spaniards, and by the summer Spanish troops had established a close siege of Antwerp, which was to go on for fourteen months, and spelt the town's ruin.

To the merchants and manufacturers on the Continent, Britain was until well into the Middle Ages, something of a "colony", an unfailing source of raw materials—foodstuffs, wool, livestock, minerals and animal products—upon which their populations and their own highly developed industries depended. In particular, it was as a source of grain, and of soft, long-fleeced wool, that the English connection was prized by the merchants and manufacturers of the Low Countries.

At a very early date England had an important dairy industry. The Earls of Lancaster are one instance of a great landed family keeping great herds of cows upon the pastures of Yorkshire and Lancashire. And large quantities of butter were sent overseas from Lynn, Boston and Ipswich. But, in spite of the large numbers of cattle that must have been in the country, hides never played an important part in the export trade. At the close of the thirteenth century the total annual export was only about 45,000. Of that number, Newcastle was responsible for about a third, and was by far the biggest exporter. Hull was probably third among the ports from which hides were sent overseas, while Boston and Lynn each handled three to four thousand each. In the next two centuries, this trade, too, fell right away, an indication, perhaps of a growing home leather industry rather than any change in rural economy.

England, too, had grain to spare, and this was sought by the traders from the Netherlands to supplement the supplies of Northern France. It also had a ready market in Scandinavia until the fourteenth century, when supplies from the newly colonized areas of eastern Europe ousted it. Lynn, with its excellent water connections, was well placed to profit from the export trade, for the areas of low-price wheat—and these were the main corn-growing countries—lay immediately south in Norfolk and Suffolk, and south-westwards in a broad band stretching to the Bristol Channel. In consequence, during the century from 1250-1350, when the trade in corn was at its height, Lynn's exports far outstripped those of any other port in the country. Yarmouth, too, had a good export business, and so too did Hull, with Boston some way behind.

The wool trade, however, outstripped everything else in importance. The really big flocks were kept on the monastic lands in Yorkshire and Lincolnshire. Flocks of over 15,000 were not unknown, and some of the most expensive wool produced in the country came from Lincolnshire. East Anglia was not noted for the fineness of its product, but it appears to have specialized in the production of a breed that produced the long-fibred wool needed for the manufacture of worsteds. All of the principal ports from Newcastle down to the Thames had a share in the trade, with Hull and Boston sharing some 38 per cent of the trade in the early fourteenth century, compared with London's 41 per cent.

Towards the close of the fourteenth century the amount of wool being sent abroad had dropped. By 1480, Hull and Boston were each exporting less than a sixth of the amount they had sent two centuries before, and the exports from Newcastle, Lynn and Yarmouth had dwindled to almost nothing. London, too, had shown a fall, although it now exported nearly as much as all the other ports in England put together. Only in Ipswich was there an increase, but the wool trade of that port was never very big.

Coal, which later played so great a part in the development of the North-east, was of little significance in the Middle Ages. Other considerations apart, carriage was a great problem, and, except for the Tyne valley, there was no district from which it was carried in amounts exceeding a few hundred tons a year for more than a few miles from outcrops. On the Tyne, ships calling at Newcastle took on supplies of coal for London, and for places across the sea from Dieppe to Lübeck. Yet, even so, the amounts shipped were small—generally between 2,000 and 7,000 tons a year—and it is unlikely that shipments often exceeded 15,000 tons a year before the sixteenth century.

The English themselves had little part in this early trade in coal. The ships that came to the Tyne were almost all owned and manned by Frenchmen and Flemings. They brought supplies of grain, of which Northumberland and Durham were always in need, and took, as return cargoes, supplies of cloth, fish and grindstones, which were the chief products of the area. Coal was taken on in place of the usual ballast to stabilize the ship. And it continued to be carried as ballast, or make-weight, throughout the Middle Ages, because the price which it fetched when sold would never have made it worth while shipping it in any other way. At the same time it was worth a ship-

master's while to jettison the sand and rubble that had served
as ballast on the inward journey, and to lay out a little money
on coal, which could be had on the Newcastle quayside for as
little as two shillings a ton. This was particularly so if he had
been able to make the necessary contacts in his home port.
There was a steady demand for coal among blacksmiths, arm-
ourers and lime-burners. But there was no single coal-merchant
in any English port, and the same was probably true on the
Continent. In London, what small stocks there were were to
be found at the ironmongers' or with the smiths and lime-
burners themselves. There was, in fact, no organized trade, and
when the need for a large quantity of coal arose, a contractor
had to organize transportation himself. So little was coal regarded as an article of commerce that the Hostmen at Newcastle, who later had a monopoly of the trade, dealt in a wide
variety of other things as well,

By the close of the Middle Ages a number of foreign communities had established themselves in these and other parts
along the East Coast of England. Among them the Dutch,
Flemings and French predominated, but Icelanders, Spaniards
and even Italians were to be found. There were undoubtedly
Germans, too, since the Hanseatic factories in such places as
Ipswich and Lynn were still maintained. Most of the immigrants were to be found in the bigger towns, but there were
some to be found even in small villages along the coast. The
number of residents must, however, have always been small by
comparison with the changing population of visiting merchants
and the crews of foreign vessels.

It is interesting to see what evidence there is that these
foreign settlers introduced new crafts, and—in relation to East
Anglia—the cloth industry. Undoubtedly, a number of foreign
workmen from the Netherlands responded to the royal pro-
clamation of 1338 inviting them to settle in England. Even
more important, there are records of master-craftsmen, like

John Kempe of Ghent, coming over with their servants and apprentices. But the surprising fact, which the tax returns make clear, is that their numbers were never sufficiently large to account for a highly developed cloth industry in the area by the close of the fourteenth century. Except at Norwich there is no evidence of a large group of foreign workers in any one of the cloth-making centres. For the most part, the Flemings who came over to settle were brewers, parchment-makers, coopers, shoemakers, brickmakers, carvers and hatters. Of the seventy-seven Flemings in Ipswich in 1485, for example, twenty-five were brewers, twenty shoemakers and twelve hatters.

Considering the difficulties they had to face, it is perhaps remarkable that these foreigners chose to stay in England. As aliens, they were, of course, excluded from the management of the town or borough in which they lived, and were obliged to pay heavy dues before pursuing their craft. At Lynn, every alien householder paid a special tax of sixteen pence a year, and every other alien sixpence, while at Norwich an alien was unable to bring a suit in the city courts against a citizen. The treatment they received varied. Sometimes, and in some places, they were tolerated; at other times and in other places they encountered hostility, or became objects of mockery and suspicion. The Flemings, with their uncouth manners, seem to have been singled out for special abuse:

> Thus are they hoggishe, and drynkyn wele ataunte.
> Farewel, Flemmynges, hay haro, hay avaunt!

With their inadequate knowledge of the language, and without protection, they were often the victims of local traders, and particularly of unscrupulous port officials, who were accused time and time again of impounding their goods and vessels until they were prepared to make some kind of a settlement. They always lived, too, under the threat of some fresh outbreak of violence which so often followed the news of ill-treatment of Englishmen abroad.

On the whole, though, the alien population along the East Coast probably fared no worse than foreigners overseas. Merchant families who acted as "hosts" for foreign merchants in this country, and who themselves traded overseas, knew the value of good relations. There is even evidence that the men of Lynn on one occasion tried to induce the aliens in the town to take up citizenship. Their motive is not clear. It may well have been no more than a temporary expedient to raise money. But for an honest alien craftsman, who was prepared to endure the indignities of his position while establishing himself in the community, foreign birth was not an insurmountable obstacle. The clearest proof of this lies in the career of John Asger, a merchant of Bruges, who settled in Norwich, and became its mayor in 1426. He did not achieve this honour by breaking off his foreign connections, and proving himself more English than the English, for he was in Bruges at the time of his election as mayor.

In England there was no social bar, as there was, for example, in France, to prevent members of the merchant class from rising very high. The de la Poles are a case in point. The architect of their fortunes was Sir William de la Pole, a Hull merchant, who by the lavish employment of his wealth in the service of Edward III, as well as by the skill and energy with which he conducted business for the King at home and abroad, gained influence at Court. The resentment of the older feudal nobility at the rise of the parvenu did not seriously affect the family's advance.

In a reverse direction, there are many instances to show that, in the pursuit of fortune, the nobility and gentry were very ready to take a share in some mercantile adventure, or even to embark upon an enterprise on their own account. There was clearly no binding tradition to bar them. Sir John Fastolf—whose name survives as Shakespeare's Sir John Falstaff, although the two characters had nothing else in common —is an instance of a gentleman lending money in usury, and he was also one of the biggest shipowners among the gentry. He used his own vessels to carry Caen stone from Normandy, and other materials while he was building Caister Castle, and to send agricultural produce from his estates to distant markets. A little later, the Pastons had a ship of their own at Yarmouth, and Sir Thomas Roos owned the *Julyan* of Blakeney, which came to grief while carrying cloth for merchants of the Hansa. Among the noblemen, the Earl of Oxford embarked upon the undoubtedly profitable business of carrying pilgrims to shrines overseas. This enterprise of the Earl's is largely known because of a disaster that befell one of his ships carrying pilgrims to the shrine of St. James of Compostella. No member of the aristocracy, however, knew better than the Duke of Suffolk how to exploit the economic possibilities of a position at Court. The full extent of his activities will never be known. But the prominence which his enemies gave to the matter suggests that the shipment by the Earl and his friends of wool upon which no duty was paid was on a scale to scandalize even that unprincipled age.

In their activities, legitimate and otherwise, the aristocracy worked closely with the merchants. The Duke and his associates were connected with the merchants of Ipswich and Lynn, while Lord Howard often sought the assistance of Richard Felaw, a merchant of Ipswich. From about 1440, too, it became increasingly common to find members of the leading families among the principle port officials. It is, of course, certain that they never performed the offices themselves. But the positions were lucrative, and the effect of their nomination must have been to draw still closer the ties between the aristocracy and the merchants.

There was nothing, either, to prevent the sons of old, and sometimes impoverished, landed families from marrying into the merchant families where the new money was to be found. "Marchandes or new jantylmen", for their part, as one of the Pastons observed, were ready to spend money on a lavish scale for the opportunity of allying with a family of distinction.

All this represented a tremendous revolution in the attitudes of the English upper classes by the close of the Middle Ages. But it would be a mistake to think that they accepted the merchants on terms of complete equality. They were ready to accept rich and successful London merchants and the leading East Anglican townsmen more or less as equals; they were willing to take a part in a lucrative enterprise or accept a East Anglian townsmen more or less as equals; they were even ready to make known their desire for a seat in parliament; and they did, of necessity, employ the merchants in their commercial affairs. But pride of class made them draw the line somewhere. The Pastons were outraged at the prospect, as one of them put it, of their sister "selling candle in Framlingham", and there are relatively few instances of county families going into business. The record of the Cloptons, who became clothiers, was exceptional, but even the Cloptons' business activities were not such as to interfere with their lives as country gentlemen. Thomas Botiller, too, had a brother who was a London draper, but for the most part families with trading connections were not in the first flight among the county families.

On this side of the North Sea a score of little ports along the east coast of England and Scotland carried on an active trade with the Continent. But most of them were unimportant by comparison with Ipswich, Yarmouth, Lynn and Boston. The pre-eminence of these four was largely assured by the importance of the regions which lay immediately behind them and their comparative nearness to the Continent. In the case of Ipswich, the development of the town was assisted by the practice of assembling merchant convoys at the mouth of the Orwell. Yarmouth was within easy reach of Norwich, and it seems reasonably certain that the Bure and Wensum carried a lot of traffic. Yarmouth would, undoubtedly, have handled much more business than it did but for the constant difficulties with its harbour. As it was, the largest and most active of the ports was Lynn. The town's great advantage lay in its easy access to a number of important inland markets, which could be reached by water from Lynn. The Ouse and the Nene, and their many tributaries, not only communicated with the prosperous regions of Cambridgeshire, Huntingdon and the Isle of Ely, but attracted the trade of the whole southern Midlands and even from regions further west. In particular, Lynn was the port of the great Stourbridge Fair, which in the Middle Ages attracted merchants from all over Europe.

The importance of the trade between this country and Holland and Zeeland is abundantly clear. Even at Lynn, where the Baltic trade was most highly developed, the cargoes moving to and from the Low Countries far outweighed the rest. The ships of Dordrecht, Bergen-op-Zoom, Kampen, Katwijk, Middelburg, Zierckzee, Brouwershaven and many smaller ports in the Low Countries figure prominently in the British records. And, by the close of the medieval period, British traders were not behind their foreign rivals in carrying cargoes to the Continent.

The commodities of Brabant and Zeeland, which found a market here, as the author of the *Libelle* says, and as the Customs Accounts confirm, were:

> Madre and woade, that dyers take on hande
> To dyen with, garleke and onyons
> And saltfysche als for husbond and comons.

And to this may be added earthenware, beer and hops. From the great manufacturing towns of Flanders came the fine cloth of Ypres and Courtrai, leather, hats, hose, utensils of metal and wood, bricks and tiles. But that was not all. In the great international ports of Bruges and Antwerp were to be met Italian merchants, Gascons, Basques and Spaniards with the more exotic wares of the Mediterranean and the Orient. Many products of Germany and lands further east found their way to Britain along this route—beer and bacon from Prussia,

Osmonde [fine Swedish iron], coppre, bowstaffes, stile and wax,
Peltreware, and grey, pych, terre, borde and flex,
And Coleyn [Cologne] threde, fustiane and canvase,
Carde, [and] bokeram . . .
Also Pruse mene maken her aventure
Of plate of sylvere, of wegges gode and sure
In grete plente, whiche they bringe and bye
Oute of the londes of Bealme [Bohemia] and Hungrye.

At the same time, western merchants were thrusting themselves with all the resourcefulness at their command into the
jealously guarded markets of Scandinavia and the Baltic. The
bid to break the stranglehold of the Hansa ultimately failed,
but at the opening of the fifteenth century the prospects of
success were bright. From a very early date there had been some
trading between Scotland and Germany, the Netherlands and
the Baltic. The east coast ports, such as Leith, Aberdeen and
Dundee and the numerous ancient and royal burghs along the
coast of Fife, such as East and West Anstruther, Kirkcaldy,
Burntisland, Crail and Dyart were all favourably placed to
participate, and figure from time to time in early trading accounts. By the thirteenth century there was a street in Bruges
called Scotland, and from the very end of the century a letter
from William Wallace, written during his brief moment of
triumph, has survived. It is addressed to the Senate and Commons of Lübeck and Hamburg, and tells them:

"We have been informed by trustworthy merchants of the
said Kingdom of Scotland that you on your behalf have been
friendly and helpful in council and deed in all things and enterprises concerning us and our merchants, though our own
merits do not occasion this. We are therefore the more be-
holden to you and wishing to prove our gratitude in a worthy
manner we ask you to make it known among your merchants
that they can now have a safe access with their merchandise
to all the harbours of the Kingdom of Scotland because the
Kingdom of Scotland has, thanks be to God, by war been recovered from the power of the English." A postscript asks the

City Fathers to further the business of two Scottish merchants mentioned.

By 1400, Scottish merchants were beginning to settle in Danzig as well, and by the end of the century they had established small settlements in almost all the cities on the coast of Prussia.

By comparison with the business carried on by the English merchants, the trade of the Scots was always small. Guicciardini, in his description of Antwerp, says that Scotland sent a great variety of sheep skins and the skins of various other small animals, especially martens, of fine quality, as well as large pearls, much inferior to those from the East. No great quantity of goods was sent from Antwerp to Scotland, partly because the people were poor, and partly because the markets were supplied from England and France. The chief exports were some spices, sugar, madder, silkstuffs, camlets, grograms and mohair, serges and mercery.

Writing in 1598, Fynes Moryson put the importance of Scotland's overseas trade with different areas in the following order: the Netherlands, Bordeaux, the Baltic and England. There can be no doubt that until the sixteenth century trade with the Netherlands out-distanced the rest. The coarse wools, which were Scotland's chief export, found a ready market in the cloth-making centres of Flanders and the Netherlands. Much of it was sent from Leith, but Perth and Inverness sent some, too. The importance of the market is attested by the establishment of a wool staple, after the model of the English wool staple at Calais. But, whereas the English Staple was a device for collecting duty on wool, the Scottish Staple, which was controlled by the Royal Burghs, was designed partly to give some protection to Scots traders, and partly to exclude interlopers. The scheme, had it been possible to implement it fully, would have given the Staple town a monopoly of Scottish trade, and in return the Royal Burghs were able to win valuable concessions from the towns where the Staple was set up. There was competition for the monopoly between Veere,

Middelburgh and (after the decline of Bruges) from Antwerp. It was, in fact, moved from time to time until 1541, when it was established in Veere (save for brief intervals) for two and a half centuries.

Scotland's commercial links with France, like its political links, were close, and, in return for cloths and skins, saltfish and wool, imported large quantities of wine, salt and a variety of miscellaneous luxury items. The Auld Alliance was politically expedient, but it appears to have brought little commercial advantage, and in the end was probably against Scotland's commercial interest. So that, in 1524, the Scottish envoy at the French court was moved to protest that since war with the English began Scottish traders had found themselves excluded from the markets of England, Flanders, Spain and other countries. "These realms," he complained, "were formerly allied with us or friendly; now, owing to our friendship, alliance and punctillious good faith with the French, we are suffering heavily. These many years past a very few of our merchantmen have succeeded in eluding the enemy ships and reaching France, the only country that professes to be friendly to us. Those who have recently braved the dangers of the sea and got through to France are being detained there an unusually long time. Our forbearance in the matter is too well known to make oral or written representations necessary: we have clearly before our minds how much we have endured for our friendship and alliance with France."

Scotland's Baltic trade, from which came her indispensable supplies of iron, pitch, tar, flax and hemp, flourished in the Middle Ages in spite of difficulties. Some of these difficulties were of the Scots' own making. For, although seamen of all nations were engaged in piracy on the North Sea, the Scots appear to have established the worst reputation in that particular area. So much so that, in 1412, the Diet of the Hansa Towns banned the import of Scottish wool and woollens, and, in 1415, when attacks continued, all trade was prohibited. The ban was not allowed to become a dead-letter until 1436. The

Above, Dutch herring busses, *c.* 1650; *below,* surrender of the *Royal Prince.* A victory for Tromp in 1666, from a sketch by Van de Velde

Two of Britain's busiest North Sea ports: *above*, Grimsby; *below*, Hull

English, too, showed considerable zeal in seeking to have the Scots excluded from the Baltic markets. In spite of that, the Baltic trade survived. The main ports for the trade were Leith, Dundee and Aberdeen, and by the middle of the sixteenth century the trade between Aberdeen and Danzig was greater than that between any other two ports in the area, although that between Dundee and Danzig was considerable. Perth and St. Andrews, too, had a considerable share, and Inverness is mentioned from time to time.

Our countrymen abroad often maintained themselves there in face of intense hostility from their rivals. In Bergen, for example, where the English had established themselves some years before, the English Staple was, on one occasion, deliberately set on fire and destroyed by their rivals.

A natural development of this rivalry in northern waters, and of the opening up of the Icelandic fisheries by the seamen of the East Coast ports, was the development of direct trading relations with Iceland. It is indeed very difficult to distinguish these fishing expeditions from trading ventures since the fishermen naturally took English commodities to exchange for the fish which the Icelanders had in abundance. But after the destruction of the Staple at Bergen had faced many of the old-established Lynn merchants with ruin, this direct link with Iceland took on all the characteristics of an organized trading venture. It was soon well enough organized for some of the Lynn traders to recognize themselves as the "merchants of Iceland", and elected two of their number to levy taxes in the same way as did the "merchants of Norway" and the "merchants of Prussia" in the town.

Trade with the southern regions of Europe and the Mediterranean at this period naturally had not the same importance for the merchants of the East Coast as it had for the traders of Southampton and the Cinque Ports. All the same, the men of Lynn and Ipswich frequented the ports of the Bay of Biscay for wine and salt, and the odd vessel occasionally made its way through the Strait of Gibraltar to the ports of the Mediterranean. The carrying of pilgrims to the shrine of St. James of Compostella in northern Spain was a subsidiary, but very profitable, enterprise. The traffic was still largely in the hands of the south-coast ports, but by the middle of the fifteenth century, shipowners from a number of east-coast towns, including Lynn, Yarmouth, Southwold, Ipswich, Woodbridge and Colchester, were taking a share.

The fortunes piled up by overseas trade were not won without strife and bloodshed, intrigue and corruption. Nor were the interests of all the merchants identical. At Lynn, for example, there was a sharp division between those who traded lawfully with Scandinavia and who sought to hold on to what they had, and those who wanted to take advantage of the illicit trade with Iceland, and who had nothing to fear from the threats of reprisals which bothered their fellow townsmen. The controversy at Lynn came to a head in 1426 when a decree by King Eric of Denmark was read before the Town Assembly forbidding all unauthorized voyages to Iceland. In the ensuing debate, which continued for several days, the conservative element prevailed, and voyages to Iceland were forbidden. The measure appears to have been effective for a time, for a vessel preparing for the Iceland voyage was put under arrest by the Mayor. In the following autumn a London boat put into Lynn on its return from northern waters. The captain appears to have poured scorn upon the townsmen for so readily abandoning the Icelandic venture. He was arrested after a complaint had been made to the Mayor that he had called the townsmen traitors, and he was released only after he had sworn on the Gospels that he had never used the word. The matter of the Icelandic trade was raised again in 1429 after the Hamburg pirate, Bartholomew Voet, had plundered Bergen. Once again the voice of the conservative element prevailed, but they were obliged to concede to the disappointed traders a share in the Bergen venture. At the same time, it is clear that some trading with Iceland continued, even from Lynn, because in the same year certain traders who had carried off, or purchased, a number of Icelandic boys and girls were compelled to restore them to their homes. The efforts of the town council were further frustrated by the practice of the Crown of licensing individual voyages while forbidding the trade in general.

An unbroken succession of cases that came before the Courts at home and overseas is evidence of the bitterness with which international trade was conducted. The quarrels with the Hanseatic merchants were particularly fierce and bloody, particularly towards the end of the medieval period, when the British were gradually being shut out of the Baltic, and competition for shrunken markets elsewhere became keener. But even in the Low Countries the mutually advantageous trade was periodically interrupted for political reasons or as a result of individual acts of violence and outbursts of xenophobia. The traders of Yarmouth, Cromer, Blakeney and Lynn all earned a bad name around the coasts of the North Sea. Sometimes, it seems, there were acts of collusion between some of them and the foreign pirates who preyed off the shores of East Anglia,[1] while the case of the sinking of the *Marie* of Haarlem suggested that East Anglian seamen had nothing to learn from Chaucer's "Shipman', who

> "If that he faught and hadde the hyer hond
> By water he sente hem hoom to every lond."

However, it was not only with the Dutch and the Hansa that East Anglian merchants found themselves at loggerheads, but with the London merchants as well. The friction became particularly acute towards the end of the fifteenth century, by which time the wealthier Londoners had abandoned the practice of making personal business trips to the Continent, and had installed representatives in the principal ports abroad. These merchants found it irksome when provincial traders

[1] This, at least, is suggested by the complaint of a London merchant that Dieppe pirates had sold wares pillaged from his ship to a group of Norwich merchants, among whom appears the name of one of the sheriffs.

arrived in the overseas markets with odd cargoes, which they proceeded to sell without waiting for the best prices, and in so doing spoiled the market for the established firms. These provincial merchants generally traded in person or sent their factors, and, in any case, preferred an immediate return on their outlay. Towards the end of the medieval period, too, there came into being a new type of ship-owner, who had no personal interest in the cargo he carried, and who, on arrival in a foreign port, desired only to discharge his ship as quickly as possible and return home.

To prevent this, and to assure their own interests, the London merchants sought to restrict the right of provincial merchants to trade abroad by the creation of a closed corporation, in much the same way as the Merchants of the Staple controlled the sale of wool. The matter came to a head in 1497, when an Act of Parliament lowered the entrance fees and ostensibly opened the Company of Merchant Adventurers to provincial merchants. But the new entrants were not admitted on the same footing as the existing members, nor could they introduce their sons and apprentices with the same facility. It was a concession which did a little to satisfy the provincial merchants who complained that their trade declined while that of London continued to increase.

During the sixteenth century the Merchant Adventurers in England established and maintained their right to a monopoly of all authorized trade, excepting wool, carried on by English subjects with the Low Countries and Germany. Even if it did not achieve all that it was meant to do, it was looked on benevolently by the Crown, which was always short of money, and which found in the dues collected abroad by the Company a useful supplement to the money granted by Parliament.

In spite of the claim of the Merchant Adventurers that they were "no Company of one city, town or borough, but a national corporation . . . dispersed all over the kingdom", and although they did, in fact, have branches in Lynn, Norwich and Ipswich as well as in a number of other ports, relations between London and the provincial centres was never easy. In some cases, local bodies had charters which conflicted with their position as members of the Company: in others, the almost universal practice among provincial merchants of engaging in retail trade brought them into conflict with the Company's rules. But much of the jealousy arose from a sense of inferiority. It could hardly be gainsaid when four London firms were between them doing as much business as all the merchants of York. In 1548 animosity in Newcastle towards London found expression in a prohibition against letting any house or cellar to a Londoner for the warehousing of goods. And some years later the merchants of Newcastle joined those of York and Hull in petitioning the Government on behalf of the merchants north of Trent who, they said, were being driven out of their own field by the London capitalists. While Elizabeth was on the throne, however, there was no likelihood that the position of the Company would be undermined.

Apart from other considerations the Company was the ideal instrument in the struggle against the merchants of Antwerp, against the Hansa and Philip of Spain. But, if the Company emerged with a fair measure of success, it did not emerge unscathed, and by the end of the sixteenth century interlopers had succeeded in entering some of the overseas markets which the Company claimed as its own. Indeed, there were even members of the Company who were to be found trading independently in European markets.

In 1604 the Report on Free Trade, drawn up by a Committee of the House of Commons, showed how far opinion in the country had moved against the Company. It would, however, be a mistake to see in this famous Report a victory for an economic theory: it was essentially an attack upon the merchants of London, who "monopolized the whole mass and bulk of the trade of England". The struggle between the Company and the "Free Traders" was long drawn out. But by the accession of Charles II individuals with capital and enterprise were knocking incessantly for a share in European trade. In 1673 trade with Sweden, Norway and Denmark was, in fact, thrown open, and in 1689 the fellowship was divested of most of its privileges.

4

THE CLOTH INDUSTRY
OF EAST ANGLIA

WHEN IPSWICH COMPILED its Domesday Book at the end of the thirteenth century cloth was already being shipped overseas from Maldon, Coggeshall, Sudbury and other places near the border between Suffolk and Essex. But the industry was much older than that. Colchester had already made a name for its cheap russets, while a number of places in Norfolk had begun to specialize in the manufacture of a lighter material of high quality, which later became known as worsted from one of the villages where it was produced. This fabric was in great demand for the summer clothing of religious orders, and large amounts were shipped abroad to the Knights Templar and the Knights of St. John. It found a ready market, too, at home and abroad for the furnishing of houses and churches.

It is impossible to say when the cloth industry began in East Anglia, but Jocelin of Brakelond, writing his *Chronicle* in the reign of King John tells how the cellarer of the Abbey of St. Edmund was accustomed to summon the fullers of Bury "that they should furnish cloth for his salt, otherwise he would prohibit them the use of the waters, and would seize the webs found there". Most certainly, then, by that time Bury was making cloth for the fair held in the town, at which London merchants were always important buyers, and where much foreign-made cloth was also sold.

The industry was thus well established before the arrival of the Flemings, who were invited to settle in England in 1336. But their arrival in the eastern counties was a stimulus, and in the latter part of the century the cloth industry made rapid strides at the expense of wool exports. The scale of this development can be measured at Hadleigh, where in 1312 two fullers are recorded as holding land. The surviving fragment of a list of inhabitants in 1381, which contains less than half the inhabitants of the town, mentions eleven cloth-workers, seven fullers, six weavers, five cutters and three dyers. This suggests that one in five of the men of Hadleigh were engaged in the industry. And it is likely that many others, listed as "artificers", were employed in some branch of the trade. East Anglia, by this time, was on the way to becoming one of the leading cloth-making areas in England and industrially the most important area along the whole North Sea coast. In 1356–8 the average output for Suffolk, Essex and Hertfordshire had been about 700 cloths: but by the mid-fifteenth century it was not less than 5,600. Whatever the reasons for the rise of the industry East Anglia was well placed to benefit. The local rivers and streams provided an abundance of clear water, and the farms an adequate supply of wool. The local merchants had easy access to the markets of London and to the East Coast ports. And the close settlement of the population in the cloth-making regions made it possible for the industry to flourish in the smallest villages without the inconvenient and expensive carriage of goods by pack-saddle and wagon.

The actual organization of the trade in the later Middle Ages is not clear. But whereas the industry had been largely confined in earlier days largely to the towns, it was now spread over the outlying villages where it was free from the restrictions of the town gilds. It is not certain how far the large capitalist cloth merchants, such as the Cloptons and the Springs, were responsible for this, but it is not unreasonable to suppose that without their direct aid and encouragement the newer centres could not have been built up.

As a result of these developments Bury slipped from its old position of pre-eminence, and by the middle of the fifteenth century ranked far below the newer centres, such as Hadleigh and Lavenham. In some of these villages there can scarcely have been a cottage without its spinning-wheel, or a street without its weaving shops, its fulling mills and dyeing vats. The clothiers' pack-horses delivering loads of wool and yarn, or collecting pieces of finished cloth were a very familiar sight in the lanes of Suffolk five hundred years ago, and the sight of the wagons taking the great bales of cloth up to London could have inspired any Suffolk man to write, as Thomas Deloney was later inspired, *Thomas of Reading, or the pleasant historie of the sixe worthy yeoman of the West.*

In Norfolk less broadcloth was produced than in Suffolk. This, however, was due to the fact that the clothiers of Norfolk found conditions there better suited to the manufacture of worsteds. Rather less is known about the worsted industry than about the manufacture of woollens. But, by the end of the fourteenth century, Norwich had established itself as the great manufacturing centre for this kind of cloth. This branch of the industry was not dependent upon ample supplies of water, and the principal centre became established to the north-west of Norwich, but worsted-making went on around Lynn and in a number of other places down to the Suffolk border.

There was no single pattern to the organization of the cloth industry. That is to be expected in an industry which had grown up haphazardly over many years with a minimum of official regulation and control. A good deal of the work was still in the hands of very small men, who owned a loom and one or two spindles and, more rarely, a dye-house. They bought their wool in the surrounding estates, and some of them appear to have made cloths on commission. The more substantial of them owned several looms, and (as their wills show) employed work-people drawn from outside their own families. But already by the close of the fifteenth century the trade was on the way to becoming an organized industry with the emergence of the capitalist clothier who bought the wool and passed it on, as it went through its various stages of preparation, to the spinners and carders, to the weavers, the fullers and dyers. By this outwork system some measure of specialization was possible on the part of the workers who worked in their own cottages, used their own tools and were paid by the clothiers as piece-workers. The part of such men as the clothiers was indispensable, for they alone had more than a local outlook, the facilities for seeking out the best market and the money to provide the long credits of six, nine, twelve and even fifteen months which the merchants demanded.

A particularly interesting feature about the cloth-making centres in eastern England was the way in which the industry was so nearly all-engrossing, dominating the lives, the interests and fortunes of those concerned. Even in the memorials and brasses which the clothiers and craftsmen left behind them the evidence of their trades is to be found. It included all sorts and conditions of people, from the young child who was set to sort the wool and the women who spun the yarn, up through the various stages of dyeing, weaving, fulling and shearing to the head of the household, or the clothier, who had the final disposal of the work. These regions had, therefore, a compactness which was stronger than other social ties. In part, this was due to the relatively large numbers of persons required for the operations of cloth-making—as many as sixteen to a length of cloth, Reyce says. And there was room, too, in the industry for people differing widely in status and wealth, but with the same common interests. For, at the close of the Middle Ages capital in this part of England had not become divorced from labour. The Springs, the Cloptons, the Martins, the Colmans, and others like them, were all local families and knew the problems of the industry as well as the people who carried out their orders. Of course, relations were not always good. There was Thomas Glene, of Norwich, for example, who "delivered his stuffe to poore folke to be wrought by a waight a great deal above the standard, deceyvyng the poore subjects". But for the most part, a community of interest fostered good relations.

In the older towns the traditional craft guilds survived. In Bury St. Edmunds no one was free to set up as a weaver until he had served an apprenticeship of seven years. "Foreigners" were restricted by a heavy admission fee, while outsiders who came into the town to collect yarn were made to contribute to the cost of the weavers' pageant. It is clear that the guild occupied much the same position in the government of the town as did the guild of merchants, the Trinity Guild, in Lynn. Within the guild itself, masters, apprentices and journeymen were all more or less of a class, a proved fraternity, though a poor one by modern standards. There was no marked division of social standards or way of life. Subject only to the general control of the town's administrators, the Guild represented the common interests of the members, managing its affairs, and fixing wages, prices and conditions of work. Outside the Guild there was, of course, a floating mass of unskilled labour, ill-paid and uncared-for. The Guild was not concerned with this human flotsam; no guild ever had been.

The migration of the cloth trade to the country was naturally unpopular with the guilds, who endeavoured to regulate the competition. The attempt failed, as it was bound to fail because of the inadequacy of the machinery of enforcement. But, as time went on there were signs, too, of the increasing influence of capitalists whose interests were not in line with those of the guildsmen. The future difficulties of the Guild at Bury are indicated by the ordinances against master weavers having more than four looms apiece, and against a group "having sufficient kunnyng and understanding in the occupateion and exersyse of the seyd craft and not being of power and havour to sette up looms". Division of opinion about restricting competition grew more marked. While the weavers were in favour of a rigid protectionist policy, the drapers and merchants, who bought and sold the cloths, wanted as much competition as possible. On the whole, the second group were the wealthiest and most influential people in the towns. On only two points was there unison—the need for restricting unregulated sales, and the need for maintaining the assizes of length, width and quality. It was a common ground for complaint on the part of the merchants that the cloths which they had bought in bulk were sometimes found to be faulty after they had been shipped overseas, and were thus liable to be confiscated.

Hand in hand with the development of the local cloth industry went the development of the local cloth markets. Sudbury, Colchester and Norwich all became, as they were long to remain, the great regional centres of the trade. This local business was also helped by the practice of the London merchants of sending their agents into Suffolk to bargain where they could for cloth.

There was nothing parochial, however, in the outlook of the bigger Suffolk clothiers, who sent much of their cloth directly by pack-horse and wagon to London, where Blackwell Hall was the celebrated market for all country-made cloth. Here it was sold to foreign merchants and trading companies, and thence found its way to "Esteland, Russia, Spaine, Barbary, France and Turkey, and other places". There was already in the fifteenth century a close relationship between the clothiers and the London merchants, some of whom were themselves Suffolk men. About this time, too, one of the biggest of the Suffolk cloth-merchants, John Tryklowe of Clare, was in partnership with a Spaniard for the shipment of cloth.

By the beginning of the sixteenth century, the East Anglian industries had become too dependent upon the foreign market for its own good, for the mere threat of an interruption to the Flanders trade was enough to frighten the clothiers. In March 1528 the Duke of Norfolk wrote to Cardinal Wolsey to tell him that he had called together forty of the most substantial clothiers from all over Suffolk to assure them that reports reaching England about merchants detained in Flanders and Spain were false and to urge them to keep their men at work. As his letter makes clear, he preferred to deal with forty clothiers than with three hundred women later demanding that their husbands be set to work. Probably because so much of the clothiers' capital was tied up in their manufactures, the industry was very sensitive to the state of trade. And, two months later, the Duke had to write to Wolsey again, this time asking him to bring pressure upon the London merchants who had refused to buy any cloth sent up from Suffolk, with the result that local workpeople would be without work within a fortnight.

The industry reached its highest point of development towards the middle of the sixteenth century, and thereafter steadily declined. How far Government regulations, forbidding the stretching of cloths beyond statutory limits, and requiring cloths to be dyed and finished before export, contributed to the decline of the old woollen cloth industry in East Anglia is a matter for debate. The regulation concerning dyeing and finishing, certainly, appears to have been disastrous so far as the Norfolk worsted industry was concerned, because the art was not so highly developed in England as on the Continent. But the Suffolk woollen cloth manufacturers had less to complain about. For, while most English cloth was exported unfinished and undyed, the reds and blues and greens of Suffolk were justly famous on the Continent. However, when in the year of the Armada, East Bergholt was asked to contribute towards the cost of a ship and pinnace to be provided locally, the village asked for relief urging "the decayed state of this poor corner, growing chiefly, if we be rightly informed, by restraint made by a statute prohibiting that no Suffolk cloths should be transported and not here dressed before they were embarked, thereby changing the accustomed gainful trade . . . with such cloths as were best saleable in Spain, and now through long want of vent into those parts we find the stocks and wealth of the inhabitants greatly decayed." Like many another petition, before and since, it cannot be taken as the literal truth. Many cloth-makers continued to find ways of circumventing the statute, and the Crown found a fresh source of income in issuing licences for the export of white, unfinished cloth. The code governing the stretching of cloths was in line with much earlier legislation requiring that cloths should bear official seals guaranteeing their length and width. The intention was entirely praiseworthy, but it did not prevent deceit, and the buyer's own judgment was the final guide. The regulation caused much outcry, and the Privy Council found it expedient later to allow some toleration in the stretching of some cloths for the Eastern market. Its immediate effect was to let in our trade rivals, the Dutch. As a contemporary said, "The excess of straining cannot be certainly limited by law, but must be left to the seller's or exporter's discretion . . . besides, if we should wholly prohibit the straining of cloth, the Dutch (as they often have done) would buy our unstrained cloth . . . strain it to six or seven yards per piece more in length, and make it look a little better to the eye, and after that carry it abroad to Turkey . . . and there beat us out of trade with our own weapons."

The attempt to force dressed and dyed English cloth upon the unwilling foreign market inevitably led to resistance and retaliation, and this finally broke the Suffolk cloth industry. And when that happened, the natural instinct, as elsewhere, was for the crafts and the representatives of different interests to draw themselves together to preserve what they had and to salvage what they could.

The restriction upon freedom to work and freedom to trade was carried to a national level, where exclusive and privileged corporations of merchants enjoyed a monopoly of trade with the regions covered by their charter. This monopoly brought the Eastland Company, which had acquired a monopoly of trade with Scandinavia and the Baltic, and handled quantities of Suffolk woollens into conflict with local interests. The Company had a branch in Ipswich, and some Ipswich members. But membership was not readily open to the local merchants, some of whom felt that they could do better on their own behalf if they were free to do so. This was brought out in the

1620s, when, at the prompting of the Crown, some members of the Company went down to Ipswich to buy cloth. The prices offered were rejected by the clothiers, although the Company insisted that these were £2 a cloth higher than they usually paid. The merchants, for their part, were inclined to think that their offer had been rejected in the hope of persuading the Privy Council to grant the clothiers a licence to export on their own account, which, if granted, they said would have an unsettling effect upon trade. In spite of their protected position, however, the number of cloths exported by the Company dropped from 3,340 in 1626 to 728 in 1627, and one leading clothier complained that he had not sold sixteen cloths in four years.

The reaction of some local clothiers and merchants, when unable to get what they considered fair prices, and when refused admission to the Company, was to resort to clandestine trade. One group, whose activities came to light when proceedings were taken against them, sent shipments of cloth from Aldeburgh and Lynn to Amsterdam and La Rochelle for transhipment to the Baltic, and received in exchange cargoes of hemp, potash and flax.

But such underhand devices did little to solve the problems of the industry, and the Eastland Company was but one of the monopolistic trading corporations. A few years later the men of Suffolk were moved to petition the Privy Council that they had £100,000 worth of cloth unsold at a time when the Merchant Adventurers sought to restrict their trade. "If the drapers become the sole chapmen," they complained, "they will compel the clothiers to sell at what price they please, and, being few in number, may easily combine to agree to do so."

While the old woollen industry foundered in a sea of difficulties, a new one grew up beside it. The making of "new draperies"—bays, says and perpetunias—was introduced by Dutch immigrants who settled in the cloth-making area along the Essex-Suffolk border in the reign of Elizabeth. The new

[79]

fabrics were much finer, and where the woollens demanded short, carded wool, the new draperies called for combed, long-fibred wool. While the makers of the old fabrics professed to despise these new flimsy textiles, they pleased everybody else. They were popular at home and abroad; a given quantity of wool provided work for four times as many people: and it utilized the long, coarse wools, which reached, and surpassed, the price that fine wool was fetching. For a century or more Suffolk prospered as a producer not only of cloth, but of yarn upon which the industry elsewhere depended.

The demand for these new fabrics revived the cottage industry. "All sorts of people," said a contemporary, "are masters of their trade and work for themselves. They buy and sell their materials that they work upon. So that by their merchandise and honest labour they live very well. These are served of their wool weekly by the wool-buyer, either merchant or other." Celia Fiennes, who was in East Anglia, in 1689 noted "the ordinary people both in Suffolk and Norfolk knitt much and spin, some with the rock [distaff] and fusse [spindle] as the French does, others at their wheels out in the streets and lanes as one passes." And, at Colchester, she noted "great quantetyes [of bays] are made here and sent in Bales to London . . . the whole town is employ'd in spinning, weaveing, washing, drying and dressing their Bayes, in which they seem very industrious."

By the latter half of the seventeenth century, however, the industry was beginning to feel the competition of the calicoes and silks which the East India Company was importing, and, in 1696, the saymakers petitioned Parliament to exclude Indian fabrics. From then on the decline of the Suffolk industry was rapid. When Daniel Defoe made a tour of the Eastern Counties in 1722, he found Sudbury very crowded and very poor. "They have a great manufacture of says and perpetunias and multitudes of poor people are employed in working them," he wrote. "But the number of the poor is almost ready to eat up the rich." Thirty years later, the industry was still being carried on in Sudbury, Hadleigh, Lavenham, Clare and Bildeston, but the anonymous traveller who wrote about it was struck by the poverty and squalour accompanying it.

The time was not far off when the machine would take over from the hand operative and the towns of the West Riding would make cheap woollens with which Suffolk could not compete. But the industry was a long time dying. For a long time the combing and spinning of yarn for use elsewhere continued. It was a poor substitute for the manufactures of more prosperous days. But when Arthur Young travelled through the county in 1804 he could still speak of the woollen industry as the most important industry of the county. There was still an industry of sorts in Sudbury and neighbouring villages until the 1840s, when the making of bunting at Sudbury was left as the sole reminder of something that had contributed so much to England's overseas trade. This, too, finally, became extinct in 1871.

5

THE KEEPING OF THE SEA

SOMEWHERE ABOUT THE year 1440 Margaret Paston wrote a letter to her husband to tell him that a band of Flemings had raided the Norfolk coast, and that in the fight which followed eight hundred of them had been killed. To this sensational piece of news she devoted just one sentence, and then reverted to the subject which was always nearest to her heart, the hope that business would not keep her husband too long away from home.

As it happened, the rumour she had heard was exaggerated, but she reported it in good faith. The interesting thing is that she dismisses in less than twenty words an incident that occurred within a mile or two of the family estates. It suggests that raids of this sort were so commonplace in the fifteenth century that it was not worth the writer's time to describe them at length.

A few years later, when Margaret Paston and her mother-in-law write again about disturbances along the coast, they do so at greater length. It is clear that they had become seriously alarmed, and their fears were shared by the whole region. There was clearly nothing that anybody could do locally to put an end to the bold effrontery of the enemy, who hovered off the Norfolk coast in ten great ships. One of the writers ends her letter, "God yeue grace that the see may be better kepte than it is now or ellys it chall ben a perlyous dwellyng be the see coast."

This contrasts strongly with the image of a fortress-island which Shakespeare puts into the mouth of the dying John of Gaunt in *King Richard the Second* :

> This precious stone set in a silver sea,
> Which serves it in the office of a wall,
> Or as a moat defensive to a house,
> Against the envy of less happier lands . . . .

The simple truth is that Shakespeare was misinformed, even if there was a passing phase of graver lawlessness around the exposed East Coast in the middle fifteenth century. The sea had never been a "moat defensive" before Shakespeare's day. Probably from the very time of the final separation of Britain from the Continent of Europe the North Sea had been an open highway over which seafarers had roamed at will. And the rich lands of Britain had a strong attraction for them. Already, three thousand years before the time when Margaret Paston was writing, the Beaker Folk of north-west Germany had descended in large numbers upon the East coast, and many years later they had been followed by Romans, Angles, Saxons and Danes.

As a general rule, the idea of intercepting the invader on the high sea was not understood, and would have been difficult to achieve. When the Romans had to take measures to protect the coast against marauders their response was to build a series of forts. The forts of the Saxon Shore, as they were called, were all built on the edge of sheltered harbours commanding important points of entry into Britain. Bradwell and Reculver stood on either side of the Thames Estuary; Bradwell and Walton protected the several estuaries by which the invader could have made his way to Colchester and St. Albans; Burgh Castle guarded the great shallow estuary which then existed to the north of it; Brancaster guarded the Wash. In the medieval period, only two kings, in rather special circumstances,

[83]

showed any understanding of naval strategy. The one was
Alfred, who assembled a fleet and used it effectively against
the lightly built craft of the Norsemen: the other was Harold,
who might have dealt a telling blow against the Normans, but
was obliged to disperse his fleet before he could use it.

There was no suggestion in the letters, which the Paston
women wrote, that the Royal Navy should be doing more to
protect the coast, because there was scarcely any navy worthy
of the name. Henry V, knowing that he would have need of
armed transports for his wars in France, had acquired some
ships of his own. But the bulk of the King's requirements were
met by the ships that the various ports were required to provide for the king's use for a specified number of days each year.
From time to time, too, this was supplemented by a general
arrest of shipping to meet a particular need. The arrangement
was unsatisfactory because the periods of service were short and
could only be prolonged by payments which the Crown could
not afford, and the ships supplied were often too small to be
of use. In any case, the idea of keeping a fleet constantly in
being was out of the question. Down in the Channel, the Crown
had struck a bargain which worked very well in the early
medieval period. By it, the men of the Cinque Ports, in return
for various privileges, were bound to engage the enemy whenever he should appear. Since nobody knew when these sporadic
raids would occur and an engagement involved only a brief
interruption of their ordinary occupations, the arrangement
suited both parties. It was not an arrangement that could be
easily introduced elsewhere.

The earliest sea battles of the North Sea are hardly worthy of
the name. Just as a fighting fleet was slow to come into being,
so naval tactics were slow to evolve. In the councils of war,
attention was focused upon the land campaign, to which any
action by the King's ships was ancillary. Perhaps, as a result,
the earliest engagements partake of the nature of land battles.
In the summer of 1213 the English fleet arrived off Damme,
which stood on an estuary leading up to Bruges, to find most

of the French fleet beached, and the remainder at anchor. The English cast anchor well out to sea, and sent the fighting men ashore in boats to destroy the enemy shipping. The Battle of Sluys in 1340, in which Edward III commanded the Fleet, was a much more famous occasion, but save that it was fought on the water, scarcely deserves to be called a sea battle, for the English and French ships were so tightly interlocked that the action might have been fought on land. The battle was won by the English knights and bowmen. Considering, however, that the only vessel was the unstable, unmanoeuvrable "round ship", which could only be sailed down-wind, and was unable to ram without sinking itself, things could not be otherwise.

Chaucer's Merchant in the *Canterbury Tales* was not alone in wishing that

> ". . . the see were kept for any thyng
> Bitwyxe Middelburg and Orewelle."

But the merchants could not rely upon the Crown to keep the sea-lanes across to the Low Countries clear. There were, therefore, three courses open to them. They could share their cargoes among several ships to lessen the risk that the whole would be lost: they could travel in convoy for mutual protection: and they could, and did, in exceptional circumstances, arrange privately for armed escort.

In spite of this, piracy remained a flourishing business in the North Sea throughout the Middle Ages. On occasions one of the Scottish Kings, or the Convention of the Royal Burghs, or even individual towns or private individuals fitted out an expedition against the pirates, particularly if they had suffered some hurt.

The Minister of Anstruther has left a spirited account of how his parishioners on one occasion revenged the wrongs they had suffered. Purchasing a commission, they rigged out a small boat, and "every man encouraging another, made almaist the haill honest and best men in all the town go in her to the sea." After an absence of ten days they were back with the story of their enterprise. In company with a great ship from St. Andrews, fitted out by the Burghs, they sailed close to the shore of Suffolk, and chanced to find "the loon, wha had newlins taken a crear [small trading vessel] of our awn toon, and was spulyin her. How soon they spy ane comin warlike, the loons leave the prize, and run their ship on land, our fly-boat after, and almaist was on land with them; yet, staying hard by, they delash their ordinances at the loons, and a number going on land, pursues and takes a half-dozen of them." At that point the local people, fearing an invasion, began to assemble. But the Scots were able to convince the local Justices of the Peace and were allowed to carry off their prize and their prisoners. Two of the Englishmen were afterwards hanged at Anstruther, and the rest at St. Andrews.

The commission to which this story refers resemble the "letters of marque" which the English relied upon so much, lacking other means to put down piracy. These letters authorized the private vessel to which they had been granted to seize any "enemy" ship that they might encounter. The letters of marque gave a small measure of protection to whoever held them. If the ship had the worst of an engagement this warrant should have proved that the vessel was not a pirate ship. And while the captain might expect to lose his ship, and whatever it was carrying, he could hope that he and his crew would not be hanged from the yard-arm as any ordinary pirate would be. Unfortunately, seamen were not always so juristically minded.

The arrangement was a thoroughly bad one, because the distinction between privateering and piracy was very fine. There was probably not a seafarer who had not got some wrong to redress, and the desire for revenge was usually greater than the desire to suppress lawlessness. A disturbing feature of the situation as it developed was that the North Sea pirates often received encouragement from the gentry and the leading burgesses of the towns, who were prepared to receive the stolen goods.

Nor were the seafarers satisfied with a single act of revenge. After John Leiper of Perth, one of Scotland's richest merchants, had been captured by the English, his son assembled a fleet of Scottish, Spanish and French vessels and roamed the seas looking for English ships. He caused havoc until he was himself finally captured by a fleet commanded by a London merchant.

Some skippers were able to make a profitable career out of such exploits. Andrew Wood and Andrew Barton of Leith sometimes commanded royal ships, and sometimes preferred "gratuitous service" against the English. Wood's ships, the *Flower* and the *Little Caravel*, figured in many episodes. He lived to become a laird, and built a fortified manorhouse with the labour of his English captives.

These skirmishes at sea were fought with incredible savagery. Bishop Leslie, in his *History of Scotland*, tells how Andrew Barton had captured many Dutch ships "and fillit certain pipis [barrels] wit the heidis of the Holanderis and send unto the King of Scotland", after complaints had been made to the Scottish court of ships captured and despoiled, crews murdered and merchants and passengers cast overboard.

Among the most daring and ruthless of the pirates who preyed upon the shipping in the North Sea were the men of Brittany, but the men of Dieppe and Honfleur had a very bad name. So much so that one fifteenth-century poet was moved to write:

> "And of this Bretayn, who so trewth levys,
> Are the gretteste rovers and the gretteste thevys.
> Thus they have been in dyverse costes manye
> Of oure Enland, mo than reherse can I,
> In Northfolke coostes and othere places aboute,
> And robbed and brente and slayne by many a routte."

One of these pirates, petit Jehan of Honfleur, was known and feared in his day on both sides of the North Sea, and has achieved the doubtful distinction of being one of the few marauders of the period whose name has passed into history.

The French and Bretons did not, however, have a monopoly of this business. Englishmen, Flemings, Dutchmen, Danes, Germans, Spaniards, and—as we have seen—the Scots were deeply involved. Even in the late sixteenth century parts of the coast were still infested. It was reported that the Island of Inchcolm in the Firth of Forth, nearly opposite to Edinburgh, had become a pirates' nest after the departure of the monks. Pirates swarmed along the coast of Fife and around every considerable Scottish port, so that the merchants of Dundee were moved to complain that they had been pillaged "gif thair war nother God in heavin nor we had King on earth to complene to."

Left largely to fend for themselves against the day-to-day risks of descents upon these shores from its own meagre and antiquated resources, the position of the English counties nearest to the North Sea would have been critical at any time during the later Middle Ages if put to a serious test. And the ease with which the invading forces of Henry Bolingbroke landed at Ravenspur is an indication that the coast was wide open to all comers. The Crown was never able to maintain a large enough standing army, ready at all times to go wherever danger threatened, and the nobility who, in those troubled times, were alone capable of putting a large body of retainers into the field, and of ensuring the active support of the local gentry, were often unable, for a variety of reasons, to give such support.

In the circumstances, the burden of providing for the defence of each region fell upon the local organizations, which from time immemorial had been charged with the obligation of assisting the Crown's officers in the execution of their police and military duties. The organization derived from the Saxon "fyrd", which imposed upon every able-bodied man the duty to take up arms in defence of the King. The Black Death, which depopulated whole regions, and the economic troubles of the later Middle Ages which caused many villeins to flee from their homes, dealt the system of tithings a mortal blow. By the fifteenth century the tithing was still useful for raising and following the hue and cry after a criminal, but was too slow and cumbersome to meet an invading army Too often, also, the high and petty constables upon whom much of the work of organization fell in the hundreds and townships were inept, or unwilling to assume the duties with which they were charged. There is a lot of evidence to show how far the village "Dogberries" fell below the standards of "respectability, integrity, activity, firmness, discretion, humanity, honesty, knowledge and ability" that they were expected to show.

To some extent, these deficiencies were compensated for by enthusiasm and numbers. In several places the village butts, where the men and youths practised their skill with the long-bow, can still be seen. A peasant force, moreover, with little more than pitchforks and hoes, could take a heavy toll of a small invading army, as the French were to learn in Spain during the Peninsular War.

One great source of trouble in the organization of local defence lay in the decline in the office of county sheriff. In the early Middle Ages, the sheriff had invariably been a great magnate with big resources of his own, and, at the call to arms, the local levies were useful auxiliaries. But by the fifteenth century matters were otherwise. The sheriffs were chosen mainly from the squirearchy, and had no comparable body of retainers of their own; their officers were few in number, and were more accustomed to making distraints and arrests than to military affairs. Moreover, although the sheriff continued to be the King's representative in the county, many important functions had slipped from his hands. The task of supervising the constables, of enforcing watch and ward, and of ensuring the maintenance of beacons was entrusted to the Justices of the Peace, while the important task of arraying the county—of inspecting the men in each township and comparing them with the lists which the constables kept, of deciding who should be trained and what costs each inhabitant should bear towards the cost of arming them—was entrusted to weighty Commissions of Array upon which the sheriff was far from being the most important member.

Of all the coast bordering upon the North Sea, the region from the Thames to the Wash was the most vulnerable. Along great stretches nothing had changed since the Romans had constructed the works to facilitate the defence of the Saxon Shore more than a thousand years earlier. And, indeed, it is difficult to see what could have been done short of setting up permanent military encampments. Few of the castles in the region were situated near the sea. Excepting Caister Castle, which was built primarily as a fortified dwelling-house, the only one was the ancient structure which for two centuries had dominated the marshes around the port of Orford. In the circumstances the Crown employed its meagre resources upon the three key points round the coast, the Orwell estuary, Yarmouth and Lynn. But Yarmouth was always a weak link in the chain. Its haven was badly silted, its walls crumbling, and its population depleted, so that the Crown was constantly having to make grants for the repair of the walls and harbour, and, in moments of danger, to appoint strong commissions to organize the defence of the town.

The configuration of East Anglia, with the impressive barriers of the Fens and Epping Forest to the west and south-west, made it particularly suitable for what a later generation would call defence in depth, and the strategically placed castles of Norwich, Framlingham, Clare and Castle Rising gave whatever party held them a considerable influence on the surrounding countryside. Some of the inland towns, too, had their part. The more important, including Norwich, Bury and Thetford, were walled and fortified, and watch and ward was rigidly enforced. The size of the towns and their corporate unity made them easier to organize, and they reacted quickly to danger, even while their loyalty could not be reckoned on. The news of the landing of Henry VI's wife, Queen Margaret, and of her whirlwind descent from the North, together with rumours of the atrocities committed by her men at Grantham, Stamford, Peterborough and Huntingdon, galvanized them into action. At Norwich, the night watch was redoubled, and certain of the city gates were locked and the guard at the others increased.

By this date, the practice of requiring a fixed number of days' service by ships from the ports which owed service was seen to be increasingly unsatisfactory. The Crown needed bigger ships and longer periods of service. The difficulty was to vary the conditions of age-old obligations without offering some promise or inducement in return. Periodically the Crown met its most pressing needs by ordering, to the annoyance of the merchants, a general arrest of shipping in the principal ports, or by obtaining promises from the leading nobility of seamen and men-at-arms. But the only satisfactory solution was to commute services for payment in cash. In 1401, the urgency of the situation led Henry IV to anticipate the action of Charles I and levy ship-money upon the inland towns as well as upon the coastal towns. By this mandate, Ipswich was instructed to provide one ballinger; Kirkley and Goseford another jointly; Norwich, Lynn and Yarmouth one barge each, and Blakeney and Cromer a barge between them. Even so, there were limits to what the Crown felt it could impose, and among the vast fleet of 1,400 ships that assembled at Southampton in 1415 for the Agincourt expedition a number were hired by the Crown in the Low Countries. Similarly, when a big fleet was required for the expedition of 1417, the King was obliged to hire nearly half of them overseas. In spite of the heavy demands made upon them there was less opposition than there had been to the lighter demands of other monarchs. Not only did the vigour and success of Henry V's campaign in France fire the imagination, but the needs of his army brought valuable contracts to the merchants. And those merchants whose business took them across the Narrow Seas from Ipswich to Flanders and Brabant had particular reason for gratitude at the King's decision to station four of the eleven ships which belonged to him personally in the Orwell Haven.

Probably the first man to have any true conception of naval strategy, and the importance of commanding the trade routes which ran down through the North Sea and Strait of Dover, was the anonymous author of the *Libelle of Englyshe Polycye*, generally thought to have been Adam Moleyns, Bishop of Chichester. He was writing at a bad time in England's naval affairs, when Henry V's ships had been sold off to pay his debts and expenditure on the navy had fallen to a little over £4 a year.

The world about which the author wrote was still a medieval one: the great voyages of discovery still lay in the future. England, as he saw the situation, had a double advantage. She grew the wool which Europe needed, and she could control the great artery of trade, if she could find the means to

". . . kepe thamyralte,
That we bee maysteres of the narowe see."

He had, however, no answer to the problem, and Moleyns could only deplore the conditions of the times which made the English a mockery.

6

THE RISE AND FALL OF THE
HANSA IN THE WEST

PARADOXICALLY, THE ESTABLISHMENT of the great League of
German commercial towns in the 1360s, which was to have a
profound effect upon the economic life of England and her
neighbours across the North Sea, was not in itself, another
vigorous step forward. Like many other associations, it was
created at a time when German trade and colonization had
ceased to expand, and it grew in political power with the need
to preserve what its members had won.

German trade with her western neighbours, however, long
antedated the establishment of the League. The merchants of
Cologne had established themselves in London by the beginning of the thirteenth century, with a guildhall of their own
and the right of admitting other German merchants on payment of a fee. It is possible, but not definitely proved, that
merchants of other German towns received royal permission
to establish their own Hansas in London. But, by the end of
the century, the Cologne Hansa had grown into the Hansa of
the Steelyard, which comprised all, or nearly all, the German
merchants in England. Along the North Sea Coast, it was, however, Lübeck and Hamburg that dominated German trade.
They were particularly strong in Lynn and Boston, but there
were also old-established settlements in York, Hull, Ipswich,
Norwich and Yarmouth. More than a century later the London

Steelyard was still seeking recognition of its right to exercise jurisdiction over all the other factories in England. Meanwhile, the English appear to have drawn no fine distinctions, and it was to the merchants of Germany as a whole that the Great Charter of 1303 gave valuable exemptions from Customs which put them in a more privileged position even than native merchants, and conferred upon them wide powers of self-government.

The Hanseatic merchants were no less successful elsewhere in winning privileges. At Bruges, the German establishment was less old than that in London, but in due course it became their principal centre in the West. It is likely that what attracted the Germans to Bruges in the first instance was the brisk trade with England in wool and other commodities. But before long the Germans in Bruges had branched out in many directions and had made Bruges a great centre of international trade.

In many towns of Norway and Sweden the Hansa had succeeded in gaining a footing. Their position in Bergen, the Staple town for the Icelandic trade and an important source of fish and oil, was to become particularly important, and later bitter struggles were fought with foreign merchants who tried to break their monopoly. In the Netherlands, too, the German merchants had built up a network of communications, designed in part, it would seem, to circumvent the more onerous tolls which had been established at points on the great waterways.

In this way, active associations of German traders grew up in the principal towns and ports on both sides of the North Sea long before the League came into being in the second half of the fourteenth century. Nor is it difficult to trace the steps by which the great German towns came to represent the interests of their merchants abroad, and how, as international difficulties grew, the towns themselves were drawn together into a political union under the lead of Lübeck.

The League at the height of its power wielded immense economic and political power. But from the outset there were fundamental differences in the interests of its members. The interests of Cologne lay primarily with England and the Low Countries, and when the interests of the League demanded action against the West the merchants of Cologne were apt to disregard the order. It was to the interest, too, of Lübeck and its neighbours to preserve the overland route between the Baltic and the North Sea upon which their fortunes had been built. And these interests were affected when the English and the Dutch began to use the route round the coast of Denmark to trade directly with Eastern Prussia. For their part, the Hanseatic merchants of Danzig preferred to trade directly with England and Flanders by sea. In this direct conflict of political and economic interests, the latter won.

The British challenge to the Hanseatic position began in the second half of the fourteenth century, even before the political organization of the League had taken its final form. It occurred, too, at a time when the Germans were beginning to fear foreign competition. In Scandinavia, which had for long been an economic backwater that the Hanseatic merchants had exploited to their profit, an attempt was being made, under Danish leadership, to awaken a sense of Scandinavian unity. In the West the Flemish cloth industry was being rapidly overtaken by the English, while both the Dutch and the English were showing activity in opening up new markets for themselves. The time was not far distant when Bruges, already handicapped by the silting up of her river connection with the North Sea, would no longer dictate the flow of goods from West to East.

It was the English penetration of the Baltic that gave the Hanseatic merchants most cause for anxiety. English merchants had frequented the great herring market of Skania —at the entrance to the Baltic—for some time, and the Hanseatic towns had taken measures against them, but the trade was fitful, and of minor importance compared with the position which the English had built up in East Prussia, where they formed an influential colony.

[95]

The trade with Prussia was of considerable importance to towns such as Lynn, Norwich, York and Hull, and they reacted to every move to exclude their merchants, but elsewhere, too, the exceptional trading privileges of the Hansa excited jealousy even while the benefits of the trading connection were recognized. It was not difficult, therefore, to gain support during the early years of the fifteenth century for the demand for reciprocal rights in German ports for British traders. The League, divided among itself, found the claims hard to counter, and on a number of occasions the English secured treaties recognizing their rights. Indeed, the Treaty of 1437 not only conceded the old rights of entry, trade and residence in Danzig, but also customs privileges as extensive as those enjoyed by the Hanseatics in England.

At this point it would have appeared that the struggle had been decided in favour of the English merchants. Yet before the end of the third quarter of the century the English had been shut out of the Baltic, and their settlements in Prussia and Scandinavia had either disappeared or been reduced to a shadow, while the Hanseatics returned to enjoy a greater share of the English cloth trade than they had had at any time before. The position which the English had attained in their trading relations with the Hansa by the Treaty of 1437 was not to be attained again before the time of the Tudors.

The years after 1437 were marked by the same clashes and disputes as during the years that had gone before. But, whereas every earlier clash had worked to England's ultimate advantage, later struggles went the other way. Our difficulties were probably due to a variety of reasons. The Wars of the Roses coincided with a long period of unstable government at home, and deprived the merchants of any hope they may have had of vigorous backing in their disputes. It coincided, too, with a period of bad relations with the House of Burgundy, with the result that the markets of Flanders, Zeeland and Brabant, which lay within their domain, were repeatedly closed to English trade. As a result, the English cloth merchants

The two faces of Lowestoft: *above,* the promenade and beach;
below, fish markets and Hamilton Dock

Above, Skegness at the turn of the century; *below,* Great Yarmouth: Scottish motor fishing vessels moored below the Town Hall in the hey-day of the herring trade during the early 1950

who could readily dispose of their cloth while the Burgundian Alliance endured, found it necessary to cherish the one outlet which the Hanseatic merchants offered. Even so, the Hanseatic challenge would have had less weight if Lübeck had not bestirred itself to unite the League and defeat the English economic challenge. If one event sparked this off, it was the capture of the Bay Fleet in 1449. In May 1449, the 110 Flemish, Dutch and Hanseatic ships which composed the Fleet, making the annual trip to the Bay of Bourgneuf in quest of its invaluable supplies of salt, were attacked and captured on their way home. To make matters worse, the English vessels engaged in the attack belonged to people close to the King's Council, while Lübeck, for its part, had no English property within its walls upon which it could distrain to compensate itself

The year 1449 was a great turning-point in Anglo-Hanseatic relations. Until this time a reason for retaining some semblance of good relationship with England had been the need to preserve intact the great Hanseatic trade route running from the Baltic, through the North Sea towards the Bay of Biscay and the Mediterranean, and for part of this journey the fleets were obliged to sail close to the shores of England. But now, by a single act of folly the English had made it clear that the Hanseatic ships were not free from molestation. Lübeck reacted by closing the Sound to English shipping. In 1458, by which time hostility might have been expected to have become less intense, the Bay Fleet was again attacked, this time by the Earl of Warwick on the pretext that the Hanseatic boats had refused to salute the English. And so things continued, as they always did in the Middle Ages, with no clear distinction between war and piracy, between commercial and political relations. In England, the conflicting parties continued to make use of the Hansa. Abroad, Lübeck failed to carry some of the more important of the League members with her in her hostility to England, and some English shipping still continued to get into the Baltic with their connivance.

In the North Sea, piracy degenerated into outright war which

D

reduced seafaring to a state of chaos, and gave the pirates who infested the area some excuse for their activities. It dragged on into the seventies, with fortune favouring now one side and now the other until the intervention of Flanders and France proved equally damaging to both the main protagonists. In the end, a strong fleet under John Howard, the future Duke of Norfolk, inflicted serious losses on Hanseatic shipping and restored the balance at sea in England's favour. But the final outcome had already been decided in favour of the Hansa. Edward IV returned to claim his throne in Hanseatic boats and under Hanseatic escort, and they, in return, received back in 1474 all the privileges they had ever enjoyed without having to concede any rights to Englishmen in the Baltic towns.

In 1475 the Hanseatic merchants returned to England. At Lynn, Boston and Hull their position was further guaranteed by the townsmen, and their claims, up £10,000, were secured against the Customs. Before long their export of cloths reached unprecedented heights, and they were secure in a position which they were to maintain until well into the Tudor period.

For the English there were no compensating advantages apart from the restoration of peace. Trade with Prussia and the Baltic had suffered a blow from which it did not speedily recover. In 1497, the first year for which the Sound toll records exist, not a single English boat passed through, while the Dutch were sending more boats through than any other nation. It did not kill British trade with the Continent, but for a time it had the effect of concentrating it through fewer channels

The reduction of the Hansards to a position of equality with other merchants in England did not come until early in the reign of Elizabeth. The action, when taken, is indicative of England's growing ability to get along without the Hansa, but is even more important as the beginning of a move to liberate English trade from the hands of privileged societies, whether English or foreign.

The League did not give up its claim to the restoration of

its ancient privileges without a struggle, and its obvious target was the Merchant Adventurers Company, which had a privileged position abroad. Pressure was brought upon Hamburg to curtail their rights. Retaliation and counter-retaliation followed, but in the end the Merchant Adventurers were compelled, in 1579, to move back to Emden, where they had been briefly established some time before. Even this did not satisfy the Hansards, who sought the total exclusion of the Company from Germany. The matter came to a head about 1595, after Elizabeth had declared a trade war on Spain, and after Hanseatic ships, which had continued to trade, had been seized. In 1597, an Imperial decree banished the Company from the territories of the Emperor. On this side of the North Sea the Lord Mayor of London was instructed to seize the Steelyard, and the home of Hansards became a naval storehouse.

Perhaps inevitably this was not the end of one party or the other. In 1603, with a new sovereign on the throne, the Hansards pressed once more for the restoration of their old privileges, but as the Venetian Ambassador observed, "the English, who are pushing their trade all over the world, insist upon open markets, and . . . succeeded in securing the rejection of the claim." The complaints which the League addressed to the Emperor in these years also show the extent to which the ban upon the English had failed. Then, quite suddenly, in 1611, Hamburg restored the Company's privileges and and a dispensation of the Imperial ban was made in favour of Hamburg. The Steelyard was restored to the Hansards and a long-drawn-out quarrel was patched up.

Time, however, was running against the Hanseatic League in its contest with the rising mercantile nations. In the late sixteenth century it had been shorn of many of its privileges in Scandinavia, and it had failed in its aim to control access to the Baltic. At home, too, political divisions and conflicting commercial aims within the Empire told against it. In 1629, Bremen, Hamburg and Lübeck were entrusted with safeguarding the interests of the League between them. In 1669, at what was to be the last general assembly of the League, an effort was made at revival. It failed, and the three cities were left to preserve what they could of the once powerful Union. The Bergen establishment survived until 1775. In London the connection lingered until 1852, and in Antwerp until 1863.

7

NORTH SEA SMUGGLERS

PARADOXICALLY, IT TOOK a royal decree to create the smuggler. For, while goods could be sent freely into and out of the country, there could be no smuggling. It was Edward I who, in search of new sources of revenue, imposed the first duty on wool, wool-fells and hides. The first smugglers, therefore, carried wool and hides out of the country. As the duty rose, as is the way with taxes, their activities became increasingly profitable. To begin with, duties were not widely applied. But, under Edward III, the French Wars were beginning to cost a great deal of money. Then, in addition to duties on wool and cloth exported, a duty of 3s 4d. on every tun of wine imported, and of 1s. in the £1 on all other goods, was imposed. This was the tunnage and poundage which a later Parliament was to refuse to Charles I.

To begin with, there was little to hinder the activities of those merchants who felt that the wool-duty was a gross imposition, and sought to evade paying it. The area which fell within each Customs district was impossibly large. The Yarmouth division, for example, stretched from Blakeney, on the Wash, to Woodbridge, near Ipswich. After attempting the impossible, the Crown contented itself with the revenues which came to it through the officers in the principal ports. Even when deputies were appointed in the lesser ports, avoidance was a simple matter. It was a long time before the Customs service added the duty of detecting illegal traffic to the job of collecting revenue.

Nor were the Customs officials themselves above corruption. Deputies in the smaller places were invariably local men, but all too often the chief officials in the major ports were themselves local merchants, whose private interests were directly opposed to their public duties. It was usually, however, only when these officials fell out among themselves that the Crown learned about the graft and corruption that went on. It was thus, in 1411, that the Crown came to hear about a case in Yarmouth, where the Searcher seized two lighters discharging a cargo of cloth from a Flemish vessel, only to have the matter taken out of his hands by the Customs Officer for Ipswich, and his brother-in-law, both of whom had an interest in the cargo. Another prominent burgess of Yarmouth, who was both a merchant and a Customs official, was Robert Pynnes. He got into trouble for converting uncustomed goods to his own use after seizing them in his official capacity. His malpractices were on such a scale that a royal commission of enquiry was appointed. There were limits even to official tolerance.

These positions in the port were clearly worth having, and whatever group was in power made use of the "spoils system" to reward faithful service. The lucky recipients of the principal posts never filled them in person, but passed them on to those they wished to favour. One of the most prominent of the Norfolk gentry, William Knyvet, of Buckenham Castle, was Customer of Ipswich between 1465 and 1468, having held a similar position in Boston between 1463 and 1464. The abuse was well known and, in due course, an order was made that officials should reside at their post, but it was difficult to enforce. In the reign of Edward VI an official at Lynn was allowed to appoint a deputy, "since he was in the service of Lady Elizabeth, the King's sister". Right down until the middle of the nineteenth century many posts continued to be filled by absentees, and many places bought and sold. There were endless intrigues for jobs. One of John Paston's correspondents wrote to him to ask that, if the Earl of Worcester should become Lord High Treasurer, Paston would use his influence to get the nomination of one of the Customs posts at Yarmouth.

> ". . . and I shuld so gyde me in the office as I truste shuld be most profit to my seyd Lord. And if youre maistirshyp lyked to gete graunt thereof, that than it plesyd you to lycense on[e] of your servaunts to take out the patent of the seyd office; and it cost v. or vi. or viii marke, I shal trewly contente it ageyn; and yeerly as longe as I myght have the offices, or any of hem, I shal geve my maister youre sone v. marke towards an haukeney [hackney]."

Feeling that the duties levied were a gross infringement of the liberty to trade, the medieval merchant had no moral scruples about avoiding paying a penny more than he was compelled to, and he often ran considerable risks in doing so. One Hull merchant was found to have gone to considerable trouble to conceal a small barrel of honey and two hundred oranges, the amount of duty on which was less than $2\frac{1}{2}$d.

The quantity of goods smuggled across the North Sea to Holland, Zeeland, Flanders and Brabant must have been very great from the start, and the first known English smuggler, Henry of Arderne, appears to have had East Anglian connections. He first appeared as an agent in the wool business in Flanders. The offences with which he was charged concerned the shipment of uncustomed wool, hidden in empty wine casks aboard the *Fynch* of Colchester and aboard an Italian vessel. He must have been smuggling on a very great scale since, after he had fled to the Low Countries, the Lord Treasurer thought it worth while pursuing the matter further, and he was brought home under escort.

In the matter of Customs-dodging the English had nothing to teach the traders from overseas, and particularly the Florentines who came to Lynn and Boston for their wool. In 1275 thirteen Florentine merchants were found guilty of shipping no less than 5,754 sacks of uncustomed wool. They readily paid the fine of £2,877—a very considerable amount at that time—and then were pardoned of the whole amount by the King. The activities of the Italians were notorious throughout the Middle Ages, but they were by no means alone. Even the members of the German Hansa, with their highly privileged trading position, were not above adding to their profits by avoiding Customs altogether. But the Dutch were soon to establish new standards of efficiency and cunning. They had acquired new skills in boat-handling and navigation in exploring the lesser waterways at home to avoid payment of tolls in the Sound and on the Rhine, and this they proceeded to put to use in exploiting the lesser ports and waterways along the East Anglian coast.

The amount of smuggling that went on will never be known. In the reign of Henry VII the Governor of the Merchant Adventurers reported that smuggled goods arrived in Antwerp on every tide. But the position was probably at its worst in the fifteenth century, when the authority of the central government was often at low ebb. In 1410 the Customs returns were only a quarter of what they had been twenty years earlier. And, an investigation made a few years later suggested that half the wool exported may have gone out of the country duty-free. The further from the capital, the greater the scope for smuggling, and traders all over the country were ready to take advantage of this. Among one cargo of fifty thousand uncustomed wool-fells shipped out of Lynn, for example, were consignments from London, Nottingham and York. Control was particularly difficult in places like Berwick, which could make some claim to exemption from regulations made at Westminster.

Vessels engaged in the coasting trade offered the smugglers much scope. The Government was well aware, of course, that such vessels could easily slip across the North Sea with a prohibited cargo. And so merchants were compelled to enter into bonds, which were only released on production of a certificate that the goods shipped had been landed in an English port.

It did not, however, rule out the possibility of collusion between the merchants and the Customs men whereby only a fraction of the cargo was covered by the bond, so that the merchant could dispose of the remainder as he wished. In the reign of Elizabeth I, when the export of corn and dairy produce was often prohibited because of scarcity at home, the port of Lynn became notorious for its corruption. It could hardly be otherwise when the senior Customs official was both one of the most corrupt men to enter the service, and also the brother-in-law of Sir Francis Walsingham, the Queen's Secretary-of-State. He could do what he liked with impunity. Inevitably, the whole Customs service at Lynn became rotten. For a consideration, a merchant's estimate of his cargo was allowed to pass unchecked; for a fee of £3 an uncustomed cargo was allowed to leave the port. Still worse, a junior Customs official borrowed the seal of the port, and had a copy made by a goldsmith in the town. From then on he was able to sell blank receipts and Customs clearance certificates, which were indistinguishable from the genuine ones. Over a dozen years or so the exploits of the Lynn officials must have cost the Exchequer thousands of pounds. The surprising thing is that the penalties were so light when they were found out.

Apart from wine, nearly all the goods that were smuggled, until the time of Elizabeth I, were goods sent out without payment of Customs duty or in defiance of prohibition orders. From that time onwards illicit imports bulk much more largely. The country was becoming wealthier and the demand grew for expensive luxury articles from abroad, for silks, satins and velvets and cloth of gold and precious stones and the like. On all these things the duty was heavy. Then, too, there were items on which there was no duty, but which were utterly prohibited—things that were hard to find in post-Reformation England, such as Catholic service-books and devotional literature, holy oil and vestments, not to mention priests of the Church of Rome themselves. In the next century, tobacco, tea and brandy became standard articles of contraband, and the demand for cheap supplies opened sources of supply. It brought into being a new type of smuggler who had little in common with the earlier trader-smuggler. James I gave the enterprise a fresh impetus with the new book of tariffs published in 1604, which raised existing duties to a more realistic level in relation to the value of money, and imposed heavy duties on a range of new luxury goods. The King's right to levy duties at will was challenged in the Courts, and although the merchant lost his case it became a patriotic duty as well as an agreeable one to avoid the imposts.

Each successive rise in the level of import duties made the smugglers' trade more profitable, and so long as every class gave tacit approval to what they did by buying their goods, they could not fail to prosper. Even so stalwart a champion of the Establishment as Samuel Pepys could not resist the temptation to buy cloves and nutmegs when he learned that there were some to be had.

Lacking public support, the preventive service had an impossible task, and they often did their duty at the risk of their lives. At Ipswich, in 1592, a too-inquisitive Customs man was thrown overboard. He was probably luckier than some fellow Customs men further along the coast, who went out to inspect a ship and were carried off to Holland, after which they were never heard of again.

Smuggling was becoming a dangerous game in which lawless and desperate men were prepared to play for high stakes. The rewards of success were certainly very big. Of one Dutch captain it was said that he had started life as a deck-hand, and later owned a fleet of ships that landed half a million pounds of tea a year along the East Coast. While there was always scope for the individual boatman running the odd cargo across the North Sea, the industry became more highly organized, with both the money to buy the help that was needed and the facilities to stay one jump ahead of the preventive services. Groups that had all the appearances of regular trading associations, with their headquarters in Dunkirk, Calais, Ostend and Flushing, sprang up. They were not content to venture small cargoes in fishing-smacks, but employed vessels of 100 to 200 tons, which were a match for any vessel that might try to interfere. As time went on, the vessels were specially built for the job, and a type was developed which was shallow in draught so that it could be run up on to the beaches, and fast enough to out-sail the revenue boats. In the later seventeenth century the development of the fore-and-aft rigged boat was a particular boon to the smugglers, since it enabled them to manœuvre in the confined waters of a creek in almost any wind. By the beginning of the eighteenth century the associations on the other side of the North Sea were running something like a regular service across the water. Nor did they lack for crews. The policy of successive administrations of allowing the Navy to fall into decay meant that there were always plenty of hungry sailors around looking for a job. The associations, too, produced their subsidiary industries. One such, in Rotterdam, Flushing and Dunkirk, was the manufacture of oil-skin bags in which tea was transported.

The wiles of the smuggler were endless, and often became known only to the authorities when one of them suffered twinges of conscience and decided to abandon the trade. One favourite device was to meet the colliers on the high sea, and to transfer the contraband to them. The boats from Tyneside were never searched, and one reformed smuggler said that he had found the system infallible. The boats that brought over onions and apples often carried much else concealed. This was rather more risky, and only English boats were employed. It was said that the foreigners were "too timorous", but it is more likely that they lacked a sufficient knowledge of the language to talk their way out of a tight corner.

From 1604 until 1671 the Customs were farmed out. By this a succession of syndicates paid the King an agreed sum for the right to collect what they could in Customs revenue. In 1671, when the Customs reverted to Crown, it became once more a matter of direct concern to the Crown to get as much revenue as it could. One step that it took was to provide the Customs men with their own cutters to supplement the "land-waiters" and informers who worked on shore. They were a valuable addition, but there were never enough of them. One boat, for example, patrolled the whole area from Flamborough Head to the Wash, and its movements were well known along the coast.

North of the Border, the regulation of imports and exports was the affair of the Scottish Crown. Duties immediately before the Union were appreciably lower than in England, but in spite of that smuggling was rampant and efforts at control feeble. It provided another ground for looking at the proposed Union with some foreboding, because, from May 1, 1707, the Scots would pay the same duties as the English. The Scots were not slow, however, to see an immediate advantage, and, in anticipation of the Union, laid in stocks of dutiable goods enough to fill forty ships, which they unloaded on the London market when it was lawful to do so.

The eighteenth century was the hey-day of the smuggler's trade, with tea, tobacco, brandy and silk the articles most frequently smuggled. It has been said, with much truth, that England became a nation of tea-drinkers on smuggled tea. It is impossible to say how much was smuggled across the North Sea during this period. In 1723, over 100,000 lbs. of tea was seized, but this must have been only a tiny fraction of the amount brought in. The bulk of it came across the North Sea from one of the ports in the Low Countries, or from Dunkirk. It was a situation that satisfied nearly everyone, except the Government and the sprinkling of "fair" dealers. The Dutch, who got their tea very cheaply from the East Indies, were making a very good profit indeed in selling the inferior grades to the English at 2s. a pound. In England it changed hands at 4s. 6d. a pound, with the better grades costing proportionately more. The retailers added their own profit, but were still able to sell it at a price only a little above the 4s. 9d. a pound that should have gone to the Government in duty. It was a sad day for the smuggler when, in 1745, the Government cut the duty to a

little over 1s. a pound, for the English smuggler was already
feeling the pinch of competition from the Dutch and Swedes,
who were undercutting him.

Brandy and gin, like tea, were usually run ashore on a lonely
beach, while tobacco and silk came in mainly through the
ports. The trade in brandy was largely in the hands of the
French, some of whom hovered all summer off the coast
between Yarmouth and Newcastle. One Calais firm had a
fleet of ten ships which between them could carry four thousand
casks of brandy, but it is not possible to say how often during
a season they disposed of their cargoes. The French were particularly keen to do business with the crews of the colliers on
the high seas, but on at least one occasion sailed into the Tyne
and Humber looking for customers. It was against this kind
of trade that the Hovering Acts were passed. But it would have
been surprising if the brandy smugglers had not found an
answer. One favourite device was to furnish a ship with false
clearance papers from its home port to Bergen. It was a piece
of make-believe that fooled nobody, because Norway imposed
a heavy duty on spirits. But it made it difficult to seize a ship
under the Hovering Act. On one occasion at least, the collector
at Bridlington, tiring of the game, put two of his staff aboard
a ship to ensure that the cargo actually went to Bergen. After
long delays, during which attempts were made to buy off the
Customs men, the ship eventually went to Bergen, where the
cargo was re-assigned to Ireland. We are not told what happened to the Bridlington men.

While the greater part of the population regarded the
smuggler as a public benefactor, the Customs men had an impossible task to perform. The surprising thing is not that some
were found to have their price, and that many more yielded to
menaces, but that so many did their duty to the best of their
ability. The risks they ran were often great. In 1727, for
example, one officer was captured by smugglers near Snape,
and had his nose cut off. In 1741 another was murdered, for
which the killer was later hanged. This was very unusual, for it

was about as difficult at that time to get a conviction against a smuggler in Suffolk as it later became to get a conviction in the Southern States of America for an assault on a negro. Very often, when the revenue men got news of a landing, and were set to make an arrest, the crowds of supporters were so great that they could do nothing but look on. On one night in 1720, when six vessels ran their cargoes up on to Aldeburgh beach, there were no fewer than three hundred people waiting to help in distributing the cargoes of spirits and tea.

The eighteenth-century smuggler is generally treated as a sympathetic character in literature, unlike the modern black marketeer or drug smuggler, although they have all been inspired by a desire for unlawful gain. Perhaps the bootlegger in the days of American prohibition comes nearest to being a counterpart, probably because both were providing something which the public felt the Government was unjustly withholding. There can be no doubt that the smugglers along the East Coast enjoyed an immense amount of support. In 1734 the Member of Parliament for Appleby, who had recently been down into Suffolk, told the House that "all the young, clever fellows in Suffolk are employed by smugglers, and have half-a-crown a day while waiting; and when on horseback, going about the country to dispose of the goods, they have a guinea a day and are well entertained. The gangs are forty to fifty strong and so well horsed that the dragoons cannot catch them." Since none of them could have hoped to have earned more than eighteenpence a day as a farm labourer, the smugglers were never short of helpers. So confident were the smugglers of their position that they did not seek to hide their identity. A complaint from Ipswich alleged that they were "very numerous and so insolent in the town and country that they bid defiance to the officers and threaten their lives." Somewhat later, a member of one of the gangs inserted an advertisement in the *Ipswich Journal* in which he begged "to acquaint his friends and the public in general that he [had], some time back, declined the branch of Smuggling, and returns thanks for all past favours." He goes on to advertise a Cart "fit for a malster, ashman, or a smuggler—it will carry 80 half-ankers or tubs; one small ditto that will carry 40 tubs; also two very good wooden Saddles, three Pads, Straps, Bridles, Girth, Horse-cloth, Corn-bin, a very good Vault, and many articles that are very useful to a Smuggler."

There was no lack of unpaid—although not unrewarded—support. Even the parson of Rishangles appears to have allowed the base of his pulpit to be used on occasion for the concealment of part of a cargo. There was also the landlady of the Crown at Snape—and she had counterparts in many other villages along the coast—whose job it was to see that the dragoons stationed with her were suitably befuddled whenever a landing was to be made, and who put a light in the dormer window overlooking the marshes when the coast was clear. There was the man who watched the movements of the local revenue officer, and the old shepherd who, when required, walked his sheep at all kinds of unlikely hours along the route that the gang had taken to obliterate the ruts made by the wheels. The gangs could rely on the tacit co-operation of more important residents. A farmer, hearing noises in his yard, and the opening of stable doors, knew from experience that it was better to turn over and go to sleep again. In the morning his horses would be back where they belonged, with perhaps a barrel of brandy to compensate for the disturbance. It not infrequently happened that the cargoes were hidden about the farms until the gangs could dispose of them. Nor did the farmers mind while they were kept supplied with brandy, raisins and tea. Generally, though, it was only if the revenue men were making a search that the contraband stayed long where it had been landed, and then it was hastily moved from one improbable hiding-place to another. At other times, it was hastened on its way to Norwich or London.

The Board of Customs and Excise did what it could to make the lives of its riding-officers bearable. It provided for their welfare if they were sick or wounded; it paid an annuity of £10 to any seamen in a revenue cutter who lost a limb; and the provision for dependents of men killed on duty was more than for the armed services. But, for all that, it was considered a career suitable only for a single man. Surprisingly, the service did not lack recruits, and it must be supposed that the pickings from the job more than compensated for the risks run.

In some respects, the revenue men got less help than they might reasonably have expected from the Government. Until nearly the end of the eighteenth century, if a revenue-officer killed a smuggler in a struggle, or if he made a disputed seizure, he had to provide his own defence and take his chance at law, knowing that if it were a jury case he would find little sympathy. Accordingly, even the most conscientious officer was discouraged from taking risks. By law, any vessel found smuggling should have been burned on the shore and its cargo confiscated. In practice, the officers took the cargo, or perhaps a part of it, and allowed the boat to go.

In theory, too, the Customs could call upon the army and navy for help. There were small detachments of foot soldiers in many of the coastal towns and villages, perhaps with this purpose in view. But the duty was not an agreeable one and they were of comparatively little use. Nor were the vessels of the Royal Navy nearly as effective as the revenue cutters in making interceptions. The attitude of Captain Chamier was perhaps typical of others. While cruising between Yarmouth and Orfordness, he chanced to intercept a smuggler in bad weather. The smuggler took the opportunity offered by a squall to break away, and ran up on to the beach at Lowestoft, where he saved his cargo at the cost of his boat and two lives. Chamier remarks, "I took the liberty of going to bed again and allowing my friend to make the best use he could of his local knowledge." The outbreak of war always led to an upsurge in the amount of smuggling. And it was always at such times that the ships of the Royal Navy were drawn away from the North Sea coast to the strategically more important Channel area. On one occasion at least—in 1745, when a French invasion was feared—the revenue cutters were withdrawn, too, from the East Anglian coast to serve as tenders to the main elements of the Fleet stationed at the Nore. In the course of six months it was estimated that more than 4,500 horseloads were run in Suffolk alone. The authorities, at their wit's end what to do, could think of nothing better than the formation of an association of local people who would undertake to buy nothing from the smugglers "without real necessity".

The enterprise was badly affected in 1784, when Pitt slashed the tax on tea and reduced the duties on many articles imported from, or exported to, France, including French wines. From then onwards tea was not worth smuggling. The Prime Minister, however, resisted pressure to reduce the tax on tobacco, which was still smuggled in great quantities. But tobacco was easier to control since it was usually smuggled into the ports and not run on to the beaches, and new port regulations introduced at this time made it much more difficult to avoid payment of Customs.

The long war with Revolutionary France gave fresh impetus to smuggling all along the East Coast. At times, between forty and fifty vessels a week entered the port of Flushing. And much the same was true at Ostend, Dunkirk and Calais. It was a dangerous game, for the crews were suspected, with some truth, of passing useful military information to the French. They were, therefore, liable to be treated as traitors if caught. But, as the crews soon found, a foreign flag and a false set of ship's papers were to be had in any Continental port, and it became the practice to enrol a foreign seaman to pose as master of the ship if need arose. And so the smugglers continued to flourish, shipping brandy and gin, and carrying émigré families and traitors, and finding a ready welcome from our enemies, the French, provided they came with a sufficient supply of golden guineas to pay for what they took away. The Continental Blockade, which Napoleon imposed to shut the ports of the Continent to British goods, did not put an end to the smugglers' trade, but it made it more difficult. It was, therefore, with relief that the gangs greeted the end of the war. It not only reopened the ports across the North Sea, but in an instant made available thousands of men on both sides of the water who were ready tools of the smugglers. The high level of war-time duties, which were still maintained, made the risks worth while.

To meet the situation, a coast blockade was established in 1818, firstly in Kent and Sussex, and afterwards along the East Coast. It called for the establishment of a chain of posts within hailing distance of each other. In Suffolk a number of disused martello towers were handed over for the purpose. A year later the Navy was asked to provide ships and men to supplement the Revenue cutters. It was expected that the new system would be efficient enough to pay its way, but here the authorities were disappointed. Seizures were almost negligible in amount. It is difficult to avoid the conclusion that there must have been widespread collusion, and it would not really be surprising if this were so, for the share which the preventive men got of any seizure was trivial in the extreme. The Government showed an ignorance of human nature, too, in the arrangements for manning the posts. At first, it was proposed to employ only Navy men, who it was thought would be less subject to intimidation and bribery than local civilians. But, in practice, the hardships entailed in such an existence made it impossible to recruit them, and civilians had to take their place. Predictably, they were unsatisfactory, and so it was that, in 1829, a joint naval and civilian force under the name of the Coastguard was formed. Two years later, control was transferred from the Customs to the Admiralty, and the service became much more of a naval, and much less of a revenue protection, force.

Within about a decade the forces of law and order had gained the upper hand, in the only possibly effective way, by proving to the gangs that the risk of capture and punishment was too high. The authorities were to some extent aided by public opinion, which no longer regarded the smuggler as a public benefactor. Smuggling did continue, and has continued, but the days when the gangs ruled the beaches were over.

The one article that continued to be smuggled into England in large quantities well into Victoria's reign was tobacco, and in every port of any size from the Baltic to the Channel firms were busy packing tobacco for the express purpose that it should be smuggled into England. The difference in the duty made the enterprise very profitable. But the smugglers were usually careful to vary their methods, and pick up their supplies from a number of ports, to lessen the risk of detection by our consuls abroad. A great deal of the tobacco came into the provincial ports, particularly on the North-east coast, to which it was carried by the colliers returning in ballast from the Continent.

The latter half of the nineteenth century and the years leading up to the First World War saw smuggling reduced to its lowest level for a very long time. There were several contributory reasons. Tariffs were low, and the country produced an abundance of cheap goods; the Customs had been reformed and offered a worth-while career; and the Service obtained valuable reinforcement from the police in the counties bordering the sea. Smuggling was very far from dead, but as a means of livelihood most old-fashioned smugglers found it no longer worth the risk.

8

THE FISHING INDUSTRY

IT USED TO be said of Amsterdam that it was built on herring-bones. The same thing could be said with equal truth of a score of other places around the shores of the North Sea. Many towns were important centres of the herring-trade long before Amsterdam rose to prominence. As early as the great days of Imperial Rome Roman merchants in Utrecht had conducted an active business in fish between the Rhine delta and the southern provinces of the Empire. And, certainly, the fisheries were a great deal older than that, although they have left no record.

The importance of the herring in the early history of East Anglia is symbolized not only by the fishes appearing on the corporation seal of Yarmouth and Dunwich, but also by the tokens that were at one time issued by Lowestoft and South-wold. At Yarmouth the autumn fishing season was important enough to attract the men of the Cinque Ports, and until the eighteenth century, when the privilege was extinguished, the Barons of the Ports enjoyed the right of holding a fair on the sea-shore there between Michaelmas and Martinmas. The herring figures also in a number of local agreements. At the time of Domesday, Dunwich paid, and had long paid, sixty thousand herrings annually to the King, while Beccles paid a rent of a similar number of herrings to the Abbey of Bury St. Edmunds.

The Mayor and sheriffs of Norwich, too, held land outside Norwich for the peppercorn rent of providing the king, wherever he might be, with twenty-four pies "containing a hundred herring, by the great hundred, in good standing pastry and well-seasoned". That this was not just an empty gesture was shown in 1629, when the city received a complaint about the quality of the pies sent.

The importance of the herring in the medieval diet, and the elaborate preparations at the approach of the autumn fishing season is illustrated time and again in the records of private households. In one season an East Anglian nobleman laid in 150,000 herring, apart from nearly 8,000 salt-fish, and over 1,500 cod and ling. And the Pastons—an ordinary country gentleman's family—would place an order for between five and six thousand herring.

An industry of this sort, calling for little outlay of capital, flourished all along the coast. But the pre-eminent position in the herring fisheries was long disputed between Yarmouth and Lowestoft, and between them the greatest rivalry existed. The fair gave Yarmouth some initial advantages, but these tended to be nullified by the constant brawls between the burgesses of the town and the officials of the Cinque Ports who had the management of the fair, and among the fishermen who attended it. Yarmouth, too, had constant trouble with the silting of its river estuary.

In spite of their equal opportunities, the English fishermen and traders showed a great deal less enterprise than did their European rivals. By the thirteenth century vessels from France, Flanders and Holland had begun fishing off the English coast, and so began the long series of struggles between local and foreign fishermen over territorial rights. By the latter part of the fourteenth century Holland's herring fleet in the North Sea had expanded still further as a result of favourable circumstances. The origin of the story that at about this time the herring deserted the Baltic for new feeding-grounds in the North Sea is obscure, and so it is difficult to gauge its accuracy.

But it seems clear that the North Sea herring fisheries assumed a greater importance, and that the Dutch were the people who profited most.

By 1410 they had developed the "buss", a large vessel carry-ing ten or more men, in which they sought out the best fishing grounds, and took in catches at which their English rivals could only marvel. According to Philip de Mezières, they were already using special boats for gutting and packing the herring, so that the fishermen could stay for the whole season on the fishing grounds. It was an efficient arrangement, which our fishermen had still not learned 250 years later when they were sailing the width of the Atlantic from Newfoundland with a single catch of cod!

Even earlier, a Dutchman, Beukelzoon, had perfected a method of gutting, salting and packing the herring, which for years to come earned him the gratitude of the nation. The idea of preserving fish by salting was, of course, not new. At the time of the Domesday Book, salt-pans in which sea-water was evaporated existed along the East Anglian coast and elsewhere. And the early trade with Sweden in herrings was only possible by packing the herrings in salt. But the salt so obtained was not perfect for preserving, and British fishermen were slow indeed to rival the art of the Dutch in producing the fine white pickled herring.

Because of their great skill in this art the Dutch were never able to catch enough to meet the demand, and Dutch fisher-men and merchants eagerly sought supplies wherever they could find them. In 1394 Richard II was moved to direct the magistrates of Whitby to prohibit strangers from carrying away supplies of herrings, because purchases along the coast of York-shire in previous years had led to shortages. It was but one among many similiar ordinances made to ensure supplies and control prices. The frequency, however, with which such orders were made suggests that they were not very effec-tive.

The English adopted a somewhat ambivalent attitude

towards the presence of foreign fishermen off the coast. On the one side there was suspicion that they were taking something that was rightfully ours, and there was a seemingly ingrained distrust of the foreigner. On the other hand they were often able to relieve a scarcity, and by undercutting, keep down prices. In Scotland, however, fishing was of great importance to the local population, and the Scots steadily opposed foreigners fishing in their coastal waters. Frequent attempts were made to exclude them entirely, or to force them to pay tithes if they were close inshore.

The Dutch had been regular and unwelcome visitors to the Scottish fishing grounds since early times. At intervals this resulted in open quarrels and the seizure of Dutch boats, to be followed by reprisals against Scottish merchants in the Netherlands. This was not enough to keep the Dutch away, and by the sixteenth century they had been joined in the Shetland fisheries by the men of Bremen and Hamburg.

The Dutch were indeed becoming formidable rivals. They had not only increased the size of their fleet, but had improved the design of their boats and their methods of fishing. By the seventeenth century the Scots had been largely ousted from their own fishing grounds. This was a serious blow to the Scots. Edinburgh, Dundee and Aberdeen had all carried on a busy overseas trade in herrings right through the Middle Ages. Nor was any aspect of the trade too trivial to engage the attention of the busy Scots Parliament. The sizes of nets and boats, the marking of barrels and the kind of salt to be used were all subjects of regulation which came up for discussion at one time and another. The legislation is not without its interest because it reflected the economic ideas of the times, as well as practical needs. Herrings, for example, were among the goods that might only be exported by the free merchant burgesses of the Royal Burghs. Another Act—this time short-lived—forbade Scotsmen to export herrings at all, although foreigners might come to Scotland to buy them. On several occasions, as in England, there were prohibitions on the export of herrings until the home market was fully satisfied. In the long run, however, the Scots were readier than their English neighbours to look squarely at the situation, and see what could be learned from their successful rivals rather than hedge the trade round with restrictions.

No less important than the herring to the medieval diet was the stockfish, the dried, salted cod, which came from northern waters. Some of it was bought in Norwegian ports, and some of the cod which the market required was caught along the coast of Norway. But the Norwegians did what they could to discourage fishing in their home waters, and after the German merchants moved into the Norwegian market conditions for British merchants became very difficult. There was a bountiful source of fish around the coasts of Iceland. But towards Iceland the Norwegians, and later the Danes, pursued a curious dog-in-the-manger policy. Having accepted the subjection of Iceland the Scandinavians proceeded to neglect it, sending at most half a dozen ships in a year to supply the needs of the islanders. And just as Spain and Portugal, at a later date, tried to insist that there should be no direct communication between a third party and their colonies, so the Scandinavians insisted that a licence must be obtained before a foreign ship visited Iceland. Such a policy was bound to fail. Having been driven from Bergen, and having, it seems, made the chance discovery of what Iceland had to offer, the British fishermen were quick to exploit the opportunity.

The first British boat to fish Icelandic waters is said to have come from Cromer, and certainly the boats of Cromer were conspicuous from the very beginning. But it was not long before other ports joined in this highly profitable enterprise. So sudden and uncontrolled was the influx that King Eric of Denmark was moved to complain to the King about the damage done by the fishermen in Iceland and the adjoining islands. As a result notices prohibiting the venture were posted in sixteen ports along the East Coast of England. If was a futile gesture. The Icelanders were not particularly pleased to see the fishermen, for they were largely bands of ruffians, who took their catches, did a lot of damage and had little to contribute. But in their wake came the merchants to whom the Icelanders gave a ready welcome.

In 1419, the Icelanders wrote to the King of Denmark, "Our laws provide that six ships should come hither from Norway every year, which has not happened for a long time, a cause from which your Grace and our poor country has suffered most grievous harm. Therefore, trusting in God's good grace and your help, we have traded with foreigners who have come hither peacefully on legitimate business, but we have punished those fishermen and owners of fishing smacks who have robbed and caused disturbance on the sea." The Norwegian Governor, who went home with this explanation of the state of affairs, did not return to Iceland, and the Icelanders proceeded to take matters into their own hands. It was not long before merchants trading directly to Iceland for stockfish against whatever the Icelanders needed formed important sections of the communities in Lynn and Hull, as more and more merchants forsook Bergen for Iceland.

So great and profitable was the trade that it over-rode every obstacle, and the King of Denmark, while insisting that visiting ships should be licensed, was obliged to recognize its existence. One factor which here, as in every other aspect of medieval life, undermined good government, was the Kings' need of money. And both the King of Denmark and the King of England, having issued general prohibitions on voyages to Iceland, proceeded to make individual exceptions in return for payment. And merchants, who could make a profit (in terms of modern currency) of perhaps £3,000 on a single trip, were prepared to pay. Others, with less at stake, took a chance on having their goods confiscated.

By the 1440s there was a great congregation of English merchant vessels and fishing doggers off the coast of Iceland every summer. The waters off the Vestmann Islands particularly attracted the fishermen, because there was to be found the best fishing. And there, it was alleged, they built houses, erected tents, dug up the ground and fished "as if it were their own property".

One complaint of the Icelanders was that shortage of wood prevented them from building boats which were a match for those of the Englishmen. And in the meantime the Englishmen were able to fish further out to sea with long lines and many hooks so that the fish never reached the inshore waters where the Icelanders waited in vain to catch them.

It is difficult to form an idea of the size of the ships which went to the fishing grounds. For, although small, they were large enough to carry as many as ten men and enough provisions to last through the whole summer while they were on the fishing grounds, and large stocks of salt for preserving the fish. In some cases the division between merchants and fishermen becomes thin, because it is clear that some of the fishing vessels carried more food than was required for the voyage, and this was traded for additional stocks of fish.

The trading vessels proper brought an astonishing variety of wares to exchange for fish. At the head of the list, naturally, came food—wheat, butter, honey, wine and beer. Then there were metal goods and hardware. For although the Icelanders had a little low-grade iron, they lacked the fuel to smelt it. And so not only iron nails, but pots and pans, knives and horseshoes, swords and copper kettles were very welcome. Lengths of cloth and linen were particularly prized, and also hats and caps, shoes, purses, girdles and gloves. So the list continues down to such trifles as needles and pins, thread, and yarn for fishing nets. For most of these articles a standard rate of barter appears to have been worked out: so many fish for a pair of shoes, a hundred horseshoes or a firkin of honey. Occasionally, a merchant would take in exchange a quantity of coarse woollen cloth, or oil or hides but the English were primarily interested in fish, and the development of these other Icelandic products, together with sulphur and eiderdown, was left to the German traders who came later.

English domination of the Icelandic fisheries was, however, short-lived. The merchants of the German Hansa, after they had gained a dominant position in the Bergen Staple, were no more pleased than the King of Denmark to see it by-passed by merchants trading directly to Iceland. From 1435, moreover, the war which had been waged between the Hansa and Denmark ended, and the Kings came to rely more and more upon the Hansa to implement their policies, since the Hansa alone had the ships to make this possible. For the moment, however, the policy of the Danish Crown was not consistent. The need for money was so acute that Christian I was driven to pawn Orkney and the Shetlands. The revenues of the Bergen Staple were urgently wanted, but if merchants would not go there the Danish Kings were quite ready to accept payment of dues in Iceland itself, and to sell licences to anyone who was prepared to pay for them.

The challenge to the English was therefore delayed, and it was the excesses of the English that finally antagonized the Hansa and Denmark. By 1460, loss of revenue compelled the Danish King to turn his attention seriously to Iceland. Orders were sent that no trade was to be done with foreigners who did not pay the heavy dues now imposed, and a Governor was sent who was bent upon imposing his authority. His resolution resulted in his death, but it also proved the undoing of the English. In 1467 he arrived with a large retinue in an Icelandic village where some Englishmen were carrying on a brisk trade. In the action that followed he was killed and his body thrown into the sea. The Englishmen then proceeded to plunder and burn down his house and to take prisoner his son, who was held to ransom.

The Governor's wife, however, was a woman of resource. She gathered together a body of men and, says a contemporary account, "clad herself in a shirt of mail, and a woman's dress over it; so she set out with her men in array. Then they came with craft upon the English, and slew a great company of them, except the cook, who got his life very narrowly for that he had before helped their son." She then set sail for Norway to lay her complaint before the King.

As a result four English ships were seized in the Sound, and sequestered to compensate the victims. It seems likely that the men of Lynn may have had a leading part in the outrage, because when the King of Denmark subsequently gave a safe conduct to English ships he excepted those of Lynn, and told English merchants who had suffered loss to seek compensation in Lynn itself.

Meanwhile, competition in Iceland was growing. As early as the 1430s some German traders who had been unable to gain admittance to Bergen had, like the English, taken to trading with Iceland directly, but this had quickly been checked by the Hansa itself. But, by the 1470s, the trade had again become so active that Bergen was moved to protest. Among the ships that went annually from Hamburg were some belonging wholly or in part to the city, and at one time so much grain was being exported that trade was prohibited and the ships were obliged to seek supplies elsewhere. Other Hanseatic towns joined in, and it was not long before the Hanseatics had succeeded even to the extent of carrying fish to London. The inevitable clash of interests between Englishmen, Danes and Germans, some anxious to bolster the privileged position of Bergen and some not, inevitably produced endless friction and countless outrages. It was, therefore, with some relief that the English learned that the Cabots had found new fishing grounds off Newfoundland. And from that time, the Iceland trade, in which the English East Coast ports had had so big a part, steadily declined.

The Dutch fisheries continued to grow at the expense of the English, in part at least, because the Dutch were better aware of the other benefits which the industry brought. The distribution of the catch provided an opportunity to seek return cargoes. And, in this way, the herring played an important part in fostering Dutch trade. The fishing-grounds were seen, too, to provide excellent training for future seamen.

Meanwhile, the English North Sea fisheries, which had never been strong, declined to a point at the end of the sixteenth century where there was a danger that the country would lack trained sailors to man the ships in time of war.

In 1549, Fridays and Saturdays were made Fish Days by Statute, in addition to the days of Lent. And, in 1563, Wednesday was added as well, and the law was enforced with greater stringency. The regulations may have given some temporary benefit to the English fishing industry, but food regulations are never popular, and were eventually abandoned.

It was at this point of time that James VI of Scotland ascended the English throne. He brought with him Scottish concepts of the importance of the industry and Scottish notions about exclusive rights in coastal waters. Quite early in his reign, in an attempt to establish British rights and to revive the home industry, he ordered baselines to be drawn between headlands round the coast, and in 1609 required foreigners fishing off the coasts to obtain annual fishing licences. In the same year, the neglect of the fisheries in favour of the more attractive coasting trade led the magistrates of Beccles to order that "none but old men, who have spent their days in fishing-fare, shall occupy the coasting business . . . and the young men shall diligently attend the fishing-craft for the neglect of the fishery is the means tending to the destruction of a nursery that bred up fit and able masters of ships and skilful pilots for the service of the nation."

Such measures were hardly sufficient to wrest much of the industry away from the Dutch. In 1620 it was reckoned that they had some two thousand vessels engaged in the North Sea fisheries. And it is clear that they had not only sunk a great deal of capital in the enterprise, but possessed unrivalled skill in handling and curing their catches. To the annoyance of the Scots they continued to arrive off the coast of Shetland about the middle of June. The fishing boats always came accompanied by one or more store ships, which lay the whole season off Lerwick to supply the fishermen with food and equipment, while a fleet of yaggers maintained a constant supply to the markets, where the herring, lightly salted, are said to have fetched as much as a shilling each.

In the seventeenth century a number of attempts were made to inject new life into the British industry, and to wrest the herring trade from the Dutch by establishing Royal Fishery Companies in both England and Scotland, which would be wealthy enough to work on a large scale and have funds to pay bounties to the fishermen. The monopolistic form of organization within the Royal Companies was, however, ill-suited to such an industry. The other weakness of the scheme was exposed by the economist, Adam Smith, writing about a third attempt to found a Company. What he has to say about the payment of bounties has some relevance today.

> "But though the tonnage bounties to those fisheries do not contribute to the opulence of the nation, it may perhaps be thought that they contribute to its defence by augmenting the number of its sailors and shipping. This, it may be alleged, may sometimes be done by means of such bounties, at a much smaller expense than by keeping up a great standing navy, if I may use such an expression in the same way as a standing army.
>
> "Notwithstanding these favourable allegations, however, the following considerations dispose me to believe, that in granting at least one of these bounties, the legislature has been very grossly imposed upon . . .
>
> "The bounty to the white-herring fishery is a tonnage bounty, and is proportioned to the burden of the ship, not to her diligence or success in the fishery; and it has, I am afraid, been too common for the vessels to fit out for the sole purpose of catching, not the fish, but the bounty. In the year 1759 when the bounty was at fifty shillings the ton, the whole buss

fishery of Scotland brought in only four barrels of sea-sticks. In that year, each barrel of sea-sticks cost the government in bounties alone £113 15s.; each barrel of merchantable herrings £159 7s. 6d."

The scheme was altogether crude and undigested. The Company never had more than forty boats of its own, which started well enough but soon made losses: management was in the hands of an unwieldly committee of 32 members, and the work of the fishermen was hampered by regulations that prevented the fishermen from beginning their season before a fixed date. Nor did the scheme help the small fisherman, who in Scotland, at least, fell more and more under the thumb of the big landowner. His boat, if it was of less than 20 tons, failed to qualify for the subsidy. And, if he were eligible, he could only claim it by taking his catch into a port where there was a customs house.

There was also the matter of salt. Salt derived from the evaporation of sea-water was unsuitable for curing herrings, and the Scots were obliged to obtain supplies from Portugal and Ireland. There were supplies of English salt, but this could only be imported for the curing of herring to be sold on the English market. A special duty of 7s. 5d. for fifty bushels was put on foreign salt provided that it was used for herrings intended for export. To prevent the wrongful use of cheap salt for home-curing, an elaborate and expensive system of customs controls was set up. So that, in safeguarding its salt revenues and protecting the English salt manufacturers much of the help that the Government intended to give the fishing industry was undone.

In 1757 the bounty was raised to fifty shillings, and the number of Scottish busses rose from three in 1758 to thirteen in 1760 and 261 in 1766. But the Fishery Company was already in difficulties, and in 1766, when the vessels returned from fishing, the crews were told that there was no money to pay the bounties. A number of boat-owners were reduced to selling their bounty-certificates to speculators. By 1770, the number of busses had dropped to nineteen.

In spite of these difficulties, the industry showed signs of improvement in the second half of the eighteenth century, and to this the little boats, which drew no bounty before the Act of 1786, made an important contribution. By 1765 well over half of the fish exported from Scotland was caught from such boats. A major enterprise, too, had its modest beginnings in 1767 when several merchants of Wick and Staxigoe fitted out two sloops to engage in herring fishing. Although Wick, at that time, had a poor harbour, it was not long before ships from other parts of Scotland were joining the vessels from there. In 1782 Wick exported 363 barrels of herring: by 1790 the figure had risen to 10,514 barrels of white and over two thousand barrels of red herrings. The Scots showed initiative, too, in holding out inducements to the men of Lowestoft to go North to teach them the art of curing, of which they had made themselves masters. So many went that the Lowestoft trade was for a time jeopardized.

The real opportunity for expansion occurred after the outbreak of the Napoleonic Wars, in the course of which the Dutch fishing vessels "were mostly all taken and the Fishery in Holland quite undone, broken and lost".

Until about 1830 fish had been caught by gill net and hook and line. But with the appearance of the fishing-smack the whole industry was transformed. For the fishing-smack used trawl-gear, which was dragged along the sea-bed. It is said that the new technique had its beginnings in Brixham, where the art may have been learned from Dutch settlers. In the early years of the century there was a settlement of trawlermen at Barking on the Thames below London, and it was not long before the use of the beam-trawl had been taken up along the East Coast.

From the middle years of the century the industry rapidly

Above, bathing at Scarborough in 1735; *below,* the North Bay, 1895

Above, the harbour at Aberdeen; *below,* the beach at Knokke-le-Zoute, Belgium

acquired a modern image. The spread of the railway system to link the ports with the main centres of population was largely instrumental in bringing this about.

One town to benefit in this was Grimsby, which the railway reached in 1848. It had been a fishing port since earliest times. Its ships had been among those that had made the long, dangerous voyage to Iceland, and later its merchants had had a share in the Greenland whale fishery. But, after 1850, it climbed rapidly in importance as a fishing port. For its harbour at the mouth of the Humber permitted the import of ice from Norway, on which the trade depended for the next forty years. It early developed a thriving trade in lobsters. In 1851 fifty thousand lobsters were taken off the coast of Norway, and two years later a pair of screw-driven steamers were in service to bring the catch quickly to port. But Grimsby owed much to the railway company, which saw the possibilities of the industry. In 1856 the first fish dock was opened. It also had a hand in the Deep Sea Fishing Company, which built ships and engaged in fishing. The company owned the first sail trawlers to operate from the port as well as a number of steamers to carry the fish to port. It encouraged the development of the port by allowing vessels to dock without payment; it offered the free transport of fish to the main urban centres, and later gave merchants free tickets to visit the principal towns to obtain orders. It was no less active in seeking to attract fishermen from other places along the coast—and notably from Hull—to settle in Grimsby. The growth of the town is reflected in the fish landings:

Grimsby: Total Landings

1854	453 tons		1900	135,000 tons
1856	1,500 ,,		1909	175,000 ,,
1890	70,000 ,,		1958	220,000 ,,

A hardly less important revolution, in spite of its simplicity, was the practice of taking ice to sea for the preservation of the catch. In a very short time it was to alter the whole pattern of the industry. By 1872 Grimsby was importing 22,000 tons of ice a year, and 90,000 tons by 1900. But by then natural ice was giving way to artificial ice. A factory established towards the end of the century produced 300 tons a day—a figure which is now more than quadrupled. But already before this Grimsby had established a distinction for prime-quality fish by the development of its "well" boats in conjunction with its drifters. These allowed fresh sea-water to pass into the well of the boat, and in this the catch was kept alive until it reached harbour.

The quality of the fish now reaching the towns fostered an unprecedented demand, and this called for a fundamental reorganization of the industry. The first experiment, tried in 1870, was the "fleeting" system, under which all the trawlers operated under the command of one "admiral". The boats stayed at sea for eight or even ten weeks at a time, and fishing went on all the year long. The catch was transferred to carriers which took it quickly to market. "Bulk fleeting" continued until 1901.

Remarkably, the industry was slow to apply steam to its boats, and when it did the experiment was at first a failure. Wire ropes had been introduced in 1870, but it was not until 1876 that the first steam capstan was used aboard a sailing trawler, and it was some time before these came into general use. It was not until 1881 that the prototype of the steam trawler was introduced. But this boat, even with the assistance of sails, had too little power to fish anywhere save on the Dogger Bank and a little to the south of it. But the advantages of steam were appreciated, and it was not long after that before vessels capable of trawling down to 200 fathoms—four times as deep as the sailing trawler—had been developed. It opened up the deep-sea fishing grounds of the far North, and by 1891 the steam trawlers were operating off Iceland.

By the turn of the century the British Isles had advanced to the position of leading fishing nation of the world, with a catch exceeding in value the combined totals of Norway, Denmark, Germany, Holland and France.

The North Sea continued, as ever, to be an abundant source

of fish. In 1908 it yielded about one million tons, of which more than a half were herrings caught in drift-nets. At that time British boats caught about two-thirds of all the herring, and nearly all the pelagic fish (which fed on the sea bottom) caught with the trawl. The statistics for 1905 show how big a share the British East Coast ports had in this harvest.

(tons)	trawl and line	drift and stake nets
English ports	300,850	152,100
Scottish ports	114,800	135,450
	415,650	287,550

In 1913 rather more than half the total British catch of herrings was landed by the 1,650 boats of the East Anglian fleet, and the preparation of the herring provided work in the season for thousands of Scottish fisher-girls who followed the fish southwards. During the First World War fishing was drastically reduced. It picked up again afterwards, but on a markedly lower level with the resumption of the Scottish and East Anglian drift-net fisheries. The most important feature of the inter-war years, however, was the increase in German competition. Before 1925, the German catch had rarely exceeded 50,000 tons, but from then on it steadily rose to reach 250,000 tons, at which point it nearly equalled the British catch.

The growth of the German fishery was doubly significant. In the first place it meant added competition for an important export market. And secondly, the Germans introduced a significant change in the method of fishing. Until this time, herring fishing had been carried on by drifters with drift-nets. The Germans introduced the trawl, using relatively large, high-powered boats. No less than three-quarters of the German catch was taken by trawlers. At the outbreak of war in 1939 only the British persisted with the drift-net. No less important for the future, while draft-net fishing was confined to the traditional grounds of the north-western North Sea and the coast of East Anglia, the trawler men fished extensively in the deep water basin of the northern North Sea and on the Dogger Bank spawning ground, and they fished for a longer period of the year.

Fishing was again curtailed during the Second World War, but rose rapidly again afterwards. In 1945 the total catch of herrings was only about 100,000 tons, but soon after 1950 it had risen to nearly 700,000 tons. Once more, the trends which had been set before the War were resumed. The Germans, who had caught under 100,000 tons in 1946, had raised the figure to over 300,000 by 1955 and had become easily the biggest herring producers. The British fisheries, however, continued to decline in the after-War years. The East Anglian fisheries dropped from 100,000 tons before the War to 48,000 in 1953, 8,000 in 1959, and even lower in 1964. The relatively small British herring trawl fleet, which had operated from the Humber and Scottish ports between the Wars, and which was revived at Aberdeen in 1945, had ceased to operate by 1955. The past twenty years have also seen a further extension of the fishing grounds to include the spawning grounds in the southern North Sea and at the eastern end of the English Channel.

The statement of the Herring Industry Board that "the belief that there could hardly be an East Anglian season worse than that of 1958 was dispelled in 1959, when landings . . . fell by 30 per cent to an all-time low level", contrasts strangely with the graph which shows total North Sea catches in the post-war years to compare very favourably with the pre-war average.

The explanation is to be found in the changed purposes of the herring fleets. The traditional North Sea fisheries were built on the demand for fresh and cured herring for human consumption. The demand has always been for mature, high-quality fish. For this the selective drift-net has been ideal. In 1945, however, there was a world shortage of animal oils, and fish meal had become extensively used for animal feeding stuffs. In consequence, "industrial" trawl-fishing of adolescent two-and-three-year-old herring rapidly developed. Danish and

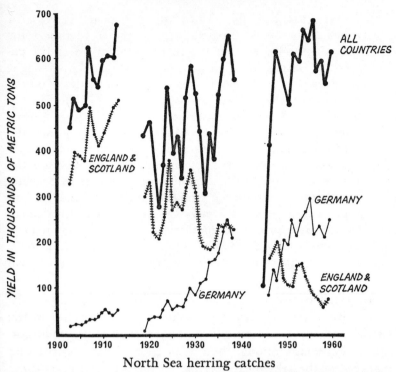

North Sea herring catches

German fishermen took a leading part, and the haul rose rapidly from about 5,000 tons in 1950 to over 100,000 tons in 1955. Britain did not find it economic to engage in industrial fishing, because the British fish-meal industry obtained what it wanted by buying offal and supplies of fish that were surplus for human consumption. A move was made at one time to extend to British vessels the Convention which permits the taking of a percentage of fish below the permitted size for conversion to meal, but the growth of the foreign fishmeal industry did not encourage further development.

The main area of industrial fishing is the Bløden ground in the southern North Sea, where vast shoals of immature herring congregate. How far this is responsible for the difficulties of the traditional industry is a matter for dispute. The Fleck Committee, which touched on this matter in 1961, noted:

[133]

"Scientists have also drawn attention to the increase in trawling for herring, particularly in the trawl fishery for spawning and spent herring in the Sandettie area [in the Strait of Dover]; and they are not agreed on relative weight to be attached to the Blöden and candettie fisheries or on the extent to which more general biological changes affecting the whole of the North Sea are responsible for changes in growth rates and in the movements of herring shoals away from the predictable patterns of the past . . . The industrial fisheries are accused also of breaking up the shoals which are the basis of the East Anglian drift-net communities by drawing heavily on the supplies of sand-eels and general small fry on which many species of demersal fish feed. Until it is demonstrated that profitable industrial fisheries are so damaging to the fish stocks as to be self-defeating, however, it would be idle to expect the countries engaging in them to give them up."

Although industrial fishing, and biological changes in the North Sea, must have had a part in causing the decline of the British industry, economic factors have been of major importance. Foremost among these was the loss of Continental markets for the salt-cured herring. In the post-war years there has been a sharp rise in costs and a decline in available manpower. The dual-purpose drifter-seiner fleet was introduced during the 30s and again after the War because it seemed commercially sound to use the vessels for herring-fishing or white fish, according to conditions. In the post-war years, it has not worked out well in practice. The change-over from drifting to seining entails the laying off of crew-members. As the Herring Board has recognized, "it is too much to expect, in these days, that the spare hands will necessarily be available when the owner wishes to revert to drifting." The trawler, employed both in herring-fishing and white-fish catching, is not faced with the same difficulties.

In 1965, the Herring Board in its Report for 1964, having experimented for three years, came out strongly in favour of the pair-trawling. It went on to add, however, that "it would be quite wrong to conclude that there is likely to be a rapid, wholesale switch from other methods of herring catching to trawling. A great deal has to be done technically and . . . financially before pair-trawling for herring can become one of the methods conventionally used by British fishermen. The great thing is that a climate of opinion favourable to this method has been created."

Landings of white fish have not suffered the same decline as landings of herring, although the catch has fluctuated considerably from year to year. In the years since the War, fishing in the remoter fishing grounds has been threatened not only by the danger of overfishing, but by the extension of international fishing limits, which have kept the British boats out of some of the most abundant fishing grounds. The vessels which have fished the waters of the North Sea nearer to their home ports have not suffered to a like extent from these restrictions, and here the declining catches of the trawlers has been offset by the remarkable increase in the Scottish seining fleet.[1]

The big firms have met the challenge in deep-sea fishing by investing in new high-powered diesel craft. These 800-tonners, up to 200 ft. overall, costing up to £200,000 each to build and capable of making a round-trip of 4,000 miles, offer the skipper all that he could ask for. His bridge is equipped with radar, radio transmitters and receivers, direction finders and depth sounders. His ship will most likely be equipped for quick-freezing of the catch. Conditions on the modern boats are good: the skipper will have his own stateroom, a private bathroom and toilet; the senior crew members have their own cabins, and the rest share. There are separate messes for the officers and crew, and the Company takes care to see that there is a good cook aboard. But, for all that, it is still a hard, dangerous and chancy life. No one who fishes the North Sea will ever trust it. It is a sea where fair weather can turn to storm with

[1]Although seine-net fishing was invented in Denmark as long ago as 1848, and its value in catching prime fish from smaller boats proved, it was not until the Second World War brought many Danish fishermen to this country that seining was widely adopted in Britain.

great suddenness. As one of the fishermen has said, "The North Sea's unpredictable, and you must respect it." Of all the adverse conditions, black frost is the worst. "It coats the decks and rigging—you can just lose your grip and you're gone. You've got to be on watch all the time. It can be 48 hours. Or three days . . ."

It is not surprising that trawler men come from families which have often been long connected with the industry. A promising man can become skipper before he is 30, and if he is successful he can earn as much as £12,000 a year. Not that there is any room in this highly competitive business for unsuccessful skippers. Such a man is soon out of a job. And finding the fish is the hardest part, for no amount of modern equipment will tell him where to look.

The method of payment varies from port to port. At Grimsby the skippers receive a share of the gross catch: at Hull they get 10 per cent of the net catch after deductions for such things as fuel, ice and dock dues, as well as £1 per cent of the gross catch as trip money. The mate also takes a share; the rest of the crew are paid wages. For that they work hard, as long as eighteen out of the twenty-four hours during the fortnight that they are on the fishing-ground, so that at the end of the day men are often too tired to eat. It is not surprising that the accident rate among men in the middle- and long-distance trawlers is so high.

Less spectacular and less financially rewarding are the careers of the inshore fishermen, who operate from most of the major ports and from countless small harbours along the coast, and who may land anything from a few hundredweight to several thousand tons of fish a year. The inshore men have a considerable share in shellfish and herring. But it is not difficult to see why men in the inshore industry would not move to the deep-sea trawlers at any price. For inshore work is essentially the preserve of individuals rather than companies. It not infrequently happens that the owner is the skipper, or the boat may be owned jointly by two working fishermen, with the crew perhaps sharing in the ownership of the nets and gear.

The skipper is his own master. He may go to sea for a few hours or for a few days. A typical inshore-man might make prawning in the Moray Firth his bread-and-butter business. Then, in winter, slip down to Aberdeen to join a friend in mid-water trawl between the vessels to catch sprats. And in summer make a five-day trip, which is about as long as a small crew can manage, in search of white fish. With the subsidy that the White Fish Authority pays, the inshore fishermen seem to do well enough at the present time. But the industry has its problems. Having so little capital behind it, replacement of equipment is a problem. With an industry organized on these lines, marketing, too, is difficult. The Authorities would like to ensure a regular flow of fish to market, and consignments of fish large enough to handle. The inshore man will not bring in fish unless he is sure the demand already exists for his fish at a price that repays his trouble.

A branch of the inshore industry which has had a long and distinguished history is the Colchester oyster trade, although oysters are bred along the Crouch and Roach as well as the Colne, and at one time around many other parts of the Essex coast as well. It has been fancifully asserted that it was the prospect of pearl fishing and Caesar's fondness for the pleasures of the table that first brought the Romans to Britain, but it is at least certain that the industry was established by Roman times. For the past 500 years the fishery rights have been held by the Colchester Corporation. Only at Colchester and Brightlingsea is the season controlled by Act of Parliament and under the control of an official Board, the Colne Fishery Board, upon which the Corporation and the dredgermen themselves each have six members. Once every year, the Mayor and his retinue come down the estuary, with the inevitable accompaniment of pressmen, and, with gin and ginger-bread and the necessary ritual, declare the season open. The actual fishery is a more prosaic affair, carried on at low tide amid the desolate marshes frequented mainly by curlews and duckshooters and Drainage Board men. The fishermen, mainly

elderly men these days, work five to a boat, each with a dredge
—a net of wire on a small iron frame towed on a rope. For much
of the year they do other jobs as well, because oysters themselves could not provide a living. Indeed, there are some who
wonder how the industry will survive when the present generation of fishermen retire. Inevitably, it is an industry that lives
on its memories. Memories of the days before 1914, when the
beds produced three or four million oysters a year. Today, they
probably produce less than 100,000, partly as a result of two
World Wars when the beds were neglected, and the floods of
1953 which caused heavy losses. But the Corporation will not
let the industry readily die; nor will the fishermen, for whom
the dignity of qualifying as a shareholder, with the possibility
of a seat on the Fishery Board, goes a long way to make up for
low wages and hard conditions.

9

THE DUTCH BID FOR
ECONOMIC POWER

BY SCARCELY PERCEPTIBLE stages and amid the stress of war,
the Dutch of the United Provinces had emerged by the beginning of the seventeenth century as a major commercial Power
in Europe. That they did so at that time was due as much to
the misfortunes and preoccupations of their rivals as to their
own efforts. The conquest of Portugal by Spain in 1580 was
disastrous for that country and its colonial empire. And when
the Dutch, who had established themselves in the carrying-
trade of Lisbon, found themselves barred, they developed
direct connections with the Portuguese territories overseas.
Nearer home, the fall of Antwerp to the Spaniards gave
Amsterdam the opportunity to become the greatest commercial city in Europe. It became a sanctuary for the scholars,
merchants and artists fleeing from the Spanish Netherlands,
and later for the Jews migrating from Portugal, Poland and
Germany. The city was fortunate in having a civic authority
alive to the opportunities, and capable of finding the money
for its plans. The result was the ordered development of the
city along lines that have earned unstinted praise.

Advancement was often won in the face of stiff opposition.
The emergence of Bergen-op-Zoom as a market of more than
local importance owed not a little to the efforts of the Dutch
and Southern German merchants to find an alternative to the

Hanseatic Kontor at Bruges. The men of Lübeck fought hard to preserve their monopoly. But, in the long run, economic forces were too strong for regulation, and the only trade that suffered by their efforts was such trade as Lübeck succeeded in controlling. In time, the Hanseatic merchants themselves were visiting the Dutch towns in the course of trade, and the cloth of Flanders began to find its way northwards through Bergen-op-Zoom to Amsterdam.

The emergence of Holland as an economic Power, however, was not so much a new departure as a quickening of processes that had long been at work. From the very earliest times the area around the delta of the Rhine had been an important commercial centre, and right into the Middle Ages the Utrecht area had an important trade in fish, corn and wine. Further south, Dordrecht—said to be the oldest town in Holland—secured the valuable economic privilege of compelling the unloading at its wharves of all goods passing to and from places on the Maas and Rhine. Leyden, too, had early developed a manufacturing industry, while in the extreme north-east places such as Groningen, Kampen and Derventer had profitable trading arrangements with the German Hansa.

A steady flow of trade had thus been maintained at all times during the Middle Ages, and there was every reason why this should be so. Living in a country set midway between the Baltic and the Mediterranean, the Dutch had many advantages. They were as well placed as anybody in Western Europe in relation to the sources of raw materials and to the centres that needed them. The Dutch, too, were by long tradition keen, thrusting seamen, as the English and Scots often learned to their cost.

What had distinguished the North from the Southern Netherlands in the early Middle Ages had been the comparative failure of its industries to respond to similar stimuli, and, in particular, the relative backwardness of that area of Holland including Amsterdam.

In explaining the great strides forward that the Dutch made

in the early seventeenth century, it would be easy to place too much importance upon the development of its colonial trade. At least as important—perhaps even more so—was the expansion of the North Sea fisheries, and the important advances which the Dutch had made in fish-curing and pickling. The insatiable demand from all parts for Dutch herrings was of the greatest importance. For not only was the trade valuable in itself, but the export trade provided an opportunity to look for return cargoes. As the Dutch put it, "the herring keeps Dutch trade going, and Dutch trade sets the world afloat."

The heavy tolls imposed along the great rivers, which found their way to the North Sea along those coasts, further helped the development of Dutch trade because it encouraged merchants and boatmen to explore the lesser-known waterways to avoid payment, and to develop craft that could be handled in confined spaces. None of their neighbours rivalled the skill of the Dutch in these arts, and they were thus able to build artificial arteries of trade, particularly between Flanders and Germany and the Baltic. Amsterdam was particularly fortunate in its overlords, the Counts of Holland, who used their authority over the Zuider Zee to promote the commercial interests of the town.

A basic factor in their success was that Holland had always been a relatively poor, unfertile country that had turned to the sea for a living. The Dutch went to sea not only as traders, but also as seamen working for whoever would employ them, and as carriers of other people's goods. In these capacities they did a useful, even an indispensable, service to some of the Hansa towns at a time when trade to the Baltic was jealously guarded. And so, unobtrusively, the Dutch were able to build for themselves a position of considerable strength in the Baltic. When, later, their position was challenged, they were able to resist successfully. As in Flanders, it was Lübeck that tried to drive them out, but it found little support from some fellow members who relied upon Dutch shipping to handle their trade.

With Holland carrying so much of the trade of other Western European countries, it was a logical, if tardy, development for her to develop industries of her own, concentrated upon the working-up of semi-finished articles for re-export. As time went on, German linens were imported in this way for bleaching, English woollen cloths for finishing and dyeing, and grain from many areas for malting and brewing. The saw-mills of Zaandam, fed by timber from the Baltic, became the most important in Europe. The manufacture of vegetable oils from linseed and colza was yet another industry of importance.

The Dutch flourished on their own successes. More trade meant more ships: more ships demanded more "ships' stores": and this, in turn, meant bigger orders for merchants trading with the Baltic. Already by 1524 the Dutch had gained a major triumph in their struggle with the Hansa when they were allowed to trade openly with Bergen. At the same time, lacking major industries of their own, the Dutch were perfecting their role as middlemen, buying goods in bulk in any market, and selling them again at a profit where they could. In time, Europe came to look to the Dutch, rather than to the original manufacturers, for supplies. This was particularly so in the case of woollen cloths, where the Dutch finished article had achieved a degree of perfection which the English manufacturer could not equal.

The share of the trade passing between the North Sea and the Baltic that the Dutch had taken for themselves grew apace. By 1640, 1,600 of the 3,450 ships passing through the Sound were of Dutch origin. Even more revealing are the figures for the Dutch share of Finland's import trade, which rose from 3% to 34% during the second half of the sixteenth century. Even later, when the East Indies began to play an important part in the expansion of Dutch trade, the North Sea and the Baltic continued to be of paramount importance, and engaged half of her shipping.

Once again, in the trade of Flanders, it was the difficulties of others that offered the Dutch their first opportunity. When the Flanders Galleys ceased to sail from Venice and other Italian ports, they left a vacuum that the Dutch were quick to fill. Dutch vessels, with cargoes of fish and manufactured goods, were soon sailing to the Mediterranean, from where they returned with luxury goods of the Levant and Far East, as well as wine and fruit and wheat from Sicily. From 1585 Amsterdam emerged as one of the great commercial and cultural cities of Europe. Its rise to fame and prosperity was powerfully assisted by the fall of Antwerp following the Spanish occupation of the southern Netherlands, in consequence of which many merchants, scholars and skilled craftsmen sought refuge in Amsterdam and other places in the Protestant North. In a century of religious persecution, Amsterdam, in particular, became a refuge from oppression for sectarians from England as well as from other parts of Europe, and for Portuguese and East European Jews as well as for Protestants. They brought with them a wealth of business experience and academic learning. A city council like that of Amsterdam, in which commercial interests were strong, might well have looked upon the newcomers as interlopers who would deprive the Dutch of business that was their own, but the authorities were awake to the opportunities which the situation offered. And, as part of their plans, they embarked on the redevelopment and expansion of their city, which not only doubled its population in a century and a half, but made Amsterdam a city of unusual architectural distinction.

These developments promoted still newer industries. With the fall of Antwerp, the diamond industry was transferred to Amsterdam, where the cutting and polishing of stones grew into an important business. A century later, the opening of the Brazilian mines gave it an additional stimulus. Holland also acquired a big market for rag-paper, after the industry had been established at Zaandam in 1606. The colonies, too, provided a range of luxury materials. The preparation of tobacco became of considerable importance and, later in the century, Middelburg became important for the manufacture of chocolate from cocoa beans.

These developments were viewed with some misgiving in England, and in particular the dominant position which the Dutch had secured for themselves in the Baltic. In the early seventeenth century the Sound acquired a significance for Englishmen as the Scheldt Question had for a later generation of statesmen. We, like any mercantile nation, were entirely dependent upon the Baltic for the timber, ropes, pitch, tallow and wax which our shipping required, and which the Dutch might be tempted to cut off. It was a thought to which Cromwell gave expression in one of the last speeches he made to the Commons: "If they can shut us out of the Baltic Sea and make themselves masters of that," he said, "where is your trade? Where are the materials to preserve your shipping?" It was the feeling out of which intense Anglo-Dutch rivalry was born, and which led to the Anglo-Dutch wars of the seventeenth century.

By this time Amsterdam's victory over Antwerp seemed complete. With the closing of the Scheldt, Antwerp had been condemned to a period of stagnation, which was to last for two hundred years. Its population fell from 150,000 to 50,000, and at one time grass is said to have grown in its streets. Even so, fears that any relaxation of the restrictions might injure Dutch trade prompted the insertion of an article into the Treaty of Munster (1648) that the mouths of the Scheldt should be closed for ever.

Holland's pre-eminence in trade and commerce was not long-lived. But her decline was long drawn out, and some sides of her economic life showed great resilience. The country had emerged still strong from the Anglo-Dutch wars and the struggle with France, and the deliberate attempts made by the British and French to eliminate her as an intermediary in their trade were demonstrably unsuccessful. The Bank of Amsterdam survived the crisis of 1672, and the statistics of

Dutch trade show that it reached new heights in 1698 and 1699, and remained at a high level through the first decade of the next century. Even as late as 1728 Daniel Defoe in his *Plan of English Commerce* could speak of the Dutch as "the Carryers of the World, the middle Persons in Trade, the Factors and Brokers of Europe . . . they buy to sell again, take in and send out; and the Greatest Part of their vast Commerce consists in being supply'd from all Parts of the World that they may supply all the World again."

The decline, when it set in, was not catastrophic. And even after the carrying and commission trade showed signs of decline, it had a remarkable ability to recover whenever circumstances were favourable. The trouble with the Dutch economy was its inability to grow while Holland's two great rivals, France and England, with their greater populations and vastly greater resources, raced ahead. With a strong central government, the Dutch might have been spared some of their difficulties. But, as it was, the country was torn by a conflict of interest between the industrialists, who wanted the greatest measure of protection for their hard-pressed industries, and the weighty interests that made their money from the carrying, commission and processing trades and who favoured the greatest measure of free trade. The conflict of interests was precipitated because the manufacturing industries, such as the textile industry at Leyden, were among the first to suffer, while the processing trades—such as cotton-printing, tobacco-cutting, sugar-boiling and the malting, brewing and distilling of imported grain—were still in a flourishing state at least until the 1730s. Moreover, in spite of what the Dutch did to prevent their neighbour and rival, Antwerp, from rising again, the city continued to survive. Its diamond, glass, silk, glove and tapestry industries flourished and money was easily raised for the establishment of the Ostend Company in 1722. Later in the century, the Austrians (the new rulers in the Southern Netherlands) attempted to reopen the Scheldt. They were thwarted by the Dutch, but Antwerp was too important to be denied for all time, and the outbreak of the French Revolutionary wars gave it its opportunity.

Inevitably, as other European nations developed their resources, dependence upon the Dutch as middlemen declined. By 1750 the English merchants had practically ceased to send cloth to Holland for warehousing and reshipment because, after paying the Dutch their commission, much of the profit had gone out of the trade. From then on, where the Dutch were engaged, they handled samples, and when they obtained orders the goods were sent directly from England to the purchaser. Similarly, the merchants of England began to go directly to Bremen, Hamburg and Altona for their purchases of German linen. And they found, too, that in these rising German ports dues were appreciably lower than in the Dutch ones. The Dutch, having put obstacles in the way of the transit trade to the Rhine, found themselves by-passed also in the Southern Netherlands, where the Austrian rulers had seen the advantages of developing the port of Ostend to handle this transit trade.

In time industrialization elsewhere affected the Dutch processing trades, too. English woollens had ceased to go to Holland for finishing and dyeing, and before long Dutch bleached linens were driven out of the English market by the subsidized linens from Scotland and Ireland, and the products of the English potteries killed the home market for Delft ware. In France, a new sugar-refining industry undermined, and finally destroyed, the Rotterdam sugar market. On the Elbe, rival gin distilleries grew up. And in a number of Baltic ports the sawn timber and refined oil could be found, of which the Dutch, at one time, had a virtual monopoly. A survey made in 1751 showed that three-quarters of all the sugar, indigo and coffee exported from Bordeaux and Nantes was then going to Hamburg, and only one-quarter to Amsterdam. Hemp and flax, from Scandinavia and the Baltic, which would at one time have been obtained from the Dutch, was now going directly to the Mediterranean in ships belonging to the French, the Spaniards and the Portuguese. Hamburg merchants who had previously bought foreign wares through their Dutch agents had also started to deal directly with agents in the countries concerned. In a small measure the Dutch were also victims of economic nationalism elsewhere, designed to throw off a Dutch monopoly. Thus, in 1736, all British vessels were required by Act of Parliament to have one set of sails made in Britain, to eliminate dependence upon the Dutch sail-cloth industry.

Amid this general recession in her overseas trade there were two areas where the Dutch remained supreme. One was the herring trade, where the supreme quality of the Dutch product defied all competitors until involvement in the Napoleonic wars destroyed the North Sea fleets. The other was the Baltic trade, where the Dutch had a strongly entrenched position. But even there, before the end of the eighteenth century, the British had succeeded in taking for themselves a slice of the Russian trade, the richest of all the Baltic trade.

The Dutch felt the effects of the recession in trade particularly in the years immediately after 1748, when Europe was briefly at peace. It was, however, easier to find causes for the falling-off of trade than to propose acceptable remedies. The business houses that depended for their livelihood upon overseas trade were ready to advocate a reduction of duties to make Dutch ports competitive with Hamburg, and favoured a complete relaxation of duties on goods imported for re-export even at some cost to the manufacturing industries.

In the end, nothing was attempted. This was partly because of the death of William IV, who had done much to restore Dutch prosperity in spite of anti-Orange opposition and the attitude of some of the rich Amsterdam merchants. He was succeeded by a three-year-old son. It was also partly due to the resumption of war in 1753, which put business again into Dutch hands. The opportunity was thus lost—if, indeed, it existed—of making fundamental changes in the Dutch economy to meet changed world conditions. In consequence the feeble manufacturing industries, which were subject to many pressures, went unaided. And new transit business through Holland to the Rhine was stifled in deference to vested Dutch interests, with the result that a new transit route was developed which avoided Holland altogether, and linked the Rhine with the port of Ostend.

One important development in the eighteenth century was the growing importance of finance houses. For some time previously the commission traders, who bought and sold on commission and advanced capital to finance transactions, had been growing beside regular trading enterprises. It was, therefore, only a step for some of these firms to abandon trading altogether and to become credit brokers and bankers. In a comparatively short time, Amsterdam had carved out for itself an important and highly profitable place in banking and insurance. The position was not without its dangers. Apart from the uncertainties inherent in international finance, there was the danger of over-extending credit. There was danger, too, in the incentive offered to Dutch financiers to speculate by the higher interest rates available abroad. The crisis came in 1763 with the end of the Seven Years War, when some newcomers to the Amsterdam money-market were unable to meet their commitments on bills issued to the warring Powers. The bigger bankers and the Bank of Amsterdam were not involved, but confidence in the Dutch money-market was shaken. Succeeding crises in 1772 and 1773 aggravated the matter.

Meanwhile, without suplies of iron ore and coal[1] of her own, Holland fared badly in competition with the growing industries of England and France. The Delft pottery industry, which had reached the highest point of its development about 1700, declined under competition from French and English ware. Shipbuilding, too, was badly affected. To this the textile industry was an important exception. It had benefited in the years after 1685 by the influx of French refugees, and through the eighteenth century it proved to be technically equal to the English industry. The Dutch industry benefited also from the re-

[1] Holland did not acquire the lignite mines of Limburg until 1839.

moval of the factories from the old urban centres to the rural districts of Twente and North Brabant, where labour was cheaper and taxation lighter.

Holland contrived to maintain an important place in European affairs until late in the century by a policy of neutrality. The critical point came in 1780 when the Dutch found themselves under the necessity of choosing between England and France, both wanting the exclusive use of Dutch transport. Wooed by the blandishments of France, and alienated from England by privateering attacks on Dutch shipping, the Dutch were mostly sympathetic towards France. The outbreak of war was disastrous. The coast of Holland was blockaded, most of Holland's trade and shipping fell into British hands, and so too did her overseas possessions. In 1782 the great Dutch East India Company collapsed, though it lingered on until 1798. With its collapse the Bank of Amsterdam, from which it had borrowed heavily, also fell. In 1795 the country was caught up once more in the wars of Revolutionary France and what was left of Holland's trade was destroyed. In 1805 the Prussian Ambassador reported that half of Amsterdam was on the poor rate. In 1815 she emerged from the war with everything to rebuild. She was fortunate in regaining most of her colonies, but in a world dominated by coal and steel Holland seemed destined to the rank of a second-rate Power. Yet she was not without certain advantages. After the Napoleonic wars, her rich East Indian colonies were restored to her, and her people possessed highly developed skills in agriculture, seafaring and commerce that enabled the nation to make a considerable contribution to the economy of Western Europe during the succeeding years.

10

THE ENGLISH COASTING TRADE

THE STORY OF the coasting trade has no obvious beginning. From the time when goods were first bought and sold, the rivers and the open sea provided what was often the easiest means of transporting them. It was a trade, too, in which comparatively small towns and villages standing on navigable water could, and did, participate. But until the period from which the Port Books survive, it is difficult to find out much about the trade between one British port and another and about the changing fortunes of the ports themselves.

There were a great many ports along the East Coast. Between the Thames and the Moray Firth there was also a number of great rivers—among them the Great Ouse, the Humber, the Trent, the Yorkshire Ouse, the Tees and the Tyne—and upon these there were many commercial towns that could be reached by deep-sea craft. Nor must such seemingly unimportant rivers as the Stour and the Witham be overlooked, because they were, and are, accessible to sailing vessels, and have had a continuing importance to the areas which they serve. The North Sea coast has been fortunate, too, in the nature of its rivers. The Tyne, below Newcastle, used to have a bad reputation for the difficulty of its lower reaches, which was aggravated by the practice in the Middle Ages of dumping ballast from visiting ships near the quays to make room for coal. But it is difficult to find instances of navigable tributaries flowing into unnavigable rivers, or of navigable upper reaches without access to the sea for ships. London, King's Lynn, Yarmouth and Hull are all instances of major ports that have been well placed on great river systems, and so able to prosper on the trade of their hinterlands. And no less important, there were few stretches along the coast without at least a minor port which made some contribution to the trade of the area.

Until the coming of the railways the coaster had no rival for the bulk carriage of goods, and even for easily divisible goods, provided that the ship carried a full load and the journey did not involve much transhipment. Even after that the comparatively low cost of carriage by water continued to keep the coaster in business. In the seventeenth century it was reckoned to be up to twenty times cheaper to send goods by water than by road.[1] In 1639, for example, the Government, with an eye to stunting the cloth manufacture which English Protestants refugees had established in the Netherlands, forbade the carriage of fuller's earth by water. The home trade was badly hit. The clothiers of York protested that the cost of fetching fuller's earth by land would be greater than the value of the cloth to be bleached. While the clothiers of Ipswich, in their petition for exemption, pointed out that it would cost £6 a ton to fetch supplies by road from Rochester, against the customary cost of two shillings a ton for supplies coming by sea. In the case of coal, its general use would have been long delayed had it not been possible to carry it by sea from Newcastle to London. In relation to its value it was the bulkiest of commodities.

The men who carried on the coasting trade until comparatively modern times were engaged in a particularly hazardous calling. They were as much exposed as any seaman to molestation by pirates and enemy warships, which hovered off the

[1] A century and a half later the same was still true in spite of the improvement of the roads. Adam Smith, in *Wealth of Nations*, writes "Live cattle are perhaps the only commodity of which transportation is more expensive by sea than by land, for by land they carry themselves to market."

coast at the approaches to the ports. For them, hugging the shore, the North Sea, with its tidal ranges, its currents and hidden shoals, and its extreme changes of mood, presented special dangers. So dangerous was the East Coast in winter that, in the seventeenth century when a great many ships were engaged in the coal trade between Newcastle and London, few ships made the journey in December, January and February. But some ships did make the journey, often under the necessity of war, and many were lost. In 1671 a correspondent reported that "the sea is so full of wreck on these coasts that those at sea are forced to look out sharp to steer clear of it." On January 13, 1673, it was reported that a hundred colliers had arrived at Great Yarmouth, "some with their sails blown away, others with masts by the board, several wrecks are seen floating, and great quantity of coals were seen cast up along the shore." It is not surprising that many sailors would have preferred the hazard of a voyage to the East Indies to a winter voyage down the East Coast.

In the seventeenth century conditions were probably considerably better than they had been in earlier centuries, when ships were much more difficult to control and the seamen had fewer navigational aids. In the Middle Ages, it seems clear, the seaman hugged the coast of necessity, navigating by sight and recognition. Chaucer's "Shipman", although a West Country man, must have found many like himself along the North Sea coast. And they, like him, depended upon their knowledge of the Moon and the tides, of currents and local hazards, and were masters in the use of the lead-line and in recognizing their whereabouts from the nature of the sea-bed which the line revealed. And they, too, knew intimately every creek and haven. Chaucer does not mention the compass of the period—the needle and stone—but that would have been available to the navigator in a ship of any size. At need, if he were carrying a cargo further afield than usual, he may have had the equivalent of the pilot-book to help him. A fifteenth-century copy of a still older text survives which gives sailing

directions from Berwick-on-Tweed round to Land's End.
About the approach to the Thames from the north-east, he
would read:

> If ye go out of Orwell Wains to the Ness [the Naze], ye must
> go south-west. From Ness to the marks of the Spits your course
> is west-south-west. And [the tide] floweth south and by east.
> Bring your marks together that the parish steeple be out by
> east the Abbey of St. Osyths. Then go your course to the
> Spits south till ye come to 10 fathoms or 12. Then go your
> course with the Horseshoe south-south-west. And if it be on
> flood come not by in 8 fathoms. And that shall bring you 11
> fathoms then go your course in to Thames with the Green
> Bank west-south-west.

He had, of course, no maritime charts to help him. The earliest
surviving chart—of the Thames estuary with its complex
system of sandbanks—only dates from the early sixteenth century. Not that that was all loss. For the early charts were very
inaccurate. Manship, the celebrated author of *History of Great
Yarmouth,* writing about 1619, corrects the existing charts.
"The town," he says, "is situated in Longitude 25 degrees and
10 minutes and in Latitude 52 degrees and 42 minutes. But, in
the Seaman's Chart, Yarmouth is said to be in 27 degrees and
30 minutes in Longitude and 53 degrees in Latitude." Even
making allowance for the fact that he was using a different
prime meridian, he was still far enough out to make his figures
quite useless.[1] It was not until much later in the seventeenth
century that navigation began to be put on a sound mathematical basis.

By that time, too, a start had been made in providing lighthouses along the North Sea coast. Some were provided by
private individuals. The two lighthouses that marked the
entrance to the Humber were provided by a London merchant,
Justinian Angell. They were maintained by a levy on shipping
that used the Humber. The lights at the mouth of the Tyne

---

[1] Yarmouth is in Latitude 52° 36′ 40″ North and Longitude 1° 44′ 22″ East.
Manship was using the meridan which passed through Ferro in the Canary
Islands. Even so, his estimate was a long way out.

were maintained by a similar levy. The lighthouses of the period were very similar to the beacons of earlier centuries. At the approaches to Yarmouth, four beacons were kept flaming every night, while at Lowestoft there was "a great fire made with coal", and a second lighthouse lit by candle. At the Naze there was a brick tower, 80 ft. high, upon which a beacon was, no doubt, lit. The usefulness of such aids must have been trifling in dirty weather, but they were a beginning, and were steadily improved with the passing of time.

The need for such aids to shipping was the greater along the North Sea coast not only because it was the most frequented of all the coasts of Britain, but also because (in spite of the number of its ports) there were few places where vessels could safely ride out the violence of a storm. Scarborough had long been well known for its harbour. And further north, the small, but busy, port of Whitby was reckoned to possess the best anchorage between Scarborough and the Tyne, partly because, facing northward, it gave better protection. So valuable was the harbour to the colliers that, after 1702, a levy was made on coal loaded at Newcastle for the upkeep of Whitby harbour. South of Scarborough there was Bridlington, which was much used by colliers in distress, and for this harbour, too, a levy was made upon coal loaded on the Tyne. South of this again, there was the Humber, which provided fine shelter, either behind the Spurn, or at Grimsby, or further up the river at Hull. But apart from that, from Flamborough Head to Winterton Ness, there was nothing. The big expanse of the Wash offered only dangerous waters and no safe harbours. In ordinary circumstances vessels would try to strike a line from Flamborough Head to Yarmouth, but, if they were caught by bad weather they were always in danger of being driven westwards and of foundering on the rocks, or of grounding on the shoals. It was not without reason that Cromer Bay was known to eighteenth-century sailors as the Devil's Throat. Boston and Lynn, important as they were, offered little hope of survival, because they were difficult to reach, and accessible only at high tide.

Further south, Yarmouth offered a roadstead and a safe river harbour, but the approach was made difficult by unreliable sand-banks, and the entrance to the narrow river-mouth was not easy in heavy weather. Further south again the coast as far as Harwich, so gentle and pleasant in summer weather, could be among the most dangerous on account of its shoals and banks.

The number of vessels lost in the days before steam must have been staggering. In the Middle Ages losses were numerous enough to make the rights of wreck among the most valuable of territorial privileges. And people living along the coast were always ready to exploit the misfortunes of distressed mariners and merchants to the full by maltreating the castaways and stealing their goods. This is illustrated in part by letters written to that eminent Norfolk gentleman, Sir William Paston, by his local representative, William Pekoc. They concern a wreck at Winterton in November 1447. From them it is clear that, in spite of the fact that five people had escaped from the ship, and no right of wreck existed, Pekoc had not only seized a large quantity of cargo, but had taken steps to assert Paston's interests against neighbours who had similarly taken goods. Defoe, writing in the early eighteenth century, noted that between Winterton and Cromer "the Farmers, and Country People had scarce a Barn, or a Shed, or a Stable; nay a Necessary-house, but what was built of old Planks, Beams, Wales and Timbers, etc." Defoe elsewhere recounts the fate of a fleet of two hundred colliers which ran into a north-east gale off Winterton after leaving Yarmouth Roads:

". . . some of them, whose masters were a little more wary than the rest, or perhaps, who made a better judgment of things, or who were not so far out as the rest, tack'd, and put back in time, and got safe into the roads; but the rest pushing on, in hopes to keep out to sea, and weather it, were by the violence of the storm driven back, when they were too far embay'd to weather Winterton Ness, as above; and so were forc'd to run west, every one shifting for themselves, as well as they could;

some run away for Lyn Deeps but few of them (the night being dark) cou'd find their way in there; some but very few rid it out, at a distance; the rest being above 140 sail were all driven on shore, and dash'd to pieces, and very few of the people on board were saved."

In times of war the coasting trade was liable to suffer both at the hands of the enemy and of the Navy. The losses to the enemy and to privateers must at times have been heavy, for, in 1667, it was worth recording officially that of the 150 colliers bound for Yarmouth the Dutch had picked up only one. The convoy was the answer, when this was possible, and Celia Fiennes, at Scarborough in 1689 records, "I see 70 saile of Shipps pass the point and so come onward at some distance off from the Castle, supposed to be Colliers, and their convoys." During wartime, when they were most needed, however, there were not always naval vessels to spare for convoy duties. In the summer of 1666 the Newcastle colliers were detained in port for want of an escort, with the result that the miners were thrown out of work. By August the shortage of coal in London was such that the brewers chartered ships of their own to fetch it, but these, too, were detained at Harwich and the Nore for two months for want of an escort. The loss to pirates may have been, at times, even greater. In 1626 Ipswich lost five ships and their cargoes worth £5,000, and the crews were carried captive to Dunkirk. But this is one odd incident among a great many. The pirates had no scruples, either, about how they got their booty. A few years earlier the Dunkirkers, disappointed at the size of their plunder, laid one of the crew on the block and threatened to cut off his head unless they got more money.

Masters and owners were often chary of the convoy, although it had much to recommend it, for the arrival of a big fleet was an invitation to the press-gang. Constant attempts were made to restrict the activity of the press-masters in order not to weaken the coal fleets too much, or interrupt the trade. In 1653 an order was made that boys under sixteen and men over forty-five were not to be taken off the colliers for service in the Navy, but the Navy's needs were urgent and there is no evidence that the order was effective. In later times the protection of the coasting trade was urged on the ground that the coal trade was the nursery of the British Navy. But that was not an argument to appeal to men likely to be pressed, and on occasion they refused to man the colliers without a formal undertaking that they would not be seized for service. Nor was it an argument to appeal to their wives, who on one occasion in the 1650s made so much fuss that fifty keelmen had to be discharged "on account of the mighty clamour".

With such risks, it would be surprising if merchants did not take advantage of other means to convey their goods. And, of course, they did, when it was feasible and economically possible, without the coasting trade being seriously undermined. But that belongs to a later date. Fine woollens were among the first consignments to be sent by land to escape the "detention and injuries" to which they were liable when sent by sea. For, in addition to the hazards already mentioned, must be added the pilfering that was rife in every port.

The ships which engaged in the coasting trade were of all sorts and sizes: small open boats, which ran short voyages between neighbouring ports, single-sailed square-riggers "low sloops, with great dull-red sails" that carried timber, up to the three-masted square-riggers that had been developed for the coal trade. But until well into the eighteenth century the coasters were all rather small. Even the colliers, which were almost certainly the largest ships engaged in the coasting trade, do not appear to have exceeded 400 tons. The collier had evolved to meet the need of the trade for a ship that would carry a particularly heavy cargo with ease of handling, and one, moreover, that would stand up to the rigours of the North Sea. As an example of shipbuilding it was singled out by Daniel Defoe. "An English Ship," he said, "will always endure more severity, load heavier, and reign (as the Seamen call it) longer, than any foreign built Ship whatever; the Examples are seen every year, particularly in the Coal Trade, the Loading of which is very heavy, and the Ships swim deep in the Water, by the Eagerness of the Masters, to carry large Burthens; and yet it is frequently known that a Newcastle or Ipswich built collier shall reign . . . forty of fifty Years."

An Act of 1685 mentions Hull, Yarmouth, Aldeburgh, Dunwich, Walberswick, Woodbridge and Harwich, in addition to Newcastle and Ipswich, as places where vessels for the coasting trade were formerly built. It is likely, too, that shipbuilding prospered in a number of other places, for the demands on local resources were not heavy. But, by the middle of the seventeenth century, many had declined. Indeed, the purpose of the Act was to impose an additional levy of up to five shillings a voyage upon foreign-built ships with a view to fostering the British industry. A visitor to Boston, in 1666, found that no ship had been built there for twenty years, and that the only craftsmen left in the town had been without employment for ten years. Even at Ipswich, which had a reputation all along the coast for the quality of its ships, the trade was in decline. Celia Fiennes, who visited the town in 1697, found it very run down, with "little or nothing minded save a little fishing for the supply of the town." The decay was not universal. The loss of Ipswich may well have been, as Defoe believed, London's gain. Some of the business, too, had gone to Whitby, which was building colliers, and where in 1734 there were 130 ships of 80 tons and upwards.

Even as late as the seventeenth century it is difficult to form an estimate of the number of ships or of the total tonnage of vessels engaged in the coasting trade. This is true even of the coal trade. In 1615 there were said to be four hundred ships engaged in carrying coal, of which one half supplied London, and the remainder other places around the coast. The number is said to have reached 1,400 by the end of the century, after which it declined,[1] although the total tonnage continued

---

[1] In 1774 a naval officer, Charles Townsend, noted, "There are supposed to be about eighteen hundred ships and vessels in the Coal trade, and about nine hundred more in what they call the Northern trade."

to increase as bigger vessels were built for the trade.

By the beginning of the eighteenth century the ports of the East Coast far outstripped any other comparable part of Britain in tonnage of shipping belonging to them, with Scarborough, Whitby, Newcastle, Yarmouth and King's Lynn the leaders in descending order. And they, more than the ports along the other coasts, benefited most from the capital's ever-growing demand for the two commodities they were best able to supply —coal and corn.

The growing influence of London is best seen in the ports farthest from the capital. In 1635 Berwick-on-Tweed struck a visitor as "a most shallow, barred haven, the worst that I have seen; it might be made good, a brave and secure haven, whereas now only one little pink of about forty tons belongs to it, and some few fishing boats." Even towards the end of the century the town's trade was almost entirely with Scotland, and it sent wrought silk and haberdashery there, receiving in return shipments of linen, eggs, oatmeal, stockings and numerous other items. But it sent only twelve shipments southwards in a comparable twelve months, and received one. The outward shipments were mainly for London, and consisted largely of hides, skins and fish, although there were some oats, wheat and cheese for Newcastle, salt for Faversham, and kelp for Whitby. The solitary inward shipment consisted of malt and barley from Wells. But forty years later, although Berwick showed few signs of prosperity, its sea-borne trade had greatly expanded. Between 1732–3, Berwick shipped 105 cargoes, and neighbouring Alnmouth 60 cargoes. Of these, 130 went to London. They consisted of nearly 30,000 quarters of oats, over 15,000 quarters of barley, wheat, eggs, butter, peas and beans, as well as salt, skins, wearing-apparel and fish. In the same year, Berwick received 20 shipments and Alnmouth 25. These latter shipments were immensely varied and included such things as glass bottles, molasses, crates of oranges and lemons, hops, soap, brandy, wooden hoops, and pots and pans.

In 1643 an Italian visitor, Foscarini, counted 98 ships "with tops" at Newcastle, and a few years later the Venetian, Gussoni, noted the 400 ships "which from Newcastle . . . transport combustible earths to all parts of the realm". But Newcastle has a special interest, quite apart from its coal trade. For already by the early eighteenth century it was on the way towards becoming an important industrial town. One visitor to Newcastle at that time found it "the Town of the greatest Trade of any in the North of England". For a long time already its sea-borne trade had consisted very largely in the outward shipping of industrial wares, and the importation of agricultural produce and a wide range of miscellaneous goods. Its three main industries were coal-mining (which was carried on to the west of the town), glass and salt-making. The salt came from South Shields, where Newcastle coal was used to evaporate sea-water. Sunderland did much the same as Newcastle, but on a smaller scale, for, like Newcastle, the approaches to its harbour were impeded partly by sand and partly by rubble discharged from ships. By 1733 it was shipping 275,000 tons of coal along the coast in a year, but the output of its ten salt-pans was never very great.

Unfortunately for the development of Whitby, the usefulness of its harbour was not matched by its land communications. This handicapped the development of Whitby as a trading centre, but did not deprive it of a generous share of the coastal trade. By 1734 the townsmen owned 130 vessels, and in addition, as Defoe found, built "very good Ships for the Coal Trade, and many of them too, which makes the Town rich". Hull, on the other hand, was remarkably endowed with inland water communications which linked it with both industrial and agricultural centres. According to the 1637 edition of Camden's *Britannia,* it was already "the most famous towne of merchandise in these parts". Even without the whale- and vegetable-oil industry, which belong to a later period, Hull was destined by its location to become a commercial centre of great importance.

By the early eighteenth century Boston had slipped some

Above, Ostend, gateway to the Continent for thousands of tourists every year; *below,* the beach at the height of the season

Above, Flushing, Holland's third port; *below,* Scheveningen, one
of Holland's most popular resorts

way from the position that it had achieved in 1204, when its merchants were taxed next after London in amount, thanks, no doubt, to its trade in wool. Defoe found it still "a large, populous and well-built Town, full of good Merchants", but it was now eclipsed by King's Lynn, which had excellent water connections. "By these Navigable Rivers," said Defoe, "the Merchants of Lynn supply about six Counties wholly, and three Counties in Part, with their Goods, especially Wine and Coals". It was, above all, a port for the shipment of grain, and large quantities were sent both to the London market and to the northern counties. For the rest, Lynn's trade was of so large and miscellaneous a kind that the alphabet would provide the only possible arrangement. Even Lynn's two small members, Wells and Burnham carried on an important business, shipping corn outwards and coal inwards, with (in addition) some salt from Newcastle and Sunderland and iron from London.

In spite of the trouble that Yarmouth had had from the early Middle Ages onwards in maintaining an unobstructed passage to the sea its very location in relation to Norwich and a prosperous agricultural region, as well as its own position as a centre of the fishing industry, ensured its continuing importance. Although here, as elsewhere, fortunes fluctuated, and the eighteenth century saw a falling-off in its trade. It had, as Defoe found, "the finest Key in England, if not in Europe". By that time, the trade in worsteds, which at one time had made Yarmouth the biggest exporter of worsteds in the country, had dwindled to very small proportions. It continued to ship Norwich stuffs, worsteds and stockings to London and places round the coast, but its outward shipments were chiefly corn and fish, which were sent as far away as Falmouth and Guernsey. Yarmouth's neighbours traded on a much smaller scale, and, in the case of Southwold, Orford and Dunwich, it was on a very small scale indeed. They were all the victims of the sea. Dunwich, which in the early Middle Ages had been a town of some size, had been the greatest sufferer, and much had already disappeared beneath the waves. By the early eighteenth century the

sea approaches to the town were so unsafe that the trade in
butter, cheese and corn which it retained was shipped from
Walberswick. Southwold carried on some business in smoked
herrings and sprats. But, in the case of all these towns, progress was hampered by poor communications. As the northern
coasting seamen, who presumably visited the towns to discharge coal, put it in a song:

> "Swoul[1] and Dunwich, and Walberswick,
> All go in at one lousie creek."

Orford, a little further south, had similarly once been a town
of importance. But when Defoe visited the district the harbour
was no longer capable of receiving a ship of any size. As he
says, "Orford was once a good town, but is decay'd, and as it
stands on the land-side of the river, the sea daily throws up
more land to it, and falls off itself from it, as if it was
resolved to disown the place, and that it should be a port no
longer."

Although Woodbridge was a "member port" of Yarmouth, it
belonged geographically to the group of ports of which Ipswich
is the chief. This was the area of Suffolk that had long been
famous for its dairying industry. It was famous for the best
butter—and, adds Defoe, "probably the worst cheese"—in
England. It was for that reason full of corn-factors and butter-
factors, some of whom were considerable merchants. Remarkably, Ipswich, which clearly had tremendous possibilities both
in the eighteenth century and earlier for trade with the Continent and other parts of Britain, did not seem capable of
realizing its full potentiality. Defoe was inclined to blame the
decline upon the nearness of London, "which sucks the vitals
of trade in this island to itself". Celia Fiennes, writing a generation earlier, was inclined to blame the townsmen themselves:

> "The town," she wrote, "looks a little disregarded, and by
> enquiring found it to be thro' pride and sloth, for tho' the
> sea would bear a ship of 300 tun up quite to the key and the

---

[1] Southwold.

ships of the first rate can ride within two mile of the town, yet they make no advantage thereof by any sort of manufacture, which they might do as well as Colchester and Norwitch, so that the shipps that brings their coales goes light away, neither do they adress themselves to victual or provide for shipps, they have a little dock where formerly they built ships of 2 or 300 tun but now little or nothing is minded save a little fishing for the supply of the town."

For all that, Ipswich did carry on an important outward coasting trade, particularly to London, in agricultural produce and cloth. Its inward trade, in which London played a much smaller part, was made up largely of coal from Newcastle and Sunderland. But, as for every other port along the coast, the remainder were both miscellaneous and varied from year to year. In one year London sent soap, wine oil, iron, groceries and a large quantity of woad. From Rochester came fuller's earth (needed for the cloth trade of the district); from neighbouring Burnham and Maldon malt and barley; pipe-clay from Poole and lead from Hull.

Colchester, "supply'd by a handsome small Channell and Haven", and Maldon both carried on a sea-borne trade that was similar in many respects to that of Ipswich. But Colchester, while the centre for the manufacture of bays and serges, had an important outward trade in cloth, and imported large quantities of wool. Neighbouring Wivenhoe also benefited in the eighteenth century from Colchester's prosperity, and sent two packet-boats a week to London laden with cloth, bringing back wool.

In spite of the changes which came with the Industrial Revolution—the coming of the railways, the opening-up of inland waterways, improved roads, the gradual replacement of sail by steam, the shifting of centres of economic importance, and so on—the coasting trade along the East Coast has remained of the first importance. Of the great fleet of merchant vessels, which so impressed the foreign visitor, and which, in 1829, totalled about $2\frac{1}{4}$ million tons, London was the registered port for a full quarter. Newcastle came second with 202,000 tons, and Sunderland was fourth with 108,000. Hull, with 72,000 tons, was seventh after Whitehaven and the Glasgow area. The ships of Newcastle and Sunderland were principally colliers, which ran up and down between their home ports and the Thames. And coal continued to figure prominently in the trade of such East Coast ports as Yarmouth, Ipswich and Lynn, whence it was carried to places nearby.

The amount of coal carried by water was so considerable that the total coasting tonnage was somewhat greater than the tonnage of the country's overseas trade. But apart from coal the miscellaneous coasting business remained enormous. For much of the nineteenth century it remained exclusively in British hands, since a relic of the Navigation Acts required that goods for home ports should be carried in British ships, manned by crews of whom at least three-quarters were British.

Much of the trade was, by now, in the hands of companies which ran a regular liner service of small ships between certain ports, but there were always the "tramps", which fitted in a little coasting work between trips to foreign ports in search of cargoes. And there were, too, the sailing barges, so characteristic a feature of every minor East Coast port down to the beginning of the Second World War, which between them must have handled an immense amount of cargo every year.

In 1910 there were about two thousand sailing-barges—by which we mean those flat-bottomed vessels with lee-boards. By 1939 their number had fallen to 750, and by 1949 to 125. Today the sailing-barge is virtually extinct, driven out by the auxiliary-engined barge which can work in conditions when the old-style sailing-barge would be weather-bound. It is, however, only with their going that their appeal becomes obvious to people who have not lived with them. For performance or beauty of line it had nothing to compare with many an ocean-going vessel, nor had its crews, in a lifetime at sea, adventures to tell that compared in drama with those of other seafarers. But in the light of hindsight the sailing-barge was a remarkable vessel, and many of the men who earned a hard living in them remarkable men.

There can have been few craft of which more was demanded from the designer, and from the men who sailed them. The sailing-barge existed to make money by the carriage of miscellaneous cargoes. It had, therefore, to be as roomy as possible, but it had to sail fast whether laden or light; it had to be handy enough to navigate a tidal river, or poke up a narrow Essex creek. And above all, it had to be seaworthy in the worst conditions that the North Sea could throw at it.

The sailing-barge, evolved over the years by the aid of experience and intuition was, with all its limitations, a handy boat, fast when lightly laden, and even capable of out-sailing, when conditions were right, boats that would have been held superior. They sailed well both light and heavy loaded, and indeed some of them handled better under a load. Being flat-bottomed, they were ideally suited to the shallow tidal creeks and estuaries of the Essex coast, which has always seemed their natural home. They were adaptable to the carrying of a wide variety of goods, and above all they were cheap to build and run. In the days before the First World War, before steel construction became common, it used to be possible to build a barge for £2,000, and sometimes much less, and to recover its cost within a year. Since their upkeep was small they were well suited to a trade where work was irregular and cargoes had to be sought, provided always that men could be found to sail them. That was still possible before 1939.

It is not difficult to imagine that the men, who crewed the barges in the days before the diesel-engine killed their interest in the job, would not willingly have exchanged their boat for a first-class liner. Since the barge rarely carried more than the captain and his mate, with perhaps a boy apprentice, there was a remarkable degree of freedom, which is lacking in bigger ships. Theirs was a job, too, which called for a high degree of skill and self-reliance. It would probably be true to say that none of these men had any formal training in navigation and seamanship. They learned the skills of their job, as they learned the capacities and limitations of their boats, by seeing how it was done. Not the least attractions of the job was the variety of experience it offered. Although these barges were primarily coasters carrying barley, coal or sand, or any of the innumerable cargoes sent by water, it was not unusual for them to make the trip across the North Sea to the Dutch and Belgian ports, and the owners were content to entrust valuable cargoes to men who could not speak a word of Dutch, French or German, confident that they had the ability to see the matter through.

11

THE GREENLAND WHALERS

IT IS SAID that the first ship to sail out of Hull in search of the Arctic whale left in 1598. From this small beginning Hull became the greatest whaling port in the world. When the whale was virtually exterminated in the northern seas, Hull turned to producing oil by seed-crushing, and from this in turn has grown the group of interdependent industries which are one of the main foundations of the town's prosperity.

But Hull was not the first in the field. The whale was being hunted in the northern seas and off the coast of Flanders in the ninth century. It was the Basques who made a speciality of the craft in hunting the Biscayan whale, and, when the home supply was depleted, began searching for it elsewhere. Their skill was such that usually one Biscayan was enrolled by any foreign vessel, and close attention was given to learn their secrets. That redoubtable old seafarer, Captain John Smith, tried on his own and later said, "We found this Whale-fishing a costly conclusion: we saw many, and spent much time chasing them; but could not kill any."

The "train oil" extracted from the blubber was in much demand in Elizabethan England, and after the establishment of the Muscovy Company the enterprise made rapid strides. The Company would, had it been able, have kept the Arctic enterprise to itself, but it was not long before "interlopers" from the English ports were fishing the same areas. In a very short time, the Dutch, too, had appeared, brought there, it was alleged, by a former servant of the Company who had fled to Holland to escape imprisonment for debt.

It seems likely that the earliest whaling expeditions were to the shores of Greenland, and that name remained long after the centre of the enterprise had been transferred to Spitzbergen. By 1613 ships from England, the Netherlands, France and Flanders were hunting the whale in the waters around the island, and bitterly disputing the others' right to be there. In the following year fourteen whalers accompanied by four armed vessels came from the Netherlands alone, and the year after that tried, unsuccessfully, by a show of force to keep the ships of other countries away from the area.

The Dutch, unlike the English whalers (who in 1617 brought home 1,900 barrels of oil), were at first not very successful. But they were persistent, and in 1623 they set out with a particularly large fleet of ships, carrying all the materials needed to build a complete whaling station. The site chosen was on the north-western tip of the island, and it was given the name Smeerenburg. This marked the beginnings of Dutch pre-eminence in Arctic whaling, which lasted a very long time. Soon more than a thousand whalers and their attendant boats were sailing northwards in the summer months from Amsterdam, Rotterdam, Flushing, Middelburg, Veere and other Dutch ports. The boom-days of Smeerenburg were, however, short-lived, because the whales which had abounded in the neighbouring bays were soon killed off or frightened away, and the whalers had to pursue them along the coast, or out into the Arctic.

Success in the whale fisheries depended very much on the size of the national effort and the amount of support given by the Government at home. The Dutch whaling-fleet was often given armed escort, and their products were protected by a tax on foreign whale products. The French, on the other hand, who went to Spitzbergen in small numbers, were regarded as the legitimate prey of every other bigger fleet. In 1636, fourteen French boats were taken by the Spaniards.

A great deal of the English effort was wasted by the disputes of the Muscovy Company with English "interlopers", whom it lacked the power to control, as well as with foreigners, and in formally taken possession of this or that area of land or sea in the name of the King, without being able to make the possession effective. Nor was the practical side of the job handled with the skill and foresight that the Dutch showed. The crews were not always equal to the fogs and storms and other hazards of the region, with the result that ships were lost. The blubber and utensils were carelessly handled, and that, too, meant loss. The Company made enemies, but was not always ready to fight off reprisals. In 1617 some of its ships were attacked by armed Dutch vessels, which captured two English ships and a pinnace, rifled them and burned their casks. The other English vessels dispersed in a panic. In 1622 the Company was put up to auction. The new owners struggled on for a few years. But, in 1625, their boats arrived in Spitzbergen to find that rivals from York and Hull had been there before them and had burned their casks, demolished their fort and houses and had stolen or ruined their boats and gear. But, apart from this, the English were finding the enterprise increasingly unprofitable. This was in part because they continued to search the bays for whales long after the Dutch and Basques had appreciated the need to hunt them further north in the open sea. In 1698, of the 189 whalers engaged, 129 were Dutch, and of the 1,968 whales caught during the season, the Dutch took 1,255.

The old whaling ships were all very much alike from whichever port they came. They were strongly built and capacious, and in consequence rather slow. They were of two hundred tons dead weight, or rather more, and carried a crew of twenty-five to fifty or more. In addition, they carried as many harpooners as there were boats, a number of coopers, two cutters, who prepared the whale-flesh for boiling, and two pursers.

F*
[169]

In preparation for the voyage, which began in March, everything that was likely to be needed, down to the wood to heat the cauldrons in which the oil was extracted, had to be put aboard.

The method of hunting the whale was extremely hazardous and not very different from the methods used in *Moby Dick*. On sighting the whale, the small boat, rowed by perhaps eight or ten men, with the harpoonist at the prow, set off in pursuit. The harping-iron was fitted to a wooden staff with which the harpoonist would plunge the iron into the whale. That, in turn, was fastened to about five fathoms of fine-quality hemp rope, which was always kept ready in the bow of the boat. The extreme danger of the job lay in the need to approach the whale closely enough for the harpoonist to plunge his weapon deeply into the flesh, with the attendant risk that the animal would smash the boat or capsize it. Having been struck, the whale plunged, carrying the line with it, while someone aboard stood ready with wet cloths to prevent the king-post smouldering as the rope hurtled round it, and someone else stood ready to attach further lines. While the hunt lasted the boat careered, prow down, through the water. It used to be reckoned that the crew would have to pay out ten lines before the whale's strength was exhausted and it was obliged to surface. Then, if all went well, the boats in the vicinity closed in upon it, and killed it with harpoons and lances. It took all the available boats, tethered one behind the other, to tow the whale back to the ship.

Three hundred years ago the whale was not dragged out of the water, but was supported by block and tackle at the ship's side so that it could be turned about as the cutting-in required. The whale-bone and tongue were removed, and then the blubber was cut away. The blubber was towed ashore in 200-lb. pieces to be chopped up and fed into the enormous copper vats, each of which held about 100 gallons. The "coppers" were set into masonry which formed the furnace. The top formed a platform along which the chopped blubber was transported and fed through holes into the vats below. When ready, the extracted oil was bailed out into the first of a succession of coolers with long-handled copper ladles, and the "frittered" whale-meat set aside to keep the furnace burning. The oil, as it ran from the lowest of the coolers, was barrelled, and set aside for shipment at the close of the season.

On the Dutch ships, and perhaps on some of the others, authority was divided between the captain of the vessel, who was in command of all that related to the navigation of the vessel, and the chief blubber-cutter, who controlled the whaling. An important part of their earnings consisted of a percentage of the oil obtained, which was a direct incentive to every member of the crew to capture as many whales as possible. It has been suggested that the comparatively poor showing of the British vessels was due to the payment of fixed wages.

From about 1630, for very nearly a century, the English virtually withdrew from the Greenland fisheries, while the share of the Danes and the French had become of little importance. Meanwhile, the Dutch went from success to success, with only the Germans as new arrivals to share it with them. In 1721, 251 Dutch ships made the journey to the Arctic, together with 55 from Hamburg, 24 from Bremen, 20 from the Biscayan ports and 5 from Bergen.

The enterprise was clearly profitable, and in a period of ten years the Dutch made a profit of 4,750,000 florins. In England, meanwhile, the price of whalebone and oil charged by the Dutch and Hamburg merchants had reached such levels that the newly formed South Sea Company determined to revive the enterprise, and, in 1724, twelve ships were sent out. The Company, however, had not reckoned on the fact that British seamen had no experience of the craft, and experts had to be hired from the Continent at considerable cost. The first results were hardly worth the effort. The cruise of 1724 brought home $24\frac{1}{2}$ whales. A year later twice as many ships brought back only $16\frac{1}{2}$ between them, and so it continued, more or less, until 1732, by which time the Company had lost £7,000.

The traditional response of the fishing industry to difficulties of this sort is to ask for a subsidy, and in due course a bounty of twenty shillings a ton was granted to all ships "fitted out in Great Britain, of two hundred tons and upwards, for the whale fishery, and navigated according to law." It did not make any appreciable difference to the number of whaling vessels, and the subsidy was increased in 1740 and again in 1749. In 1755 the Government began paying the bounty to vessels under, as well as over, 200 tons, while stopping the bounty on vessels over 400 tons. In order to qualify, vessels had to carry one apprentice for every 50 tons.

The improved grant was sufficient to attract the fishermen of some of the ports. Prominent among the newcomers were the ships of Whitby and Hull, and of Leith, Dunbar and Dundee. By the 1760s as many as sixty vessels were making the journey to the Arctic. In 1772 the *Volunteer* of Whitby sighted no fewer than forty whaling vessels at one time. It is clear, too, that there were still whales to be caught for on one memorable day the *Gibraltar*, the *Manchester* and the *Molly*, all out of Hull, between them caught twenty-seven.

By the early nineteenth century the whale was making an important contribution to the economy of Hull, and the Englishmen were feeling sufficiently confident of their position to attack and capture the vessels of the Dutch when they could be found.

The early whale-men were more familiar with their craft than with the pen, so that they are largely unknown, and the story of whale-fishing in northern waters is poorly documented. An important exception was William Scoresby, of Whitby, a contemporary of that even more famous Whitby man, the explorer Captain James Cook. Like Cook, Scoresby's decision to go to sea was almost fortuitous, for neither came from a family of seafarers. But having chosen the career, he was not only industrious, but showed a remarkable intuitive skill, which marked him out for early promotion. But he, too, was to prove that a captain is no better than his crew, and he returned from his first cruise without a single whale or barrel of oil. Before his second cruise, in 1792, he made it a condition of his continuing command that he choose every member of the company. On this occasion he caught eighteen whales and returned with 112 tons of oil, which was about five times the average catch for a ship. From then until the turn of the century his ship, although smaller than some of the others, was the most successful. He stayed for a shorter season than anybody else, with the result that the oil he carried was that much fresher when he reached port. His early successes at first provoked amusement and wonder, but when they continued year after year, it was clear that luck was not the only ingredient. In 1798, by which time he was working for another owner, he brought the *Dundee* into the Thames with 198 tons of oil, having caught the astonishing total of 36 whales. He was never to surpass that number, although he obtained bigger cargoes of oil on several occasions. By 1803, when Scoresby—tired of separation from his family—returned to Whitby to take an eighth share in a new company and the command of a new vessel, the *Resolution,* he was on the way to making a modest fortune. The succeeding years were equally successful, as the accounts for the first eight voyages show:

Total expenses	£37,657	4s.	2d.
receipts	£53,777	9s.	11d.
profits	£16,120	5s.	9d.

A profit of £2,000 a year—multiplied to make allowance for the changed value of money—was very good business and represented a continuing return of 25% on the initial investment in the company. These were years of war with France, when the cost of provisions and wages were high. A calculation of the net profits of the thirty voyages undertaken by the Scoresbys, father and son, between 1791 and 1822 shows the total net profit to have been between £80,000 and £90,000.

There can have been few industries that yielded a comparable return on so small an initial outlay.

But already before the retirement of the elder Scoresby there were signs that the best days of the whale-fishers had gone for ever. As his son says:

> "Superior knowledge of the Arctic ices, and consumate skill in penetrating and navigating the compact or tortuous interruptions to the usual retreats of the whales which with [my father] were so characteristic, were now no longer available. So greatly had the whales been reduced, apparently by the enormous slaughter of their species during the last quarter of a century; and so much scattered had the residue been by the perpetual harrass and attacks to which they had been subjected, that the positions, wherein the opportunity for making a successful voyage used to be constantly afforded, were now almost entirely deserted. Hence the enterprise and skill, enabling the fisherman to take a lead in penetrating the ice, which had been wont to be eminently rewarded, had now become of little avail. No one could calculate on the positions in which fish might be found ... Within about half-a-dozen years of this time the whale-fishery of the Greenland seas proved so utterly unremunerative, as to be all but abandoned as a distinct commercial enterprise. The port of Hull, for example, which during the whole period of my Father's command of a whaler, had, on an average sent out 22 ships annually to the Greenland fishery,—in 1828, only five years after he discontinued the pursuit, had only one Greenlandsman, and the year following none."

12

THE NAVY IN THE NORTH SEA FROM THE TUDORS TO NAPOLEON

THE RÔLE OF the Navy everywhere was changed under the Tudors as a result of a development for which Henry VIII was personally responsible. It came about as a result of the King's passion for big guns. Having seen for himself the devastating effect of the work of the German gunsmiths, the thought occurred to him to put such weapons into the royal ships. It was, of course, totally impractical to put guns weighing several tons into the turrets of the ships that then existed. To have carried them would have caused the ships to capsize in a heavy sea; to have fired them there would have sent the gun crashing through the superstructure on the recoil. The only place to put them was on the cargo deck, and the only way to fire them was to cut holes in the side of the ship. The shipwrights were commanded to try it, and it worked. England now had ships that were, in theory, capable of destroying any ship they encountered, and they were reasonably seaworthy. They still lacked manœuvrability, and tactics had not been evolved to make use of the broadside in an engagement. But, unobtrusively, and almost by chance, the ship had become a weapon, and not merely an armed transport.

Across the North Sea, the political situation was meanwhile turning against England's favour. At the very end of the fifteenth century the Netherlands, which had for long been

Burgundian territory, had become by descent and marriage part of the possessions of the rulers of Spain. It is possible that Henry and his Council, bent on playing France off against Spain, never appreciated the potential danger in a situation in which a great Power, with whom our relations were uncertain, was in a position to threaten our position at both ends of the Narrow Seas. But by Elizabeth's reign, with the growing threat of a Spanish invasion of England, the Crown could not fail to be aware of the great army which Spain kept in the Southern Netherlands, and which Philip would use, if he were allowed, against England. Possibly then, for the first time, we became aware of the importance of the Southern Netherlands for England's security. James's sincere, if unrealistic, attempt to live in peace with Spain had two unforeseen and unfortunate results. With the Fleet laid up and the crews disbanded, the seas around Britain were made safe once more for the foreign privateer. Year after year, fleets of North African pirates sailed up through the Channel, capturing English vessels and enslaving their crews. On occasions they even entered the Thames estuary. Along the East Coast the Dunkirkers, privateers in name, but indistinguishable from pirates, in their small, fast boats, continued to bring fear and ruin. In 1619, when a national subscription was called for to restore the haven of Dunwich, Southwold and Walberswick, it was stated that the cause of the poverty of the towns was the losses occasioned by the pirates. At one stage, the Dunkirkers established a virtual blockade of the Thames, levying a toll upon the ships that entered and left. Some of the Armada fleet still lay in the Medway, but without masts, guns or crews. Parliament talked and complained, but the ravages continued as they had done for a long time, and would continue for several years to come. And, meanwhile, not a few English sailors, lacking employment, were taken on by the "Turks" and Dunkirkers as additional crew.

A consequence of James's policy of peace towards Spain which was not immediately obvious was the denial to British merchants of a share of the trade which was falling from the grasp of the Spaniards. The Dutch had no such inhibitions and prospered greatly by carving out vast trade monopolies, particularly in the East at the expense of Spain's protégé, Portugal. There was little room for sentiment in seventeenth-century trade, and the Dutch, who enjoyed a particular reputation for sharp bargaining, proceeded to build up a monopolistic position in foreign trade to which they made no exception, even to the English, to whom so recently they owed a great deal. The inevitable clash would probably have come in the days of Charles I had the Civil War not occurred. To his successor, Oliver Cromwell, who, like Henry V, needed a popular and successful foreign venture to distract attention from affairs at home, the idea of war with Holland was attractive. He had, moreover, the advantage of a Navy in being, and the backing of the City.

In 1651, before war broke out, the English Parliament passed the famous Navigation Act, which forbade the importation of goods into England except in English ships or in the ships of the country which produced the goods. The Act, reinforced by subsequent measures, remained in force until superseded by a stronger Act in 1660. How effective it was against the Dutch carrying-trade, against which it was directed, is a matter of dispute but it inaugurated a period of hostilities that went on for more than twenty years.

Although Holland, as a wealthy nation, and a great sea Power, appeared at the outset to have great advantages over England, the position was not so one-sided. The wealth and power of Holland depended upon her overseas trade, and geography decreed that to reach her overseas Empire Dutch vessels must pass down the North Sea and through the English Channel where the English had a tactical advantage. England, which was still largely an agricultural country, suffered from no such disadvantage. In this war the issue was plain. It would decide who would command the Narrow Seas. Many of the actions were fought for the protection of convoys of merchantmen, and they were fought with considerable fierceness. The First Dutch War was sparked off by a collision off Dover over the question of saluting the English flag. The first North Sea battle was fought off the Kentish Knock in September 1652, and in the succeeding months the North Sea was the centre of activity. Orwell Haven became a base of first importance, and the neighbouring towns had their subsidiary part. The rush of volunteers from the coastal towns is clear evidence of the war's popularity. But as time went on the local seamen found that there was more to be made in private merchantmen, and the Navy had to resort to the press-gang to man its ships. Nor, as the sick and wounded and prisoners were put ashore, were the local inhabitants pleased to find that they were expected to house them without any guarantee about when they would be paid. When the war was over there was at least one bill for £1,883 owed at Aldeburgh and one for £3,838 at Ipswich. The treaty which brought the war to an end let the Dutch off lightly. They agreed to salute the English flag in the Narrow Seas and to pay compensation for English claims abroad, and the English undertook to recognize the freedom of the North Sea fisheries.

The quarrel with Holland, however, was about trade. As General Monk bluntly put it, "The Dutch [had] too much trade, and the English [were] resolved to take it off them." And this was a matter that the First Dutch War had not resolved.

In the years which followed, English overseas trade grew, but not as rapidly as had been hoped. And, in spite of her defeat Holland continued to retain the bulk of the carrying trade. In the prevailing jingoism that pervaded the Court and City in the '60s war could not be long avoided, and, in fact, the English went out of their way to provoke it. Samuel Pepys, who, as Clerk to the Navy Board, was better able to assess our ability to wage war at that moment, observed, "They are ringing the bells now, soon they will be wringing their hands." In 1665, when the Second Dutch War broke out, he would have found few in the City to agree with him.

The pattern of action was much as before, with the English Navy surprisingly successful in battles which showed that on balance they were a match for the Dutch. In a hard-fought battle off Lowestoft in June 1665, at least twelve Dutch boats were destroyed, at least fourteen captured and over two-thousand prisoners were landed at Southwold. In the following year, after the Four Days' Battle which the Dutch should have won decisively against the divided English fleet, but which they were glad to break off, the English put to sea again within seven weeks and won a resounding victory on July 25th. The English Admiral continued to cruise unmolested along the Dutch coast as far as Texel, where he sent a detachment into the Vlie. It destroyed some 150 ships as well as a town in West Terschelling in an operation known as Holmes's Bonfire.

But already Parliament was counting the cost of the war, and, without waiting for the conclusion of peace, the main fleet was laid up in the Medway. The Dutch were not slow to see their advantage. Arriving off North Foreland in June 1667, the Dutch Admiral, De Ruyter, captured the unfinished fort at the entrance to the Medway, smashed the chain defence at Gillingham, and had the Royal Fleet at his mercy. When the Dutch penetrated the Thames to Gravesend, the sound of their guns threw London into a panic. It was a day that Englishmen did not quickly forget, and which seemed to throw away nearly every advantage previously won. Fortunately, the Dutch wanted peace, too, and, fearful of French designs on the Low Countries, were less disposed to drive a hard bargain. The Navigation Acts were modified in favour of the Dutch, and we surrendered the last of our spice islands in the East Indies. As a sop, the Dutch gave us a settlement of little importance on the North American continent. It was known as New Amsterdam, and later re-named New York.

England had as much reason to fear Louis XIV's plans for French aggrandizement in the Low Countries as the Dutch themselves, even if the nature of the menace was not fully appreciated at that time. Nor could England be indifferent to the possibility that France might seek to take the place of Holland as a great mercantile and naval Power. Every instinct should have prompted the English to stand neutral, if they were unwilling to aid the Dutch in any war between France and Holland. But Charles II's need for money was such that he contrived an alliance with Louis, trusting always that the recollection of past bitterness towards the Dutch would be sufficiently fresh to make his policy acceptable at home.

In this way, England found herself committed in 1672 to war once more with the Dutch. With French support, the English should have had a convincing superiority, but events turned out differently. In May 1672, the Dutch caught the English fleet at anchor in Southwold Bay, and used their fireships to good effect. The French squadron, so they said, misunderstood their orders and sailed off. A year later, the English fleet found itself again in a hard-fought action off Texel, and again the French left it in the lurch. But this time the public was less ready to accept explanations, and Charles was forced to make peace. The war on land between France and Holland continued for another four years, during which the English were free to penetrate the markets which the embattled Dutch could no longer hold, and over which the two countries had fought so long.

In November 1688 the ships of the British Navy which had been assembled at the Gunfleet, off the Essex coast, could have inflicted serious losses, had it been so minded, upon the cumbersome fleet of William of Orange. But it chose to remain inactive, and the great fleet ran unhindered before a fresh easterly breeze while crowds of watchers on both the French and English looked on from the cliffs above the Strait of Dover. The accession of the Dutchman, as William III of England, inevitably resulted in a re-orientation of our national policy and inaugurated a period of Anglo-French wars which were not unpopular because it seemed that our obligations were in line with our national interests.

During the 125 years that we were fairly regularly at war

with France, the principal naval engagements were mainly fought out further south in the Channel and Atlantic, or far away from the shores of Britain. We did, however, become increasingly conscious of one sensitive area of the North Sea coast. This was the Scheldt estuary, over which Louis XIV, in his wars of aggrandizement, was determined to gain control. To prevent this, we were prepared to send a succession of armies overseas. The importance of the area was as evident to Napoleon as to his predecessor. Antwerp was, he declared, "a loaded pistol that I hold against England's throat". In 1803 he decreed the construction of two basins there capable of holding 52 ships of the line, and he set about making Antwerp the greatest naval base in the French Empire. To neutralize the base, England sent an expeditionary force to the Scheldt in 1809, while Napoleon was otherwise occupied in Austria. Unfortunately, it wasted itself upon the island of Walcheren. But that was not the end of our interest in the area. The securing of the ports from the Scheldt to the Seine became a basic maxim to every British strategist. Wellington's concern for the safety of the North Sea ports caused him to misinterpret Napoleon's intentions, a mistake that nearly cost him the battle of Waterloo. And, not least, it inspired the guarantees that Britain gave to Belgium before the First World War.

After Trafalgar, it was clear that an invasion of Britain was impossible, and while the British Navy tightened its blockade on enemy coasts, Napoleon's thoughts turned to the idea of an economic blockade of Britain. The position seems paradoxical, but the idea was not so novel as has sometimes been supposed. Nor was French weakness at sea an insuperable obstacle to success. The economic notions current at home, which measured national prosperity in terms of a favourable visible trade balance and an influx of gold, were current also in France. And from the outbreak of the Revolutionary Wars French industrialists and traders had welcomed every attempt to interrupt our trade with Europe, and so to cripple Britain economically. The efforts ended in failure, but not before serious hardship had been inflicted on this country. Britain needed, in particular, grain and timber from Europe, and when the normal channels dried up, she sought for others. Between 1789 and 1800 the trade with Prussia and Russia was expanded, and the trade with Bremen and Hamburg expanded six-fold. It was less easy for France and her allies to find alternative sources of the colonial goods, the textiles and iron-ware which Britain had been in the habit of supplying. The first French efforts achieved the opposite from what was intended. In the last decade of the century, British exports doubled, while her imports increased by 64%.

The position in Europe in 1806 was, however, radically different from what it had been in 1800, with France now master of all Europe, and Russia an unwilling confederate. In November 1806, therefore, by the Berlin Decree, Napoleon declared that the British Isles were in a state of blockade, and that no vessel coming directly from Britain or her colonies should be admitted to any port under French control. Moreover, to maintain control over goods imported into Holland, Spain, Italy and Switzerland, it was required that these should be marked with the country of origin. The Decrees had an immediate and serious effect upon Britain's economy. Exports, which in 1806, had been £40.8 million, dropped in 1808 to less than £35.2 million, while grain imports in 1808 fell to one-twentieth of the level of the previous year.

It looked for a time as though the French measures might achieve all that was hoped of them. Distress in the industrial areas of England was further aggravated by the consequences of the Government's counter-measures, which sought to control the trade of the neutral Powers with Europe by introducing a licensing system. Napoleon reacted with the Milan Decrees of November 1807, which now ordered the confiscation of all ships that had called at English ports, and directed that many commodities were to be reckoned British unless it could be proved that they were not. The Americans, who were caught in this dilemma, reacted by placing an embargo upon trade with both sides. But, in fact, the British were the only sufferers, since British industry was heavily dependent upon American cotton, and relied upon American ships for the carriage of some colonial wares.

The hardship and social unrest was particularly evident in England, but the very efficiency with which Napoleon's port officials applied the Decrees in every port from the Baltic to the Mediterranean ensured their ultimate failure. Within a year, French Customs receipts had fallen to a sixth of what they had been in 1808, and exports had declined by more than a quarter of what they had been in 1806. Moreover, French manufacturers, who at first felt the benefit of relief from British competition, had begun to feel the need for raw materials. French farmers, too, as well as those of Eastern Europe, felt the pinch when they were no longer free to ship their surpluses across the water to England. France, like any other country in time of war resorted to substitutes for what was readily obtainable, but they were expensive and not entirely satisfactory. Moreover, what was tolerable to a patriotic Frenchman was scarcely bearable to France's subject populations. In 1809 Holland opened her ports to American ships, provided that the cargoes were stored in bond under French supervision. It was the beginning of the collapse of the whole system of Continental blockade. Scarcely less important was the oversight that allowed English bills of exchange to be freely negotiated in European banks, and permitted the English to subsidize her allies, and feed her armies.

By 1810 colonial wares were again in plentiful supply in Frankfurt, and Leipzig had become the centre for trade in English goods with eastern Europe. The French, too, partly to pacify the farmers, had to some degree relaxed the blockade, with the proviso that vessels trading with France should take more out than they brought in. Consuls in all the ports which France controlled began the indiscriminate issue of licences, with less regard for the regulation of trade than for the revenue accruing from the licences, in which they themselves shared.

The conditions were favourable to the development of smuggling and the establishment of a black market of enormous proportions.

In the summer of 1810 the Emperor, alarmed by the course of events, sought to win the support of the United States by agreeing to rescind the decrees affecting neutrals, provided that Britain would relax its control, and at the same time tightened the measures against smuggling. A tightening of the blockade was followed in 1811 by a succession of bankruptcies all over Europe, and growing commercial difficulties among France's allies, which contributed to Russia's decision to break with her ally. In France itself, the industrial towns of Rouen and Lyon were almost at a standstill, and the financial houses were feeling the strain. But the situation had a corollary in England, where bad harvests added to the difficulties. The interruption of the export trade across the North Sea and Channel in 1811 reduced business with France and Northern Europe to 20 per cent of the volume of the previous year. Our exports to all countries for the year amounted to £39.5 million, compared with nearly £61 million in the previous year (admittedly, an exceptionally good year) and about £48.5 million in 1805.

The Emperor had succeeded, probably beyond his expectations, in exposing the vulnerability of England, and he did so without command of the sea and without important resources outside the Continent of Europe. By the early part of 1811 it must have seemed to many informed people in Britain that it had become a question of who could hold out longest. But Napoleon, too, was subject to heavy pressures, and he threw away a trump card when he allowed shipments of corn to England. We, for our part, allowed quinine, cotton and coffee into France, and a brisk business in export licences developed.[1]

1 Even the French Government took a hand in breaking its own blockade. When fifty thousand overcoats were wanted for the army in Poland, they were ordered from England and paid for. The army, however, never received its overcoats, as the consignment was intercepted by the Royal Navy while being shipped to Hamburg.

During 1812 exports were 28 per cent better than in the previous year. The opening of direct channels of trade was an incentive to illicit business, and smuggling flourished wherever the French were unable to prevent it. It was in the summer of 1812 that the Emperor began his ill-fated Russian campaign, and economic matters took second place to political and military questions. Had he succeeded, the economic blockade of Britain would certainly have been tightened once more. As it was, the spectacle of a contest between a powerful maritime country, with complete command of the sea against a land Power able to deny access to the ports from the Baltic to the Channel, was never played to a conclusion.

13

THE SEASIDE RESORTS

THE MIDDLE YEARS of the eighteenth century saw the beginnings of a fashion, which was to have a lasting effect upon the fortunes of many towns and villages along the East Coast. It was the sudden enthusiasm for sea-bathing.

The seaside, until then, was little appreciated (the very word, in its modern connotation, dates from only 1797). Those who lived beside the sea, and made a living from it, turned their backs on it and sought protection from wind and water by building their houses as far inland as they could, taking advantage of any natural shelter. There was no attraction in a good sea view. The ports and fishing villages along the coast offered little, as a general rule, to encourage the visitor to prolong his stay, and the traveller, passing to or from the Continent, did not linger longer than he was obliged to do by wind and tide.[1]

Fashionable society, in search of relaxation and a "cure",

---

[1] Even as late as 1787 the author of the *Guide to Scarborough* thought it well to reassure the intending visitor:

"The approach to sea ports are seldom particularly beautiful . . . Here often (but most frequently in summer) a vapour, arising from the sea, condenses, and obscures by a thick foggy kind of cloud, everything around. Sad, gloomy, and alarming is such an aspect, at such a season, to the earlier apprehension of the infirm visitor, and those of tender health.—But nothing pernicious is to be feared;—the common precautions of a great-coat and a handkerchief, insure safety from every danger."

found what it needed at one or other of a number of spas. The better known, such as Bath, Tunbridge Wells or Harrogate, attracted the gentry in their hundreds during the seasons, and elaborate arrangements were made to make their stay enjoyable as well as beneficial.

Most of the spas were inland resorts. But there were exceptions, and Scarborough was one. The merits of its mineral spring had been long established. It naturally drew most of its visitors from the East and North Ridings, but its reputation extended well beyond. It was providential that among the natives of the town was a Dr. Wittie, author of the first book to draw attention to the merits of sea-water as a cure. His book, published in 1660, recommended its use, both internally and externally. It was, he urged, unsurpassed for "drying up superfluous humours, and preserving from putrefaction; [it] kills all manner of worms". The idea was taken up by other physicians, both locally and in London. In the early eighteenth century, Dr. Peter Shaw published his *Dissertation on the Scarborough Waters,* which ends with directions for bathing in the sea. This was followed by a book by the eminent London physician, Sir John Floyer, on the history of cold bathing, which traced the medical prescription of cold baths from classical times and told of some remarkable cures achieved in this way. A second edition was called for, and in a much expanded version, written in conjunction with Edward Baynard, the author recommends the use of cold water for practically everything from consumption to rupture, from deafness to insanity.

The idea attracted attention, and Scarborough, which could offer the amenities of a spa, was able to take advantage of it. By 1730 the town was on the way to begin a new career as a watering-place.

A Journey from London to Scarborough, published in 1734, gives a lively impression of the early days of the first seaside resort. "It is the Custom," we are told, "for not only the Gentlemen but the Ladies also, to bath in the Sea. The Gentlemen go out a little way to Sea in Boats (call'd here Cobbles) and

jump in naked directly; . . . The Ladies have the Conveniency
of Gowns and Guides[1]. There are two little Houses on the
Shore, to retire to for Dressing."

The morning dip was something of an ordeal to be got over
with as quickly and as early as possible. The hours between six
and eight were recommended. It was essentially a medical
treatment, to be undertaken under medical advice. And perhaps that was as well, since the coldness of the water was regarded as a virtue, and many visitors came in winter and early
spring when the sea was at its coldest. Later, the bigger resorts
provided covered baths with hot and cold sea-water, but these
did not yet exist at Scarborough.

The sea-bathe over, there was still much of the day to fill. And
Scarborough had much to offer. The spa waters continued to
be drunk, and a visit to the spring was enlivened by the dubious
witticisms of Dicky Dickinson, the deformed cripple, who was
in charge of the spa waters. At low tide, there was a good stretch
of sand:

> "The Recess of the Sea leaves a beautiful Parterre upon the
> Sands, of two Miles, the whole level as a Bowling Green;
> and at that time all sorts of sprightly Exercises and genteel
> Diversions go forward there; particularly Horse-racing, fre-
> quent at the Season, either for Plate given by the Town, or
> by contribution of the Company. Great Numbers of Coaches
> and Saddle-Horses are seen scouring over the Sands every
> Morning."

The town had a coffee-house, where for a subscription of
half a crown the visitor could read the latest papers and have
the use of pen, ink and notepaper; there was a bookseller's in
Long-Room Street and a theatre where plays were performed
in the afternoon; there was a Presbyterian church and a Quaker
Meeting, as well as a church of the Church of England (which
had already become far too small for the congregation at the
height of the season).

[1] The ancestors of the formidable Victorian "bathing-women".

The point upon which social life revolved, however, was the Long Room. "Here," says the author of the *Journey,* "are Balls every Evening, when the Room is illuminated like a Court Assembly (and, indeed, for the great number of Noble Personages present, may very justly be called so); Gentlemen (only) pay for dancing one Shilling; on one side of the Room is a Musick-Gallery, and at the lower end are kept a Pharô-Bank, a Hazard-Table and Fair Chance; and in the side Rooms, Tables for such of the Company as are inclined to play Cards; below Stairs you have Billiard Tables . . . There is no Ordinary [table d'hôte] here, but Gentlemen may have anything dress'd in the most elegant manner, the House being provided with Cooks from London."

Nor—although these are not mentioned—did this exhaust the pleasures of a visit to Scarborough. "As a pleasant change, and of an unusual kind," says another author, "ladies and gentlemen (with well-stored panniers) take a cold repast among the grotesque rocks of Clowton-Wyke, four miles from Scarborough. A boat provided with bait, rods, lines, etc., should be ordered round in waiting: the landlord at Clowton public house is a ready guide through the fields to the cliff, and finds many requisites for the completion of the day's enjoyment."

Dr. Richard Russell's famous book, *A Dissertation concerning the Use of Sea Water in Diseases of the Glands,* and the treatment which he offered at Brighton, did much to spread the fashion. It only required royal patronage to put the resorts on the road to prosperity. Before the century was out, any town or village with anything to offer was bidding for custom. Among the smaller places, Wivenhoe and West Mersea both had accommodation to offer, while Harwich was advertising "a newly invented Salt Bath" and "a Crane Chair . . . for such who have not the Strength or Courage to leap in." By 1790, Lowestoft was boasting a six-week season, and Yarmouth offered fishing as well as bathing.

From the very first, there was a note of self-advertisement about the descriptions of the resorts. And, as the profit which

lay in the new fashion became more evident, advertisement
sometimes took the form of disparaging rival resorts. "The sea
[at Scarborough]," says one puff for the town, "is many degrees
cooler, in the month of August, than at Brighton, and possibly
than at Weymouth, or any place southward of the Thames."
From Bath, on another occasion, malicious rumours were
spread of the deaths of several persons of distinction at Scarborough during the season, while Margate's early public relations man, in drawing attention to the bathing-machines,
"happily calculated to preserve the modesty of the female
sex", could not resist the temptation to add ". . . very different
from the marine sentry-boxes at Brightelmstone".

Nor were the writers slow to draw attention to some of the
incidental attractions of a visit to the seaside. Referring to the
opportunities for horse-riding, Scarborough's bookseller, John
Schofield, added: "While, to the South we read such or such
a treaty of marriage is "said to be *on foot*"; here we find them
happily on *horseback*;—and now, as in the times of ancient
chivalry, a knight, or an esquire, is considered as appearing
nowhere more manly, or more acceptable, in the eye of his fair
"Lady Love", than on a handsome, well-caparisoned steed,
obsequiously ready to escort and attend, wheresoever her
pleasure may direct the route."

Nor did the writers overlook the mild sensual exhileration
of the sea-shore, whether the visitor was attracted by the opportunity to laugh at the antics of bathers being ducked by the
bathing-women. There were plenty of admirers, too, whose
poems fill the magazines and guide-books of the time:

> "D'you think, what ancient Bards suppose
> That Venus from the Ocean rose,
> Before she did ascend the Skies,
> To dwell among the Deities?
>
> Yes sure; Why not? Since here you see
> Nymphs full as beautiful as she
> Emerging daily from the Sea.

The Nymph that captivates my Love,
Gay PASTORELLA, there, will prove,
That her perfections cannot die:
She, in her turn, will mount the Sky
And reign the lovlier Deity."

Scarborough flourished, and by the end of the century there
were twenty-six bathing-machines for the use of visitors. Two
bathing attendants were at hand for each lady, and one man
for each gentleman. There was also a lad with a horse to draw
the machines in and out of the water. The use of the machines
was not, by the standards of the time, cheap. It cost a shilling
a time, to which had to be added a tip for the staff "as a recom-
pense for the uncomfortable, fatiguing amphibious life they
lead; and as a reward for their—in general—very civil attention." By that date, too, a second Assembly Room had been
added for the entertainment of the crowd, and a Master of
Ceremonies had been appointed to regulate the public functions. In this, Scarborough had seen the wisdom of following
the general lines which Beau Nash had laid down for the running of the spa at Bath. This not only provided a full programme of entertainment, but made it easy for the newcomer
to fit easily into the society of the town, and prevented the ex-
ploitation of the visitors.

Margate's rise from being a small fishing village to becoming
one of the country's most popular resorts was due entirely to
its proximity to London. By 1765 the sailing vessels which
carried wheat up to London were each taking sixty or seventy
passengers down to Margate on some of their return journeys.
By 1802, the eight or nine "hoys" between them carried over
twenty thousand passengers in a season to or from Margate. In
fair conditions, the journey from London took eight or nine
hours, but against a head-wind it might take a whole day and
night. And there were occasions when the vessels were carried
clear past their destination and out into the North Sea, from

[191]

whence they made port with great difficulty. A guide-book to the town written in 1789 says that few people "in genteel life" travelled by water "unless recommended by their physicians to do so in order to experience sea-sickness, which is thought to be very beneficial in some cases." But it is clear that, for all the discomforts, the river trip was popular with people of all sorts.

Until well into the nineteenth century a number of the old bathing establishments stood on the west side of Margate High Street, backing on to the sea. Here the bathers assembled, and, having had their names entered on a slate, awaited their turns for the bathing-machines. In the meantime, they read the papers, gossiped or passed the time at the piano, which stood in one of the rooms. The *Description of Thanet*, written in 1763, adds: "The bathing rooms are not large, but convenient . . . The guides attend, sea water is drunk, the ladies' dresses are taken notice of, and all business of the like kind is managed. There are three of these rooms, which employ eleven machines till near the time of high water, which at the ebb of the tide sometimes runs two or three hundred yards into the bay. The sands are so safe and clean, and every convenience for bathing is carried to so great perfection that it is no wonder that this place should be frequented by such multitudes of people, who go to the sea either for health or pleasure."

Margate not only quickly acquired the bathing-machines, but also the theatre, the assembly rooms, the hotels and hostelries, and shops and booksellers and everything else that an up-and-coming resort required to house and entertain its visitors. It also acquired the Royal Sea-Bathing Infirmary—the first of its kind— which was opened in 1796 as a place where poor patients might take the sea-water cure. The building was provided with a "solarium", and probably entitles the hospital's founder, Dr. John Coakley Lettsom, to be looked upon as "the father of all open-air sanatoria".

The town was, from the start, a cheerful sort of place. The essayist, Charles Lamb, reminiscing in *The Old Margate Hoy*,

Above, another popular Dutch resort, Zandvoort; *below,* the Danish port of Esbjerg

Reclaiming the Netherlands from the North Sea. *Above,* an aerial photograph showing the Dutch method of drainage; *below,* constructing a road on some of the reclaimed land

wrote, "We have been dull at Worthing one summer, duller at Brighton another, dullest at Eastbourne a third, and are at this moment doing dreary penance at—Hastings!—and all because we were happy many years ago for a brief week at Margate."

Meanwhile, on the other side of the Thames, Southend, with seemingly every advantage—notably a shorter journey from London and a smoother boat passage—was having indifferent success. Although, when George III ascended the throne in 1760, it was still a "poor hamlet of fishermen's huts' at the south end of Prittlewell parish, it attracted bathers who liked a quiet resort. This was especially so after a chemist had set up a laboratory there to crystallize salts from sea-water. There was, moreover, as the century moved on, a growing demand for a quiet resort from people who found Margate a little boisterous, and who were offended by Brighton's scandals and want of propriety.

But, for some reason, Southend never quite succeeded. The mile-wide mud-flats which were exposed at low water, and the difficulties of getting ashore before the pier was built were minor inconveniences. But for success in competition with the established resorts, Southend needed, simultaneously, crowds of fashionable visitors, and all the amenities to house and entertain them. And above all, perhaps it needed royal patronage. To begin with, it had none of these things.

When a new start was made, it was decided to build a terrace of fine houses and a new hotel on the cliffs overlooking the sea, rather than in the old village farther east. By the summer of 1793 new Southend was receiving visitors. The hotel was opened on July 8th with a ball attended by 150 guests. Dancing went on till midnight, and then, after supper and a concert, dancing was resumed until eight o'clock in the morning. In the "seasons" that followed, the hotel became the centre of the resort's social life. The Old Town at the Southchurch end also continued to attract visitors, who found prices there very much cheaper, and in 1795 the Old Town opened a covered baths similar to those at Brighton and Margate.

The time, however, was not propitious for so bold an experiment. Many visitors, who might have come, were deterred by fears of a French invasion. In the summer of 1797, Thomas Holland, one of the more prominent sponsors of the new resort, could not meet his commitments, and his property in new Southend was sold off. In spite of that, people did still continue to visit the resort, and it had its moment of fashion when the young Princess Charlotte was taken there in 1801. Three years later, her mother, Caroline, Princess of Wales, also spent a holiday in Southend.

The town's hopes of becoming a fashionable resort were, however, short-lived. The coming of the steamer, which made the journey to Margate less of an ordeal, dealt a serious blow. And, to judge from Jane Austen's *Emma,* written in 1815, the resort had acquired a reputation for dampness and for promoting agues and fevers. In the 1850s its population was still less than 2,500, and a contemporary writer speaks of "quiet, dull Southend . . . with half a dozen bathing-machines and its two dozen or so bathers."

Meanwhile, the character of the resorts was changing. This was true even at Scarborough. There was no invasion of the seaside by the masses. But wealthy manufacturers, bankers and stockbrokers, and well-to-do members of the farming community were caught up in the fashion and began to invade the places which had been the preserves of the aristocracy. At Margate the change was much more complete. For the steam-boat made the resort "popular" even before the coming of the railways. In 1830 nearly 100,000 people are said to have landed at Margate from London.[1]

Inevitably, the resorts began to acquire a social grading.

1 The growing popularity of Thanet after the coming of the Steamboats is shown by the figures of visitors to Margate and Ramsgate:

1812-13	17,000
1815-15	21,931
1820-21	43,947
1830-31	98,128
1835-36	105,625

This is reflected in "The Tuggses at Ramsgate", one of the stories in Charles Dickens's *Sketches by Boz*. There, the Tuggs family, having come into some money, decide to go on holiday. But where? Gravesend, on the Thames, was dismissed as "low". Margate? "Worse and worse . . . nobody there but trades people". Finally, Ramsgate was agreed upon as "just the place of all the others".

Sea-bathing remained popular, but the original purpose of going to the seaside for a cure was soon lost in the quest for relaxation and enjoyment.

The donkey-ride, which was to be a feature of many a child's seaside holiday for the next century, made its appearance at Margate about 1800. The donkeys were particularly popular with the ladies, and the proprietor in the High Street who kept them had a sign engraved over his door which read:

> "An Angel honor'd Balaam's ass,
>   To meet him in the way,
> But Bennett's troop through Thanet pass
>   With Angels ev'ry day."

The prudent author of the *Guide to Thanet* advised visitors to engage the donkeys by the journey if they were proposing to go a long way, and by the hour of they were merely riding for pleasure.

Bigger crowds, of a lower social level, inevitably meant that something would be done about sea-bathing. The men's carefree habit of bathing nude lingered on,[1] although at some resorts groups of women seem to have found an effective weapon by stationing themselves at intervals along the beach, thus separating the men from their clothes. But this was the eve of an era when mock-modesty was in favour, and the women were the first to succumb. It was perhaps not proper for woman to be seen bathing at all. And at Margate, a Quaker, Benjamin Beale, came to the rescue of their modesty by inventing a

---

[1] This was the cause of Mr. Jorrock's' embarrassment when he lost his trousers, although Surtees is not explicit.

canvas cover which fitted on to one end of the bathing-machine and could be lowered whenever a lady entered the water, screening her from public view.[1]

Then there was the matter of mixed bathing. It was gradually discouraged, and people who thought mixed bathing harmless were obliged to go to a Continental resort right down to the First World War.[2]

By present standards, the steam-boat journey to Margate was not cheap, although it was cheaper than by coach. One of the better cabins cost twelve shillings and a fore-cabin ten shillings. In spite of that, the trip down the river from London was very popular, and by 1827 there were five boats making the run during the season. The saloons were said to be comparable "to a London coffee-house", and were provided with books, newspapers, cards, backgammon, chess and a band. A very vivid picture of the Margate boat of the period is to be gained from the chapter in *Jorrocks' Jaunts and Jollities* in which Mr. Jorrocks makes a trip to Margate. Perhaps even more surprising than the cosmopolitan nature of the passengers which the *Royal Adelaide* carried was the fact that Mr. Jorrocks's companion appears to have made a practice of going down to Margate for the week-end, because he found Sundays with "the old folk in Tooley Street" more than he could bear. *Jorrocks* is, of course, a work of fiction, but Surtees would clearly not have put in anything that his readers would have thought too remote from everyday life.

Charlotte Brontë provides another clue to the popularity of the seaside in the deep romanticism of the early Victorian. Speaking of seeing the sea for the first time on a visit to Bridlington in 1839, she wrote, "The idea of seeing the SEA—of

---

[1] Beale's invention was copied at many resorts, but he did not reap any benefit from it and died a pauper. He is usually credited with the invention of the bathing-machine, but as John Setterington's engraving of Scarborough in 1735 makes clear, there were bathing-machines long before Beale's time.

[2] Blackpool would not tolerate mixed bathing from the outset. A bell was rung when it was time for the ladies to take to the water, and any man found in the vicinity was fined!

being near it—watching its changes by sunrise, sunset—moon-light—and noonday— in calm—perhaps in storm—fills and satisfies the mind." She was overpowered by the first encounter and shed some tears before she could bring herself to speak.

Children are conspicuously absent from most of the guides to the resorts written before about the middle of the nineteenth century, but some of them were taken to the seaside all the same. In 1803 William Hutton wrote, "To observe the little animals, in the greatest degree of health and spirits, fabricating their pies and their castles in the sand, is a treat for the philosopher," and a little earlier John Schofield in his *Guide to Scarborough* makes a passing reference to them. But the early pleasures of the seaside were not devised with the children in mind. It was not until the early years of Victoria's reign that the public discovered that the seaside, with its unlimited areas of sand and water, its donkeys, sea anemones and shells, sea-weed and pebbles, was a child's paradise.

When, in 1841, Dr. A. B. Granville prepared a map of the principal bathing places in England, his list of 36 included no less than 14 on the East Coast. They were Tynemouth, Hartle-pool, Seaton, Redcar, Whitby, Scarborough, Flamborough, Bridlington, Yarmouth, Lowestoft, Aldeburgh, Southend, Margate and Broadstairs. It is not clear by what criterion he judged a place a resort, for the Census of 1841 shows holiday visitors in quite a number of other places. Their numbers were always very small, but the Census was taken in June, which is not a favourite month for holidays in England, and the numbers were everywhere smaller than one would have expected.[1] Cleethorpes had 186 "for the annual feast and sea-bathing": there were 50 at Cromer, 44 at Skegness, 60 at Bridlington, 28 at Alnmouth and 50 at Cullercoates. Another generation was to pass before Clacton received separate notice in the Census returns.

The great expansion of the seaside towns waited upon the

[1] Even Margate is only credited with 1,586 visitors.

coming of the railways, and in the 1840s they had not arrived. Except in the case of Margate and Broadstairs, the visits of working people to the seaside were limited to day-trips to nearby resorts: few stayed longer.

One of the earliest railway excursions was arranged by the organizers of a church bazaar at Grosmont in 1839, who persuaded the local company to issue cheap tickets to Whitby on their horse-drawn trains. But the possibilities which the railways offered were not at first appreciated. As the Select Committee on Railways found in 1844, "Fares were fixed just low enough to preclude the possibility of competition, and to give the railways the advantages of what might be called the latent coach traffic, developed by a slight advantage in economy and an immense advantage in point of time and facility, but not low enough as to call into play an entirely new description of traffic." The outcome of the inquiry was the "Parliamentary train", which obliged the railway companies to provide accommodation for passengers at the rate of 1d. a mile. The railway companies were not long in discovering the profit in the third-class passenger and the excursion train.

"It has been alleged," wrote Dr. Granville, "that the being wafted through the air at the rate of twenty or thirty miles an hour, must affect delicate lungs and asthmatic people: that in such as are of a sanguineous constitution and labour under fulness of blood in the head, the movement of rail trains will produce apoplexy; that the sudden plunging into the darkness of a tunnel, and the emerging out of it suddenly, cannot fail to make work for the occulist; and finally, it has never been doubted but that the air in such tunnels is of a vitiated kind and must give rise to the worst effects; while at the bottom of deep cuttings or excavations, being necessarily damp, will occasion catarrhs and multiply agues." Granville was clearly not persuaded by the arguments he set down, nor was the general public. A number of resorts had still to wait several years before the railway reached them, but when it came the change was sudden and complete, and the phenomenon of the English seaside resort which has often puzzled foreigners, and some-times pleased them, was on the way to its fullest development.

The middle classes were the first to adopt the idea of an annual seaside holiday. And just as the Tuggs family had had its criteria in choosing a resort, so now the newcomers had standards of their own. By the late forties, Walton-on-the-Naze was advertising itself as "a most healthy watering-place, and but little known", and a score of other small towns and villages along the coast found that they could offer just the kind of pleasant relaxation which some holidaymakers sought. To some ancient ports and decaying fishing harbours, such as Whitby, this new-found popularity was also a new lease of life.

The railway companies, too, found a new source of profit in the holiday traffic, and began to promote the stretches of coast which they served by offering excursion fares and family tickets, and by themselves advertising the resorts or providing sites on which such advertising could be displayed.[1]

It is clear from Mr. Jorrocks' adventures that the London crowds had radically altered the character of Margate by 1830. Its most insistent feature was noise.

At Margate, the great event of the day was the arrival of the London boats, and, on a Saturday, the arrival of the "Husbands' Boat", which brought the men-folk to join their families—"the stayers"—for the week-end. The Saturday Boat always drew the crowds, not only of wives and children and sightseers, but of touts and musicians and street-sellers, and of course the local wags who could always be reckoned on to find victims for a few bawdy jokes about goings-on in Town while the wife was away. Lord William Pitt Lennox, who was in Margate in 1857, thus describes the town:

"The jetty was nearly blocked up with elderly gentlemen and antiquated dames in bath chairs; nursery maids with their numerous charges; porters conveying the baggage to and from the steam-boats, showing little respect for the pedestrians;

---

[1] Probably the best known of all these advertisements is the "Skegness Is So Bracing" poster designed, some years later, by Arthur Hassall.

"would-be yachtsmen" with duck trousers, blue jackets, fancy boating-shirts, glazed hats and long telescopes; young ladies dressed in the extreme of fashion with attendant beaux, more exaggerated in their costume than their fair companions; middle-aged females "got-up" in the most juvenile fashion with knowing hats, short petticoats and those fawn coloured boots so peculiar to the visitors to the Isle of Thanet; ragged urchins offering their services as carriers of carpet-bags and cloaks; boatmen recommending a sail round the forsaken hulk of the "Northern Belle", as if an ill-fated ship would furnish agreeable reflections on a pleasure trip, the town band playing all the popular airs to the delighted multitude—and all multitudes are delighted with music, especially when they can have it for nothing.

> "If the jetty was alive, the streets were equally so—flymen, goat- and donkey-drivers, owners of children's perambulators and chaises, vendors of cakes, Bath buns, apples, pears, cherries, strawberries, pologne sausages, lollipops, brandy balls, imperial pop, periwinkles, shrimps, red herrings, gingerbread, nuts and roast potatoes; saleswomen offering lace embroidered collars, worked sleeves, antimacassers, crochetwork, worsted ornaments for the table, children's socks, garters and night-caps; salesmen with shoes, boots, slippers, bootlaces and blacking-balls; fishermen crying fresh soles, lobsters, whiting, shrimps, Pegwell Bay prawns, Mackerel 'all alive'."

At the height of the season, eating-houses, pastry shops, taverns and the bathing establishments were full to capacity, and there was not an apartment to be had in the town. The Assembly Rooms—now more like a popular London concert hall in Surtees' description—had Genge, "the sweetest of tenors", who appeared nightly to a packed house. A number of London stars were booked at the Theatre Royal, and an American Circus was billed to give two evenings and two matinée performances "in which stupendous elephants, magnificent, highly trained horses, talented riders, unequalled acrobats, daring tight-rope dancers, clever ponies, educated mules, dashing female equestrians and jocose clowns" would take part.

Most of the essential features of the popular seaside resort until the First World War were already there in Lennox's description, but not, surprisingly, the Nigger Minstrels, who made their appearances about the 50s and were a popular feature everywhere until just before the turn of the century when the blackened faces gave way to the pierrot troop.[1]

Writing in August 1860, a *Times* correspondent noted:

"Our seaport towns have been turned inside out. So infallible and unchanging are the attractions of the ocean that it is enough for any place to stand on the shore. That one recommendation is sufficient. Down comes the Excursion train with its thousands—some with a month's range, others tethered to a six hours' limit, but all rushing with one impulse to the water's edge. Where are they to lodge? The old 'town' is perhaps half-a-mile inland, and turned as far away from the sea as possible, for the fishermen who built it were by no means desirous of always looking at the sea or having the salt spray blowing in at their windows. They got as far back as they could, and nestled in the cliffs or behind the hill for the sake of shelter and repose. But this does not suit the visitors whose eyes are always on the waves, and so a new town arises on the beach. Marine Terraces, Sea Villas, 'Prospect Lodges', 'Bellevues', hotels, baths, libraries and churches soon accumulate, till at length the old borough is completely hidden and perhaps only reached by an omnibus."

There was a good deal of profit to be made from the holiday trade, and in the resorts which sought it public and private enterprise combined to give the public what it wanted. A good promenade was of the first importance, and so too was a pier, even when this served no practical purpose as a landing-place. Ornamental gardens and bandstands followed. The public

---

[1] Scarborough had its pierrot party in 1896, five years after the first group appeared at Cowes.

was also becoming more demanding about such basic things as sanitation and water supply.

The seaside towns within easy reach of London that sought to profit from this explosion developed enormously in the years that followed. The railway reached Southend in 1856, and by 1861 was only an hour's run from town.[1] But there was a feeling that anywhere north of Walton was rather far for a week's holiday, and even Yarmouth's miles of golden sands did not attract Londoners in the same way as the South-east resorts. It did, however, attract the Midlanders, and went on to build a big holiday business.

Scarborough grew from about 13,000 in 1851 to just over 38,000 at the turn of the century, but since then has remained fairly stationary. Felixstowe, Southwold, Cromer, Hunstanton all had their devotees but never became popular resorts. Further north, Bridlington was popular with day-trippers from Hull, and enjoyed a busy, if short, season. Tynemouth benefited from its proximity to Newcastle, and Roker developed as a suburb of Sunderland. The Lincolnshire resorts were particularly late in developing, although Skegness, Mablethorpe and Cleethorpes were to establish themselves as quiet resorts.

Although the essential features of the English resort were repeated from town to town, and change such as it was seemed to take the form of adding yet another amenity to attract the visitor, the observant might have noticed minor changes over the years. The bathing-women were the first to go. Then, the horses that drew the machines down into the water, and the men that looked after them. The machines were at first stationed at high-water mark, and later put right at the back of the beach. Shortly before the First World War the machines themselves began to disappear, and were replaced by tents and afterwards by more permanent huts. The change, however, was

---

[1] In 1871 its population was still less than 3,000. It grew to under 8,000 in 1881, to over 12,000 in 1891, and to nearly 63,000 in 1911.

slow, and the machines on wheels were still to be seen well after the First World War.

The War itself did not bring the resorts to a standstill. Husbands and sons might be away, but families continued to take their summer holiday. Along the East Coast there was the constant reminder of the war at sea in the jetsam from sunken vessels on the beaches, from the occasional floating mine and the barbed wire spread out in improbable places by local enterprise against the possibility of a German invasion. The East Coast had to take the brunt of enemy attacks on civilian targets. In December 1914 Scarborough, Whitby and Hartlepool were bombarded by German warships, and a month later some of the first bombs to fall on English soil were dropped by a Zeppelin on Yarmouth and King's Lynn. From then on, the coast was always liable to attack by aircraft on the way to, or coming from, the big industrial targets. But the danger was never very great. Most holiday-makers accepted it as the inevitable consequence of war. And, in fact, most resorts were little marked by enemy bombardment. With the Armistice and demobilization, the resorts were among the first places to benefit from the general desire to return to "normality". It was, however, a return with a difference. Accepted conventions of public behaviour tended to be looked at anew, and, although not abandoned, were modified. Mixed bathing became more common; women abandoned the knee-length bathing costume and floppy mob-cap for close-fitting costumes of a more abbreviated style, rubber swim-helmets and brightly coloured wraps. And, as the years between the wars rolled on, and the German craze for sun-bathing was taken up in Britain, costumes for men and women shrank still further. There was, too, a gaiety, a desire to make up for lost years, giving life at the resorts a momentum probably not known at any other time. More people, too, were taking holidays. By 1934, half of the working families in London were taking holidays away from home. Places such as Southend and Margate, which catered for the crowd, benefited especially. Just before the outbreak of war in 1939, Southend was attracting 5½ million visitors during the season, and Margate one million.

The holiday camp is said to have existed in Britain since the '20s, but it made little impact upon the resorts until Billy Butlin opened his first camp at Skegness in 1936. But the Butlin Camp immediately appealed to thousands of Britons as offering the kind of holiday they had been looking for. By the time war broke out, Butlin had already seen his ideas copied by a host of competitors, so that in 1939 there were some two hundred camps, large and small, round the coasts.

In the late summer of 1939 the resorts were filled with visitors of a different kind. These were the school-children who had been evacuated from the industrial areas which were likely to be targets of enemy attack. They were removed, however, from the East Coast towns after a few months when it was seen that these resorts, too, were vulnerable.

In this war it was less easy for the resorts to carry on as usual. Too many people were personally involved, rationing was introduced earlier and more widely, and the North Sea coast was more heavily bombed. Finally, from April 1944, a ten-mile-wide stretch of coast from the Wash southward, and certain areas round the Firth of Forth, were declared prohibited areas to all save those who lived there, or who had valid reasons for entering the zone during preparations for D-Day.

After 1945 the resorts, no less than their former visitors, were anxious to get back to normal as quickly as possible, in spite of the many difficulties. And none were better able to do this than the holiday camps, some of which had been used during the War by the Armed Forces.

In the years immediately after the War, the resorts did very well. Not only had people saved money which they had been unable to spend, but an ever-increasing number of them were taking holidays. This more than offset the increasing numbers going abroad. And, of course, some of the more conveniently situated towns, such as Margate and Ramsgate, benefited from traffic in the opposite direction from Continental visitors who found nothing comparable to the popular British seaside resort in their own countries.

The coming of the automobile and the development of coach travel has been responsible for some of the biggest changes since the war. The bigger resorts are now drawing their visitors from much greater distances. Margate, for example, which even fifteen years ago drew 70% of its summer visitors from London and the Home Counties, now draws 60% or more from the Midlands and the North. The changes have not been all to the advantage of the resorts, and particularly to the seaside landlady. There has been a tremendous increase in the number of day-trippers, and a growing popularity of the caravan and holiday camp.

The resorts have met the changed social conditions in various ways. Many of the boarding-houses and small private hotels have been converted into holiday flats. In other places the seaside landlady has held on by adding new amenities and services, such as baby-sitting, television and better cooking. In some places, too, and particularly in some of the smaller resorts on the North-east coast, the force of conservatism has been strong. In Bridlington, for example, there are landladies who have had the same visitors for seasons on end. Visitors not only like things the way they are, but often look upon the landlady as a family friend.

It is safe to say that the seaside will go on changing, as it has constantly changed over the past two centuries. The direction of some of the changes can already be seen. Southend, which is too near London for more than a day trip, even for London's East Enders, is likely to find its future prosperity in a growing residential population, in its airport and light industries. Yarmouth, and a number of other resorts, are already finding new wealth in North Sea gas. On the other hand, the upsurge of new sports—particularly sailing—is bringing week-end yachtsmen and their families in their hundreds to places such as Burnham-on-Crouch, which had until recently been quiet backwaters.

14

THE HARWICH PACKET
SERVICE

THE STORY OF the Harwich packet service begins almost exactly three hundred years ago, although clearly that did not mark the beginning of a mail service between England and the Continent. For centuries before that, messages must have passed regularly between merchants in this country and their agents, or members of their families, resident abroad. Indeed, the *Cely Letters* are perfect examples of just this type of correspondence. Much of it was entrusted to the captain of a convenient ship, or to a trusted courier. The needs alike of Crown and merchants led to the development of a regular foreign mail service in the reign of Henry VIII. But for a long time the Crown pursued a curiously ambiguous policy. It was to be regarded a privilege to use the royal mail service. But, on the other hand, the Crown did what it could to prevent the use of private couriers, partly, no doubt, to prevent treasonable correspondence. Foreign merchants were allowed their own messenger, provided he carried only business letters in one of their own vessels and that the approval of the Master of the Posts had been sought. The Merchant Adventurers and other English merchants fought for, and obtained, similar rights. For the rest, the mail intended for the Low Countries and Northern Europe seems to have gone by way of Dover and Calais. The service was not particularly rapid, and there were complaints of mail taking eight to eleven days to reach Antwerp. Here, by the early seventeenth century, the Continent was already setting an example by introducing a *staffeto*, or express packet service, which travelled by night and day, and departed immediately with the arrival of the mail.

The return of Charles II from exile in 1660 introduced a period of stability into the affairs of the Post Office, and is in some ways a point of new departure. In 1661 an arrangement was entered into with the Dutch for the establishment of a packet service from Harwich to Holland. A few years later there was a twice-weekly service sailing on Tuesdays and Fridays, and "so many also . . . return weekly, but their arrival being (as the weather) uncertain forceth the Clarkes to perpetuall Attendance". The terminus on the Dutch side then, and for a century after, was Helvoetsluis, on the south side of Voorne, at the mouth of the Maas. On occasions Brill, on the north side of the island, was used, but the former was the better harbour. An English agent, appointed in each, was responsible for loading the mails, checking the passes of passengers and arranging for the passage of "poor soldiers" up to the capacity of the boats.

At first the Dutch preferred to use their own boats on the service, and this appears to have continued for some time even after an agreement had been made in 1668 that the mails should be carried in English packet-boats. It is not surprising that they should have preferred to do so. The number of letters carried at that time could often be counted in tens rather than in hundreds, so that the carrying of passengers was important. The tiny English hoys that were in use then must have given everyone a very uncomfortable passage, save in the best of conditions. In 1669 the Post Office recognized that the Dutch hoys were better suited "to avoid the shelves and sands" of the Dutch coast, and bought three of them. There were other grounds for preferring the Dutch boats. In 1675, an official complaint was lodged that the English boats were "nasty, ill-provided and out of order", while their rivals' were "neat and exact". The Dutch could not do anything about Harwich which, as Defoe reported, was "far from famed for good usage to strangers". But, in fairness, Helvoetsluis and Brill were not well famed either!

The value of the mail service was such that it continued uninterrupted during the Third Dutch War of 1672-4, and, on occasion, boats even sailed through the Dutch fleet to reach their destination. There were naturally moments of anxiety. Harwich once reported that its packet-boats had not returned, and that one had been gone ten or eleven days. A similar thing happened a few months later, when it was suspected that the Dutch were detaining the English while allowing their own boats to sail.

With the accession of the Dutchman, William III, as King of England, the Harwich packet became more important than ever, and steps were taken to improve the service. At the King's suggestion, new boats were built. They carried neither freight nor armament, and relied for safety from attack upon their speed. They proved capable of outsailing the French privateers, but in every other respect they were unpopular alike with crew and passengers. Being without guns made the ships vulnerable in the eyes of the crew, but equally it prevented them from the profitable engagement of a weaker enemy, and that counted for more. They were also uncomfortable in all save the calmest weather. As the Post Office said in a memorandum to a Secretary of State. "It was necessary that they should be low built, but by the experience we have had of them we find that in Blowing Weather they take on so much water that the men are constantly wet during the whole voyage, and can noe ways go below deck to shift [change] themselves, being obliged to keep the Hatches shut to save the vessel from sinking." They did, however, keep the postal service open at a time when war with France, and the activity of French privateers, closed the service from Dover to France and Flanders.

With the end of the war with France the Harwich boats were replaced by hoys of 60 to 70 tons. Something had to be done for passengers comfort, for revenue was falling as travellers switched their custom to the new passenger service that had begun to operate from the Thames to Rotterdam. The ships were again armed, and passengers were again at times the unwilling attendants at a chase. In 1704 the Postmaster General was writing to the Agent at Harwich to complain, "In our whole experience the passage of mails was never so inconstant as it has been this past year." And, a few days later, he was writing to inquire why two boats had been respectively two and three weeks late although they had had favourable winds. There was no prize in tow to be explained away, but the practice was to take a bill of ransom from the defeated captain, and the captains do not seem to have found it difficult to find excuses to explain the delay of the mail on that occasion.

The packets most certainly did not always get the better of such encounters, which were frequent, particularly in time of war, and their general instruction was: "Run when you can, fight when you must, and, when you can fight no longer, destroy the mail before you strike your colours." It was the practice, therefore, when an action was unavoidable, to put the mail near a port-hole and weight it with pieces of iron. It was put in the charge of a sailor whose job it was to drop it overboard if the enemy looked like winning.

In the later eighteenth century, at least, it was the practice at Harwich for the captains to be the legal owners of their ships, and as such responsible for the mail at sea. The actual ownership was often divided between officials in London and the ports. The captain received a fixed amount for the hire of the ship, out of which he paid the crew and met the cost of minor repairs. In addition, he received the profits from the carriage of passengers and freight, and was free to trade on his own account. It was a lucrative position, and at Harwich it was considered "as good as a Vice Admiral's place". In some ports the job tended to become hereditary, and there was a great deal of wire-pulling. Sometimes a ship's captain was appointed on merit, but often the Treasury recommended the appointment of someone who had had no service at sea. Experience was thought not to matter. Navigation was always left to the ship's master, and there were cases (although the Post Office Board disapproved) of captains who regularly stayed ashore.

The crews were recruited locally, and sometimes included a number of the captain's relatives. At Harwich, where wages were higher than elsewhere, the ordinary seaman was paid about thirty shillings a month in the late eighteenth century, and from this a shilling was deducted for pension. Something more was made by a little smuggling. This was so common that it was regarded as one of the perquisites of the job, and when, in 1788, the Post Office Board ordered its abolition the result was an immediate strike. Wages were raised by way of compensation, but the practice still went on. At Harwich, which was also the base of a division of the revenue cutters, as well as the Royal Navy, the practice had the effect of damaging relations between the services still further. The packet-boat crews were not under naval discipline, and the captains were, therefore, held personally responsible for any contraband found.

With the outbreak of the war against Revolutionary France, there was no possibility of an understanding such as had existed with the Dutch when we were at war with them. The closing of the Dover-Calais service threw an extra burden on Harwich, and between 1795 and 1801 the service was transferred still further north to Yarmouth. The capture of the ports of the Low Countries by the French raised further problems. For a time the mail was smuggled out of Katwijk, but afterwards Cuxhaven and Hamburg were used, although in a severe winter, like that of 1798, Hamburg could not be reached, as the Elbe was ice-covered for weeks on end. Later, an agent was stationed at Bremelehe, at the mouth of the Weser, so that ships could use either the Elbe or the Weser.

When peace was restored in 1802 the service between Harwich and Helvoetsluis was restored, but the Post Office decided to retain the service to Northern Europe by way of Cuxhaven. When war broke out again, the Post Office for no obvious reason hoped that the French would tolerate the mail service to Holland. They were mistaken, and three of the Harwich packets were captured in harbour at Helvoetsluis. The captains and crews, together with the Post Office agent and a British envoy, were lodged in prison at Brill. One captain and a number of seamen managed to escape, but the rest, with the agent at their head, were marched off to Verdun where they spent nine years or more in confinement. After that the packet-boats were thrown back on Cuxhaven. But this was soon closed to them and Husum in Schleswig was tried, and when, in the winter of 1803–4, this too was closed, they went to Gothenburg.

These were long, hard years for the service, "attended with more Labor, more Difficulties, and fewer Advantages". The crews particularly disliked entering the Kattegat during winter when few other vessels attempted it. Some mail was smuggled in through Altona and Husum. But relations with the Danes were not cordial, and it was perhaps less than tactful to use the *Lord Nelson* on the run, seeing that Nelson had so recently been responsible for the destruction of the Danish fleet at Copenhagen.

With the return of peace in 1815, Harwich continued regular mail services to Helvoetsluis, Cuxhaven and Gothenberg, but the days when a captain's job was worth a Vice-Admiral's place were over. With the fall in passenger receipts, the Post Office was obliged to supplement the captain's emoluments. There was an inevitable falling-off in efficiency, and it was not unknown for a vessel, on seeing another approaching port, to shorten sail to give the other the right to turn about first. Colchester, too, which had started a packet service to Ostend, was cutting into the profitable Harwich trade. To judge from the local press, Colchester took every opportunity to boost the superiority of its services over that of its rivals, not to mention the merits of its hotels, its road connections and the reasonableness of its porterage charges!

The end of this stage of the history of the Harwich packets came with almost dramatic suddenness. The question of converting the service to steam was considered by the Post Office in 1822, and rejected as uneconomical. Until the coming of the railway, Harwich was comparatively remote. When steamers began to make regular trips across the North Sea from London they could make the journey much quicker than the mails that went by road to Harwich and by sailing-craft from there. Nor were they liable to be weather-bound in harbour for weeks on end as the older vessels had been. And so the General Steam Navigation Company, sailing from London, was given its first postal contract in 1831. In the following year the regular mail service to Hamburg and Holland was transferred to the Company. Two years later, to the disgust of the *Essex Standard* which saw in it a Whiggish plot and an example of Lord Grey's glaring nepotism, the Swedish service was transferred to Hull.

Harwich did not give up readily. At one time there was talk of setting up a European Steam Packet Company, which would run a daily service to Hamburg and the Hague, and it was proposed to ask the Admiralty to spend £30,000 on a deep-water pier. Delays in providing a railway link—it did not come until 1854—were fatal to the plans.

Within a few years economic developments on the other side of the North Sea offered the possibility of again running a paying service from Harwich. In 1863 the Belgian government bought up from Holland the right of levying toll on shipping using the Scheldt, which was the last obstacle preventing the development of Antwerp. And from that time, navigation on the Scheldt became free. At the same time, the Harwich boats regained a contract to run a weekly mail service to Rotterdam. From then until 1939 the service developed without interruption. To Antwerp and Rotterdam were added sailings to Flushing, Esbjerg, Hamburg and Gothenberg. Towards the end of the century the development of Bruges demanded the construction of a deep-water port, and the port of Zeebrugge, which was opened in 1907, has since become the terminus of the Harwich train-ferry. It is, in fact, the only service which now runs directly from Harwich, for the railway authority preferred, as time went on, to develop its own quays at Parkeston.

15

THE EAST COAST IN THE
INDUSTRIAL AGE

In 1800 THE highly industrialized areas around the Northumberland and Durham coalfields were for the most part still rural. Only where good household coal could be easily mined within a few miles of a navigable waterway were there collieries and industrial establishments and groups of workers' houses to change the appearance of this essentially agricultural area. Nor were these industries new. The coal trade was already centuries old. It developed greatly from the seventeenth century onwards, however, and as it did so the old centres grew in size, and new centres grew up among them. But the cost of wayleaves and the laying down of rail-roads for the horse-drawn wagons discouraged the opening of more distant collieries. The Sunderland coal-trade, which gained a footing in the London market when supplies from Newcastle were interrupted during the Civil War, was similarly expanding, but there, too, mining was limited to a small area. The salt industry of South Shields, where at one time there were two-hundred salt-pans employing a thousand men, was already past its peak, but there were a number of other industries offering work. A glass industry, too, had been established at the mouth of the Tyne in the early seventeenth century. There was pottery-making, iron-working and shipbuilding, roperies and other industries subsidiary to shipbuilding also in the vicinity. But the great industrial expansion in the area came later; much later, in fact, than in other parts of the Midlands and Northern England.

Some of the processes, however, which were to lead to a ten-fold increase in the population along the North-east coast (from 200,000 to 2 million) during the nineteenth century, and which were drastically to change the character of the region, were already at work. The roads, which early travellers had found so bad, had already been improved, and this was important since good communications were a prime necessity for the development of the region.

It would, however, be a mistake to think of the development of the North-east as a story of steady progress. Some places like Blyth and Seaton, were run down because of the decline of their salt industry, or their poor harbour facilities. Even in the prosperous, expanding areas, an incident like the exhaustion of a workable coal-seam could lead to large-scale movement of population. Among those to be so displaced was George Stephenson, the inventor of the railway engine, who moved from Willington, outside Wallsend, to take up a job as engineman at a colliery at Killingworth, a few miles away.

During the first quarter of the century, however, the prosperity of the region was increasing. The coal-trade was expanding, and the building of wooden ships at South Shields, iron-working at Newcastle and Gateshead and glass-making along the Tyne were all flourishing industries, able to absorb the high natural increase of the local population.

The great development in the next quarter of a century was due primarily to the great advances in metallurgy. Britain, which had relied upon imports of German steel, became an exporter in the years after the Napoleonic Wars, making possible not only engineering, as the term is now understood, but increasing the demand for coal. This, in turn, lead to a considerable influx of miners into the coalfields, especially from the lead-mines of Derbyshire, which were at that time going through a period of depression. As a result the population rose from 300,000 to half a million between 1831 and 1851.

If one single event has to be singled out for the transformation of the North Sea coast, it was the coming of the railways. The Stockton and Darlington line was opened in 1825, with the object of developing the small pits of the area, by making it possible for them to ship their output. Once it was shown that the railway engine was a practical invention, other schemes were rapidly carried out. One of the first industries to benefit was the iron industry, which had previously been restricted to areas where suitable coking-coal and iron ore were both available.

The first iron ships were built on the Tyne in 1850, and the Armstrong engineering works were established three years earlier. But of more immediate importance was the development of related industries—wooden ship-building, chemicals, iron-founding and the like. There was an ever-growing demand for stationary steam engines for collieries, components for iron bridges, and, as time went on and the steamship became more common, for ship-machinery. In 1829 a shipyard with a patent slipway was opened at Jarrow, and a sail-making factory was opened nearby. The alkali trade was introduced to Britain, when a factory was opened on the Tyne in 1806, and the industry went rapidly ahead after the repeal of the duty on salt in 1823. There was already a copperas industry on the Tyne as well as a number of other similar firms. Only the coal industry in the immediate vicinity of Newcastle did not share the development. Many of the old pits were worked out, and the mining families drifted away. This was all to Wearmouth's profit, however, since it was able to take some of the London household coal-trade in which the Midland's fields were not yet able to compete.

For the most part the new industrial establishments were still small. But there were already signs of the great industrial transformation. The Hawthorn works at Newcastle are said to have begun in 1817 with less than a dozen workmen. By 1830 they were employing more than two-hundred, and as many as nine-hundred in 1850.

The influx of population made radical changes in the appearance of Britain's towns. This was, however, particularly so at Newcastle, where the demolition of the city's northern wall made possible a vast scheme of redevelopment. The feature, however, that singles out Newcastle from many other industrial towns was the foresight to carry out a great scheme of town-planning. Whole new streets lined with buildings in the classical style were created. At one time in the 1830s two-thousand workmen were engaged on the work.

In the 1850s and '60s many areas of the East Coast were reached by railway for the first time. The effect was profound. In Lincolnshire the coming of the railway finally broke the isolation of the area. Cleethorpes, Skegness, Mablethorpe and Sutton-on-Sea, as well as smaller places such as Chapel St. Leonards and Ingoldmells, whose sandy beaches and bracing air were to attract holiday-makers from the Midlands and Yorkshire, all owe their early development to the opening of the railway. No less important, the completion of the link across the Trent enabled coal, foundry-iron and other materials from the Midlands and the North to reach the nascent engineering industries of the area, and (as in East Anglia) provided an outlet and new markets for the flour-mills, the malting and brewing industry and the fish trade.

No part of the North Sea coast, however, developed as rapidly as the North-east where industry continued to encroach upon areas which until then had been entirely rural. It continued to attract population from outside the immediate area, and among those who came—besides Irishmen and Scots and Cornish mineworkers—were workers from the depressed agricultural areas of East Anglia. Even new competition from the Midland coalfields, which supplanted the north-east in the London market, did not cause a set-back, for a new and increased demand for household coal was created by the gas industry. The great boom, however, was in coking-coal, which industry demanded. The development of the Tees-side iron industry was followed by renewed activity in the south-western corner of the coalfield. Further north, the area immediately west of Durham City was developed for the first time, and the area north-west of Bishop Auckland was rapidly expanded. By 1880 there was little scope left for further expansion in the coalfields, and such development as has since taken place has been the result mainly of improvements in techniques or in communications, as in the port of Blyth, which made possible the development of the Ashington area.

By 1850 the North-east was served by an adequate network of railways. Shipping facilities, however, both here and along the whole North Sea coast had failed to keep pace. This was reflected in the statistics for the coal trade. The Tyne, which had neglected the interests of shipping, lost a proportion of its export trade to newer ports in Northumberland and Durham. In 1850, however, the Tyne Improvement Commission was set up, and was followed two years later by the Tees Conservancy Commission. In the course of a decade, important works were carried out at Sunderland, Seaham Harbour and the Hartlepools. On the Tyne, the bar was removed and the channel dredged, new docks were begun and a start was made on the construction of new piers at the river mouth. In this way the North-east ports were put into a position were they could cope with an ever-increasing export business right up to the First World War. In the case of coal, the demand rose from 8½ million tons to nearly 35 million tons.

The first iron ships were launched in the 1840s, but little progress was made until Sir Charles Mark Palmer launched his first iron screw collier. After that the industry, which was to do much to change the physical appearance of the industrial North-east, went rapidly ahead. The *John Bowes* had been launched in 1852, and this was soon followed by the first iron battleship, which was also built at Palmer's yard at Jarrow. After that there was a steady demand for armour-plate, stimulated by the outbreak of the Crimean War. The war also brought the demand for guns, and in 1859 Armstrong turned his Elswick works over to ordnance work. The demand for

steel was met by the establishment of an iron-smelting industry on the Tees, where, by 1856, there were 21 furnaces in
operation at Middlesbrough. On the Tyne, the Tees and the
Wear more and more of the river banks were taken over for the
needs of shipbuilding, graving-docks and marine engineering.
On the Tyne, the industry was at first concentrated below the
town, but the substitution, in 1876, of a swing bridge for the
low stone bridge permitted the industry to develop higher up
the river. During the period up to 1914 employment in the
industry on the North-east coast increased from 5,000 to nearly
50,000. Even the tremendous development of shipbuilding and
engineering in Northern Germany in these years did not halt
the progress.

In company with marine engineering, general engineering
continued to flourish, and in particular there were large railway locomotive and carriage works in the area. In the '80s electrical engineering works were set up at Hebburn and Heaton
and rapidly expanded. Some of the older industries, however,
had reached the peak of their development for the time being
or had actually declined. At Blyth and Seaton Sluice the salt
and chemical industries were already moribund at the beginning of the nineteenth century, and along the Tyne several
firms making glass and chemicals were tempted to close down
by the high prices offered for good river-front sites. In spite of
that, in 1863 nearly half the chemical industry of the United
Kingdom was still concentrated on the Tyne, and by the time
the local industry reached its peak in the early '70s it employed
nearly 7,000 workers. It was not until the First World War that
the perfection of the technique of the fixation of atmospheric
nitrogen led to the establishment of the I.C.I. plant at Billing-
ham, and chemicals were added to steel as the mainstay of
Tees-side.

Of the 2 million who lived in the North-east coastal industrial area in 1913, roughly three-quarters of a million lived in
the urban areas of Tyneside, another 275,000 along Tees-side,
and about 170,000 along Wearside. By that time, the whole

economy of the area was dominated by mining, the iron and steel industry, shipbuilding, heavy engineering and chemicals. Over 60 per cent of all the working population was directly engaged in one or other of them. And to this some percentage of the service industries must be added—notably, the power and transport industries, upon which the key industries depended. The heavy industries, however, offered practically no opportunities for the employment of women. There were dangers in this industrial concentration, particularly in some of the smaller towns where the entire labour force was concentrated in a single industry, and even in one firm. But before the matter was put seriously to the test, the War came, and there was an unprecedented demand for all that the North-east could produce.

It is perhaps natural to think of Lincolnshire as essentially an agricultural area with a flourishing bulb industry, and it comes as something of a surprise to find in Scunthorpe an important steel-making town. It is a town that owes everything to the railway, which supplied the area with South Yorkshire coal and coke, and to the rail and road connections linking Scunthorpe with Sheffield and other steel-using centres. Until 1864, when the first furnaces were lit, the local Frodingham ore had been sent to Barnsley for smelting. Scunthorpe's early development was not sensational. In 1890, when steel was first produced there, the population of the united villages of Scunthorpe and Frodingham was just over 3,000. But in the present century the town has gone steadily ahead. By 1931 its population numbered 34,000; by 1951 it was 54,000 and it has now reached over 70,000. This is another town whose prosperity is entirely bound up with the steel industry. It has been estimated that nearly 50 per cent. of the employed population is engaged directly in the industry. And many of the town's other firms, such as those engaged in making fertilizers and chemicals, in tar-distillation and the making of road materials as well as engineering, are all very dependent upon the steel industry for the materials they use. Fairly recently, some light industries such as clothing and footwear manufacture have been introduced to diversify the economy and more particularly to provide employment for women in what is essentially a man's town.

In Scotland, in contrast with England, the Industrial Revolution led to no shifting of the centre of economic activity away from the Forth-Clyde Valley although within that area Glasgow steadily grew as the economic capital. Textiles have an important place in the industrial history of Scotland, and the chief centre of the flax industry was the eastern Lowland strip, especially Angus. After linen became a factory product, the home supply of flax was inadequate. By 1845 Dundee was importing more than 400,000 tons a year from the Baltic. The finer damask wares were a speciality of Dunfermline. The kindred manufacture of jute began in a tentative way with the import of a few hundred tons from India by a Dundee manufacturer, and later developed to a point where it was one of the products with which the name of Dundee was primarily associated. As time went on Eastern Scotland lost some of its linen trade to Ulster, but gained more in jute than it lost in flax. Coal had been worked for centuries in Fife and the Lothians, but a patriarchal system and heavy royalties reduced it to a secondary industry for a long time. In the 1830s there was greater demand than could be met owing to the phenominal industrial development in the West of Scotland, but in spite of new developments in Fife and elsewhere the coal industry followed an irregular course through the century.

In the years following the First World War the North-east was highly vulnerable. It had too many eggs in one basket. Balance of payments problems, industrial developments in other countries, and nationalist policies hit the area hard. Among the first to feel the effect of the changed conditions were the coalfields of Northumberland and Durham which had relied very much upon their overseas markets. Other industries felt the effect of the falling-off of orders, but they were often able to adjust themselves to new types of work. The Tyne ship-yards, finding the demand for naval vessels severely cut, turned to building other types of vessels and particularly tankers. Tees-side, too, began to produce a greater proportion of steel, for which there was demand, and rather less pig-iron.

The North-east attracted its share of the newer industries, such as electrical engineering. But the area needed more than that, and there was little that it could offer to tempt manufac-turers to go there. The newer industries required few of the old skills. Existing factories, too, were old and specialized, and not always suitable for conversion. In human terms, the prob-lem was a very serious one. For many of the men there was no suitable work. The tankers, which took the place of the war-ships on the Tyne slipways, were much simpler to build, and took fewer men. There were not many openings for men thus displaced, nor were these highly skilled craftsmen always easily trained for other jobs.

The full impact of the situation was not felt until the Depres-sion of 1930. Within two years 37 per cent of the population was unemployed, and the percentage of unemployed in the North-east continued for a long time well above the national average. Distress was not equally spread. Newcastle got off fairly lightly, but lower Tyneside, Sunderland and Hartlepool, which depended more heavily on shipbuilding, all suffered severely.

The town whose story epitomises the economic and social problems of the North-east, and whose response touched the conscience of the nation, was Jarrow. It was a town that had long grown familiar with the ups and downs of industrial life. When there was shipbuilding to be done the money was good: when there was none, the men went on the dole. For after the

Jarrow Steel Works closed down in 1921 the famous Palmer's Works, where they used to say that iron ore went in at one end and came out as a first-class battleship at the other, provided almost all the work for the town. In 1933 Palmer's too, was closed down, and, worse still, the company which bought the property for scrap made it a condition that no shipbuilding should be carried on at Jarrow for forty years. The effect was to throw 85 per cent of the town out of work, and to put 23,000 of Jarrow's 35,000 on public relief. Worse still, perhaps, was the lack of hope that conditions would improve. Those were the days when two hundred men applied for one roadsweeper's job, and the unused return half of a ticket to London was worth having because it offered prospect of some casual work. The desperate situation had its epic climax in the march by two-hundred unemployed men to London. The Crusade succeeded beyond expectation, and the Government was put in a difficult position. But then, at the last moment, it was saved by the well-meaning action of one of Jarrow's friends, Sir John Jarvis. When it appeared to everybody that the Government was cornered, he announced that £40,000 had been raised, and that men would be set to work laying out the Jarvis Park and Sports Stadium in Jarrow. Later, ships were brought in to be broken up in the Jarrow yards, and later still Sir John provided a new steel tube works. Fine though it was, it was not nearly enough, and the announcement, coming when it did, gave the Government the opportunity to do nothing. Jarrow, it seemed, had accepted Lord Runciman's advice and had set about working out its own salvation.

The worst days were, however, over. It had become evident that the North-east could not solve its problems unaided, and a North-east Special Area was created, incorporating most of County Durham and Tyneside, but excluding Newcastle and Tees-side. With Government help, trading estates were established and financial aid was provided to tempt firms away from more favoured areas. The scheme had a measure of success, although the amount of employment created was small in relation to needs, and did not provide much work for men from the heavy industries.

The outbreak of the Second World War put an end to the immediate problems of the North-east. Firms engaged in ship-building, engineering, metal-working, chemicals and explo-sives were all engaged at maximum capacity and the labour force in these key industries increased by nearly 100,000 during the early years of the War. It is improbable that anyone was concerned to ask how long this would last, or possessed the facts to make an appreciation of the situation. It is now clear, how-ever, that the number of new jobs, created by the demands of war, was relatively less than in some other industrial areas of Britain, while its geographical position was a handicap rather than an advantage.

In the post-war years the inherent problems of the North-east have engaged the attention of successive governments, who have sought ways to bring prosperity to the area, and support what is being done locally.

East Anglia, too, has been subject to change. By the mid-nineteenth century, its textile industry had all but ceased to exist in competition with the products of Yorkshire. Even its agriculture was badly hit by the increasing competition of foreign grain. The period between 1870 and 1939, in particu-lar, were years of depression when many acres of arable were turned over to grass. The War reversed the position and made agriculture once more a prosperous industry, and there was a big drop in the acreage of permanent grass. The centre of the region is one of large farms, almost entirely cultivated, with wheat on the heavier soils, and barley (for malting) and feed on the lighter soils. Sheep, once so important in the economy of East Anglia, are now comparatively few. The turnip, too, with which the name of "Turnip" Townsend of Norfolk is linked, has given way to the sugar-beet, particularly in the neighbour-hood of the region's sixteen sugar factories. East and West of this belt there are important differences. Mixed farming, where income is derived from dairying, fattening beef cattle, and pigs and poultry is found along a belt stretching from the Thames to the Wash and again in the southern part of the Lincolnshire Wolds and on the north Lincolnshire coast. On the peat fens of the Isle of Ely, in Holland (Lincs.) and the Trent valley farming is more intensive. The agricultural population is denser, and wheat, sugar-beet and potatoes are the main sources of income. But some regions have concentrated upon more valuable horticultural crops. Spalding is the centre of a thriving flower-bulb industry, while the Wisbech area has concentrated on soft fruits.

In recent years industry has become increasingly important in the area, and has attracted in the first place neither by local demand or the supply of raw materials, but rather by cheap factory sites and a cheaper source of labour. The manufacture of electrical goods, radio and electronic apparatus, metal goods and paint and varnish are new, but some, such as furniture-making, saw-milling, brush- and basket-making are old industries brought up to date, and no longer dependent on local materials. Agricultural engineering, so well established all over the region, has a long, and in some cases continuous, history. One firm dates from 1789, when Robert Ransome, a Norwich ironmaster, set up a small foundry in a disused malting shed in Ipswich to make ploughshares for local farmers.

Above, the Grand Fleet patrolling the North Sea during the First World War; *below,* Rotterdam, thriving after recovering from the effects of the Second World War

Above, an Anson of R.A.F. Coastal Command keeps watch over a wartime North Sea convoy; *below,* Dunkirk, 1940. Troops wading out to an evacuation vessel

16

THE NAVY IN TWO WORLD WARS

For the greater part of the nineteenth century, after the close of the Napoleonic Wars, the North Sea enjoyed a period of peace without precedent. Upon its waters the British Navy rode unrivalled and unchallenged. For much of the time, in the cosy security of Victoria's earlier years, it must have appeared that this had become the established order of things. There was no serious reason to think that British mastery would be challenged, least of all as a result of technical change. Ships, guns and naval tactics remained essentially what they had been for centuries before. Britain not only had naval superiority over any European rival, but with her wealth and experience could outbuild any possible competitor.

The position changed suddenly, although the significance of the revolution may not have been immediately grasped, and although its immediate effect was neither to undermine the Royal Navy nor to lessen the respect with which it was held abroad.

In the space of a few years the introduction of steam power and screw propulsion and the use of iron and steel in ship construction made existing vessels obsolete. "The science of naval architecture," as Professor Marder has said, "underwent a greater change in the latter half of the nineteenth century than in the preceding ten centuries combined." Together with this

H

went the introduction of the explosive shell for the cannon-ball. These new developments offered enormous scope to the experts in ship design and armament and to the metallurgist, but it also engendered a not altogether healthy state of watchfulness and mistrust, and, as time went on, a growing feeling of insecurity as it was realized that the whole future of the country depended upon untried ships and weapons of war.

For much of the time attention was fixed upon France as a potential enemy. Germany was hardly considered. In 1860 a *Punch* cartoon had represented Britain as a warm-hearted, indulgent seafarer giving a toy boat to a small, bespectacled German, and telling him to "run away and play with it". After the unification of Germany in 1870 the situation changed rapidly, but people in this country were slow to note it, and the authorities were slower still to act upon it.

The significance of the Big Navy Movement, which the Emperor launched in February 1895, in a lecture to the War Academy, was minimized by the refusal of the Reichstag to provide funds for abnormal expenditure on the navy. And the importance of the opening of the Kiel Canal in the same year in doubling the potential German North Sea fleet was lost sight of by commentators, who saw the event as another guarantee of peace.

It was not long after this, however, that growing estrangement over events further afield, as well as the vast increase in naval credits voted by the Reichstag, awakened the more perceptive of British journalists to the realities of the German threat. As one anonymous writer in the *Saturday Review* put it, "Here is the first great racial struggle of the future; here are two growing nations pressing against each other, man to man, all over the world. One or the other has to go: one or the other will go."

From the strategic point of view the emergence of Germany as a naval Power, raised the North Sea area to a position of prime importance, such as it had not had even in the days when the Dutch were our principal opponents. For possession of the key position in the Strait of Dover no longer gave us a stranglehold over a fleet that could just as easily reach its home ports round the north of the British Isles. Moreover, the practice of the German navy of concentrating its main units in home waters made questions of the size, composition and distribution of the British forces increasingly urgent.

The public campaign for a naval base on the East Coast of Britain and for a North Sea squadron reached a climax in the winter of 1902–3. It was given powerful backing, and in March 1903 the Prime Minister announced that a new base would be established in the Firth of Forth. Construction had, however, not advanced beyond the point of surveying and planning as late as 1905, and the work had still not been completed at the outbreak of war. The responsibility belongs in part to Sir John Fisher, the First Sea Lord, although the reason for his opposition to the construction of the Rosyth base is not clear. At the same time Fisher embarked on a far-reaching policy of bringing the Navy up to date and preparing it to fight a modern war. None of his plans yielded a more speedy benefit at the outbreak of war than the plan to keep the reserve fleet in a permanent state of readiness with nucleus crews. One division of the reserve was stationed at Sheerness, and a modern Home Fleet in the North Sea was built up after 1905 by the expedient of sending the Dreadnoughts, as they were completed, to join the vessels already at Sheerness.

Although Germany had taken the initiative, and had as its Chief of Staff to the Navy's High Command, Admiral von Tirpitz, a man of exceptional ability and energy, the advantage did not lie entirely with our potential enemy. Understandings with France and Japan permitted the strengthening of the British Fleet in Home waters, while in Admiral Sir John Fisher the Government possessed a man who appreciated the significance of the mine and torpedo as weapons of war, and possessed the vision to bring the British Navy up to the requirements of the twentieth century. The introduction of the Dreadnought, an all big-gun battleship, made all existing capital ships obsolete at a stroke, and initiated a period of feverish construction during which, as von Tirpitz said (if with some exaggeration), "every ship became obsolete by the time it was finished." If Britain was unable to maintain her numerical advantage in big ships over Germany, the advent of the big ship so far affected the balance of strength in the North Sea area that the Kiel Canal had to be deepened and widened before the heavier German capital ships could move between the Baltic and the North Sea.

The strategic advantages and disadvantages of England and Germany could not have been more different. The North Sea coast of Germany, hemmed in by Holland and Denmark, was barely 150 miles long. It was a situation admirably suited for defence, and every device had been used to improve upon Nature. The estuaries of the Ems, the Weser and the Elbe had been developed as the home ports of the High Seas Fleet, where it could lie in complete safety. Thirty miles offshore from the nearest point on the mainland lay the island of Heligoland which formed an apex to the so-called "Wet Triangle". After Germany had acquired it in 1890 from Britain in exchange for Zanzibar it had been transformed into a fortress, armed with long-range guns which dominated the approaches to the German coast.[1] Nearer to the mainland, the coast is screened by many small islands. The deep channels were few. Elsewhere the water was shallow and made impassable by dense minefields.

The British Home Fleet, on the other hand, was responsible for the defence of an area extending from the Channel to the Orkneys and beyond that to the coast of Norway. While it maintained its superiority it had all the room it needed for manœuvre, and could deny the German High Seas Fleet free access to the Atlantic both through the Channel and by the

---

[1] Heligoland was formerly Danish territory. The British seized it during the Napoleonic Wars, and it was used as a base from which to break the Continental blockade. It was formally ceded to Britain in 1814.

Northern route. Moreover, it could, by simultaneous thrusts from north and south, put the German High Seas Fleet in a hazardous position if it ventured into the North Sea since the Germans had no choice of route by which to regain their home ports. The British High Command was however very conscious of the weakness of its defensive position. Not only were many miles of coastline exposed to the tip-and-run raider, but in 1914 Germany had a Fleet which was a match for the British Navy, and which at any moment, as a result of single disastrous action, might become superior to our own. During the decades, moreover, during which France had been Britain's principal enemy, the shore defences of the South Coast had been strengthened, and those of the East Coast neglected, and this neglect had not been remedied.

By the time Fisher retired in 1910 plans for the redeployment of the Fleet had been laid on the soundest lines, but plans for its employment, particularly in conjunction with an Expeditionary Force, had not been worked out. The advent of Sir Francis Bridgeman, Prince Louis of Battenberg and Winston Churchill was in this respect of the first importance.

It was probably not a matter of chance that in the summer of 1914 German's fourteen battleships and six of her battle-cruisers were in harbour at Kiel and Wilhelmshaven. The British authorities, however, showed no sense of the imminence of war when it ordered the Second and Third Fleets to return to their bases after the Spithead Review, and arrangements were made for the discharge of their reservist crews. The continuing deterioration of the political situation, and Churchill's bold decision to defer the discharge of the reservists, put Britain in a better position to meet the crisis than she would otherwise have been in. On July 26th, summer leave for the First Fleet was cancelled, and three days later, during the night of 29-30th July, the main units of the Fleet were despatched to take up their war-stations. "We may picture this great Fleet," wrote Churchill, "eighteen miles of warships running at high speed and in absolute darkness through the Narrow Straits, bearing with them into the waters of the North Sea the safeguard of considerable affairs."

The Grand Fleet was stationed as far north as possible, at Scapa Flow in the Orkneys, to seal the passage by which units of the German Fleet might make their way into the Atlantic. It was supported by the 10th Cruiser Squadron, which patrolled north and east of the Shetlands. Soon afterwards a second cordon in the north was formed by cruiser squadrons of the Grand Fleet, and later a battle squadron, based on Cromarty. The lighter, and speedier, battle-cruisers had their base at Rosyth. Harwich, which was suitable only for light craft, had destroyer and submarine flotillas, which were to make a notable contribution in North Sea patrols and offensive action against the enemy coast. Between these key-points, a variety of light craft, working from the main estuaries, contributed to the security of the East Coast. To the south of Harwich again, the strategic picture was completed by the Second Fleet, built around a nucleus of pre-dreadnought vessels, and a reserve Third Fleet of still older ships.

At the outbreak of war the Grand Fleet consisted, in all, of 21 dreadnoughts, 8 pre-dreadnoughts and 4 battle-cruisers. Attached to it were 8 armoured cruisers, 4 light cruisers, 9 other cruisers and 42 destroyers. Opposing it, and stationed mainly in the Jade, was the German High Seas Fleet of 13 dreadnoughts, 16 pre-dreadnoughts, 5 battle-cruisers, 15 light cruisers, 2 cruisers and 88 destroyers. A light force of cruisers was based on the Ems, and a smaller patrol force was based on Sylt and Heligoland. With these formidable fleets in being, it is not difficult to appreciate the force of Churchill's remark that "a single false move could jeopardize the whole future of the British Empire in a single afternoon."

Although the Grand Fleet, as the stronger force, might have resorted to blockade, the British Navy hoped that von Tirpitz would make good his boast to meet and humble the British Navy. With this in mind, and to ensure freedom of navigation in the North Sea to British shipping, Jellicoe was ordered, on August 4th, to begin a series of sweeps, returning to Scapa only to coal. Whatever may have been von Tirpitz's intentions, the ultimate authority remained with the Kaiser, and he, in July 1914, made an Order allowing the High Seas Fleet to go beyond a line from the Horn Reefs to Terschelling only "if a favourable opportunity to strike offers itself": otherwise, it was to engage in guerrilla tactics until such time as the British Fleet was weakened sufficiently for the German Fleet to venture out safely. The reasoning was based, in part, on the false assumption that the British Fleet would impose a close blockade of the German coast, where it would be exposed to submarines, torpedoes and mines. The action in the Heligoland Bight on August 28th, 1914, in which the German cruisers *Mainz*, *Ariadne* and *Köln* were sunk, confirmed the Kaiser in his opinion that the High Seas Fleet should not be risked in any action where the result was not certain victory.

The course of events gave the British Commander-in-Chief cause for concern. It was impossible to keep the Grand Fleet permanently at sea, with only the briefest intervals for coaling. Before long there would be need to withdraw units for refitting, while in the meantime the Fleet was weakened by losses to submarine and mine, as a result of inevitable accidents. The alternative, of confining the Fleet to harbour, had few attractions. At the outbreak of war, none of the four bases—Scapa Flow, Cromarty, Rosyth or Harwich— was secure against submarines, and at Scapa and Cromarty there was only light armament. The Orkneys, had indeed, been chosen as the main base for the Fleet in the belief that it was beyond the range of German submarines. But this was soon seen to be inaccurate, and two false alarms in the early weeks of the war sent the Fleet scurrying to gain the security of the open seas. The Germans lost an opportunity to cause tremendous havoc among the ships at anchor by giving the British Navy credit for having taken the safety precautions that they would have taken themselves. As it was, the Grand Fleet was in a sufficiently nervous state to move temporarily to Loch Swilly and Galway Bay on the north and west coasts of Ireland, where it was certainly not well placed to contain the German Fleet if it had emerged into the North Sea.

No less important—as was to become clear as time went on—was the effect upon crew morale of the deadly monotony of life amid the barren windswept wastes of Scapa.

By the end of October a number of painful losses to submarine and enemy mine had forced Jellicoe to certain positive conclusions about his strategic and tactical plans:

"... The Germans have shown that they rely to a very great extent upon submarines, mines and torpedoes, and there can be no doubt whatever that they will endeavour to make the fullest use of these weapons in a fleet action, especially since they possess an actual superiority over us in these particular directions ... They cannot rely with certainty upon having their full complement of submarines and minelayers present in a fleet action unless the battle is fought in the southern area of the North Sea. My object will therefore be to fight the fleet action in the northern portion of the North Sea."

Jellicoe went on to point out that if, in a desire to bring the enemy to action, the British Fleet allowed itself to be led on by the enemy, "it is quite within the bounds of possibility that half our Battle Fleet might be disabled by underwater attack before the guns open fire at all."

Jellicoe's memorandum cannot have made agreeable reading to the Admiralty, although his views were known and his reasoning sound. For, as recently as August 5th, Battenberg and Churchill had waived the requirement that two regular divisions should be retained in Britain, so confident were they that the Navy could protect the East Coast against invasion.

In the light of hindsight, it is difficult to understand the fear of invasion which was entertained, even at the highest levels, during the early months of the war. The possibility never

appears to have been discussed in Germany.[1] But, in the very
first weeks of the war there was serious concern lest the enemy
attempt to disrupt the departure of the British Expeditionary
Force by a diversion against the East Coast. On August 12th
Jellicoe was warned, "We cannot wholly exclude the chance
of an attempt at a landing during this week on a large scale
supported by the High Sea Fleet . . . extraordinary silence and
inertia of the enemy may be prelude to serious enterprises."
Early in October, Kitchener voiced his fears lest a deadlock
in the land war should liberate 150,000 to 200,000 men for an
invasion in force. Germany, he felt, had shipping for such a
venture, under cover of the German Navy and Zeppelins. Yet
another invasion scare swept Whitehall in November, and
the period from the 17–20th of the month was pin-pointed as
the most critical. The 3rd Battle Squadron was brought up the
Channel, arrangements were made for the sinking of block-
ships in undefended harbours along the East Coast, and some
300,000 half-trained troops were deployed in danger areas.
Jellico, after pointing out that enemy submarines made it impossible to keep the German coast under close watch, and so
made it improbable that the Grand Fleet could intervene
promptly in an emergency, went on to offer advice on such
things as the rapid destruction of jetties by explosives and the
use of petrol for creating fires on water. It was finally agreed
that the Grand Fleet should concern itself exclusively with the
destruction of the High Sea Fleet, "taking [its] own time, choosing [its] own method, and not troubling [itself] at all with what
is going on in England."

The nearest thing to an invasion was the bombardment of
Yarmouth by German cruisers in November 1914, followed by
the bombardment of Hartlepool, Whitby and Scarborough in
the following month, and of Lowestoft in May 1915. Casualties

---

[1] On the contrary, the German High Command was convinced, in September
1916, that a British landing in Jutland was contemplated. They appear to have
obtained information about plans that had been discussed and long since
abandoned.

were few and damage insignificant, but the psychological effect was very great.

Neither Churchill nor Fisher, who had been recalled from retirement, were men to whom a policy of inaction would appeal. As the Assistant Director of Operations wrote, early in August 1914:

> "We have the game in our hand if we sit tight, but this Churchill cannot see. He must see something tangible and can't understand that naval warfare acts in a wholly different way from war on shore. That Fleet in the North dominates the position . . ."

Uppermost in their minds in the early months was the idea of forcing an entry into the Baltic to unite with the Imperial Russian army and attack Berlin from the north. The idea was discussed of sending a force of destroyers to the Elbe to blow up the Brünsbuttel locks at the southern end of the Kiel Canal, and of attacking Kiel harbour. Apart from navigational difficulties and minefields and submarines, the naval experts pointed out the practical difficulty that there were two gates to each lock, and that it would be necessary to smash the outer to get at the inner. Nor were they prepared to risk any reduction in the strength of the naval force. The alternative idea of an amphibious landing in Schleswig-Holstein, with the intention of capturing the canal, presented difficulties that were no less great. The Lords of the Admiralty then reverted to the idea, which had been discussed and rejected before the outbreak of war, for a close blockade of the Heligoland Bight by the seizure of a convenient base. Churchill favoured the seizure of Ameland, a Dutch island between the Texel and Borkum. He was very disappointed to find his plan dismissed as a "strategical and tactically futility" by the naval experts, who pointed out that it would antagonize Holland and the Cape Dutch and could lead to a Japanese attack upon the Dutch East Indies (which would not have pleased the Australians). Strategically it would accomplish nothing, and, in any case, the harbour would not contain a substantial force. For a time the idea of an attack upon Heligoland was entertained, and then Borkum and Sylt. But the troops were not available, and in the face of the experts' arguments and the glowing attraction of the Dardenelles, the idea was quietly dropped.

Meanwhile, Jellicoe's caution, and the Kaiser's restrictions upon the use of his navy, deferred a clash between the two fleets for nearly two years. The delay was destructive of morale. The crews at Rosyth, within easy reach of Edinburgh, were not badly off, but the men stationed at Scapa Flow and Cromarty reach a point of boredom and frustration where even the prospect of a sea-going exercise failed to rouse them. On the whole the minor engagements between British and German forces at this time went in favour of the Royal Navy. The seemingly uncanny precision with which the British were able to divine the movements of enemy warships must have been very damaging. For this the British had to thank their superior wireless direction-finding equipment and the lucky chance that put the German code-book into British hands. In the light of subsequent events, however, it would have been better if things had gone less well for the Royal Navy at that stage. For the damage inflicted on German vessels lulled the Admiralty into believing that our shells possessed greater penetrating power than they did in fact possess, while the damage to the *Seydiltz* in the Dogger Bank action alerted the Germans to the danger of detonation from shell-flash in the magazine, and enabled them to remedy a fault in design. The British remained in ignorance of this danger, as well as of the vulnerability of their deck-armour, and of the superior gunnery of the German Navy. The lessons were painfully learned at Jutland.

The Battle of Jutland was fought over a vast area of the North Sea westwards of the North Jutland coast. It was a protracted battle, beginning in the middle of the afternoon of May 31st, 1916, and going on until the following morning, although the main elements were in contact for a bare half-hour.

As a battle, Jutland has the unusual distinction of being

celebrated by both sides as a victory, and it has been the subject
of earnest analysis and discussion for the past fifty years. In
terms of tonnage lost, and the number of casualties, the fight
went heavily against the British, as the following table shows:

VESSELS LOST	British	German
Battleships (pre-Dreadnought)	—	1
Battle-cruisers	3	1
Armoured cruisers	3	—
Light cruisers	—	4
Destroyers/Torpedo-boats	8	5
	14	11
	(115,025 tons)	(61,180 tons)
CASUALTIES	6,945	3,058

But it was the German Navy that ran for harbour, and, in
doing so, exposed itself to grave danger. Had luck been on the
side of the Royal Navy it would have marked yet another
Glorious First of June in its proud record. Admiral Beatty later
referred to it, in a letter to his wife, as "That terrible day when
we might have accomplished so much". In contrast with the extravagant claims of the German communiqué there were no
illusions of victory among the German crews, and the Fleet
crept into harbour as though it had been soundly thrashed. But
it was the German communiqué that gave the first news of the
battle to the world, and the subsequent Admiralty statement
did not completely dispel the gloom and state of shocked
surprise that settled upon Britain. But, as Lord Hankey wrote,
"On the morning that followed the battle, Jellicoe found himself in undisputed possession of the North Sea without a sign
of the enemy, and, to all intents and purposes, this state of
affairs continued." The measure of British success only became
apparent later. The battle has the further distinction of being,
undoubtedly, the last great battle in which the principal units
of two great modern Fleets engaged at close quarters in a gun
duel.

Second only to the outcome of the battle was the evidence that

Jutland provided of the performance of the Navy in battle. It revealed serious inadequacies in design. Decks needed heavier armour, and sensitive points, such as the magazine-rooms, needed protection from cordite-spark. British range-finding had proved far inferior to German, while the passing of messages and information from ship to ship during the Battle had been incredibly bad. There was much, too, for the British to learn about the deployment in battle order of fast-moving ships. It was not realized at the time, and has only become apparent as a result of recent research, how much responsibility for the course that the battle took rested upon the Admiralty who had inhibited the initiative of its Fleet Commanders with a mass of Battle Orders. Through them ran three basic ideas: the subordination of offensive plans to the need to take precautions against mine and torpedo; the engagement of the enemy in single line astern, with the heavy gun as the sole decisive weapon; and the concentration of all authority and initiative in the Commander-in-Chief. It is more difficult to understand and excuse the failure of the Admiralty to pass on to Jellicoe the information which it had about the disposition of the German fleet while the battle was in progress. Had it done so, it would have put Jellicoe in a position to intercept the enemy before the enemy had retreated to safety. The Commander-in-Chief was left to rely upon his intuition, which served him well. But, as he wrote to the Prime Minister, "The whole position was difficult to grasp. I had no real idea of what was going on, and we could hardly see anything except flashes of guns, shells falling, ships blowing up, and occasional glimpses of an enemy vessel."

It has often been said that, after Jutland, the German High Seas Fleet never put to sea again. But this is not true. It made two abortive sorties in August and October 1916. Only then did the Kaiser accept Scheer's contention that "even the most favourable issue of a battle on the high seas will not compel England to make peace. A victorious termination of the war can only be attained by destroying the economic existence of

Great Britain by the employment of submarines against commerce."

On February 1st, 1917, unrestricted U-boat warfare was declared, and the submarine flotillas of the High Seas Fleet were withdrawn for service elsewhere. Deprived of its "eyes", the German navy was severely handicapped. But the British were not in a position to exploit the situation. For, while the German Fleet was in being, the Royal Navy was unable to establish a close blockade of the Heligoland Bight and could not prevent the movement of enemy vessels by an effective system of minefields and destroyer patrols. Nor, as long as the War lasted, was it possible to disperse the capital ships stationed in the North Sea area lest the German Fleet made a sortie.

The cardinal importance of an economic blockade in applying pressure on Germany was well understood, and, in fact, German commerce carried in German ships practically ceased in the early days of the war. But large quantities of contraband continued to reach Germany in neutral shipping and through neighbouring neutral countries. Control over shipping entering the North Sea by way of the Strait of Dover was easy to enforce. It was less easy in the case of the northern route, where the Northern Patrol had to police 450 miles of sea between the North of Scotland and Iceland and a further 160 miles between Iceland and Greenland. The service, exposed to the cold and frequent gales of the northern North Sea, must have been among the most trying to which the Navy was exposed. It is not, therefore surprising that the Patrol was indignant about the number of shipments that the Government released, for fear of upsetting the neutrals, after the ships had been intercepted at considerable risk. The feeling was shared by Jellicoe and his officers.

Nine days after the Armistice the German Fleet emerged from harbour for the last time. Two days later it was met on the high seas by the Grand Fleet and escorted to the Forth pending internment. While the victorious Allies decided its fate, the German crews were permitted to remain aboard. On June 23rd, 1919, a few days before the signing of the Peace Treaty at Versailles, on the secret instructions of the German Commander, the sea-cocks were opened, and one by one the vessels listed and sank into the waters of Scapa Flow.

The High Seas Fleet died in the waters of Scapa Flow. In the 1930s, when Germany began once more to build a navy, it did not build a fleet to challenge the Royal Navy in home waters. The "pocket battleships", which were built within the tonnage specifications of the Treaty,[1] were essentially powerfully gunned, speedy commerce-raiders, designed to operate far afield and to reinforce the action of the U-boat in destroying Britain's sea-borne trade.

In 1939 Britain started the war with a numerical advantage in naval aircraft, but many of the units were approaching the end of their useful life, and the rebuilding programme had not been geared to match Germany's output. The same degree of unpreparedness for war was apparent elsewhere. Of the aircraft earmarked for service with the Navy, not more than two-thirds were available. In the event, high priority was given to the allocation of planes for North Sea reconnaissance, although the aircraft allotted, the Anson, was to prove inadequate for the job. In the matter of bases, the Navy was handicapped by a change of plan. In the latter stages of the First World War, the main units of the Fleet had been transferred from Scapa Flow to Rosyth, and it had been decided that this would remain the principal base. But, in 1938, it was appreciated that the approaches could be easily mined, and that Rosyth was too far south for ships to maintain an effective blockade of enemy ports. It was a long job to re-equip Scapa Flow, for neither men nor materials were to be found locally on this lonely outpost. As a result the work was not completed at the outbreak of war. In October 1939 a German U-boat managed to slip into the

[1] In fact the displacement of some of these ships was greater than the published figure, and made them a match for some of the older British battle-cruisers.

Flow, where it torpedoed the battleship *Royal Oak* before slipping safely out to sea again.

Since 1918 two developments had modified the position in Home waters. The one was the development of the aircraft, as an instrument of attack and reconnaissance: the other was the development of a high-speed surface craft, which experts accurately foresaw would be a considerable menace to our East Coast convoys. Fortunately, before the outbreak of war, the long-standing coolness between the Royal Navy and the R.A.F. had been resolved, but the shortage of suitable aircraft remained for some time.

As in 1914 Britain entered with some problems to which only practical experience would provide an answer. Foremost among these was the question whether enemy bombing would obliterate the towns and ports of the East Coast and make bases untenable, and whether our aircraft could similarly take over the role of the capital ships in destroying enemy installations. Some weighty naval opinion was sceptical about the damaging effect of bombing upon adequately defended bases, and in the instance it was proved right.

On the question of what would happen if the flow of Britain's trade down the East Coast and the Channel were interrupted in time of war, none of the Government experts had been able to do more than hazard a guess. But, as the threat of war grew greater in the 1930s, it had become urgent that the responsible Ministries should obtain the best advice, and that they should make plans in case shipping were prevented from reaching London and the East Coast ports. The matter was more important to Britain than to any other nation. For, although the sea-lanes of the North Sea and the English Channel carry the ships of every merchant fleet, there is no nation so dependent upon them as the British.

So much is commonplace, but a fact which was not fully appreciated, even by the Government's experts before 1939, was the significance of London and the North Sea ports. There are many other ports and harbours around the coasts of the British

Isles, but the trade of many of them is local, and fairly small in amount. The bulk of our trade passes through comparatively few of them, and a very big proportion is carried by ships passing through the North Sea and the English Channel.

This is partly to be explained by the immense importance of London as a commercial centre. But a great deal of imported iron-ore is carried to the Tyne and Tees, and large quantities of imported grain and oil-seed go to Hull. The list could be extended, but a few figures for the import of oil and petroleum products will make the point better. Between 1927 and 1929, out of an average annual import of 56.25 million tons, approximately 15.4 million tons came to the Thames, 10 million to the Humber, Tees and Tyne, against 12 million tons to the Mersey and 8 million to the Bristol Channel. Apart from the Clyde (3.3 million) and the Firth of Forth (3 million), no other group of ports reached even the 3-million-ton mark.

It was not through stupidity on the part of the Government Departments that these basic strategic facts were not realized. The detailed analyses of the movement of trade in and out of the ports had never been made. The German occupation of the coast-line from the Skaggerak to Cherbourg provided a unique demonstration of the strategic importance of these sea areas.

At the outbreak of war, it was generally assumed that this would be the signal for the intensive bombing of the more accessible towns and ports. To avoid loss, ships were accordingly diverted from the East Coast during the first fortnight of September 1939 and again during the last fortnight of October. On neither occasion was diversion complete, and in October only 25 per cent were in fact diverted (and not 75 per cent as estimated before War started). When the expected bombardment did not take place, the arrangement was abandoned until September 1940. Then, following the blitz on the London docks, ships bigger than coasters were forbidden to enter any port south of the Humber. From that time onwards E-boats and mines in the North Sea, and air attacks upon shipping in the North Sea and Channel, together with the bombing of the ports, made the whole East Coast extremely dangerous to shipping. It virtually closed the port of London to larger vessels until the end of the War. After the initial interruption, the shipping of coal from the North-east ports to London and the South Coast was resumed, but on a reduced scale.

It was well appreciated by the Government that every day lost by diversion, or by delay in handling cargo, was as much in the enemy's favour as a ship sunk for that length of time, but the authorities were not prepared for the degrees of disruption which resulted when their plans for the redirection of shipping were put into operation.

In the case of meat shipments, the bigger of Britain's two cold-storage depots was in London, and the ports of the West Country were soon at a loss to know what to do with the perishable cargoes unloaded there. They had no storage facilities of their own, and the railways could not supply a sufficient number of insulated vans. Similar problems arose over the handling of iron-ore intended for Middlesbrough, which needed 2 million tons annually to keep its blast-furnaces going, and over the handling of oil-seed, of which London took nearly a quarter, and Hull nearly a half of the $1\frac{1}{2}$ million tons imported annually.

In the West Country, as anywhere else, the roads and railways existed to meet the limited needs of the area. When extra demands were made upon them, they were quickly extended beyond their capacity. Nor was it practical, at that time and in those circumstances, to think about any major re-organization of Britain's transport system. The ports in the West of England, too, were in general no adequate substitute for those of the Thames and Humber. For the most part they were too small, and had insufficient depth of water. Some had no quay big enough for the berthing of a big ship. Many vessels, therefore, had to be unloaded by lighter, which was a slow business and immobilized many ships. Nor were these ports organized for the quick sorting and clearance of cargoes. As a result, ships often stood in the fairway, unable to unload because the transit sheds were full. It frequently happened, too, that some bulky article had to remain in the ship's hold because there was no crane in the port capable of lifting it. And, again, many important loads were left at the quayside because there were no railway trucks available to carry an over-size article.

In nothing was the effect of the closing of the East Coast sea-lanes more quickly felt than in the coasting trade. Not the least important of the things which the coasters carried was coal for the power-stations and factories of the South Coast. Many of these plants had been built to receive their supplies largely, or entirely, by sea. In any case, the railways, already over-burdened, were unable to accept the traffic which would normally have gone by sea. Stocks of coal kept locally were never large, and within a few days of the first attacks on shipping off the East Coast a serious situation had arisen in the South Coast towns. It was quickly decided that coasters would have to be risked, and after that sufficient coal continued to come south by sea for the duration of the War.

The problem of the West Coast ports could not be solved. "Everything," it has been said, "went wrong in every direction." While the crisis lasted, delays caused the loss of approximately 3 million tons of imports. Eventually, the Admiralty decided that the loss of imports outweighed the possible loss of ships. The ban on movement to ports on the East Coast was lifted for ships under 8,500 tons, provided that they were not carrying especially valuable cargo, and provided they were not fitted with diesel engines, since such engines were liable to detonate acoustic mines. In spite of attacks and the difficulty of maintaining an effective air patrol over the North Sea in winter conditions, convoys continued to sail along the East Coast for the duration of the War.

Although it did not have to meet the challenge of a German High Seas Fleet, the turn of events, and the enemy's employment of the long-distance U-boat and aircraft, imposed an impossibly heavy task upon the ships and aircraft based in North Britain. The German conquest of Norway, followed by the occupation of Denmark, Holland, Belgium and France, gave the enemy access to a long coastline, making the task of enforcing the blockade and impeding the use of enemy coastal waters very much more difficult. With the entry of Russia into the War the hazardous duty of escorting the convoys bound for Murmansk and Archangel was added. To this extent, the bigger units of the Fleet reverted to the Navy's earliest role of armed escort. At the same time an increasing share of the duty of hunting the U-boat packs that menaced the convoy routes, of watching enemy ship movements and invasion preparations, as well as of attacking enemy ports, fell to the Royal Air Force. It was the R.A.F., too, that ultimately found and destroyed the *Tirpitz*, the *Scheer* and the *Lützow* in harbour.

The War, as it developed, placed duties and burdens upon these services which the most far-sighted and the most pessimistic of the planning staff could not have foreseen in 1939. In retrospect, it can be seen that too much importance was given to heavy-gunned ships at the expense of aircraft carriers, and that not enough had been done to heal the division which existed between the Navy and the Air Force until 1937. In the long run, the issue of the War was decided elsewhere. But, at its most critical stage, the Royal Navy and the Royal Air Force between them prevented the enemy from gaining control of the Narrow Seas, without which the German army was condemned to frustration and inactivity; they ensured the continued passage of coastal convoys and the supply of war materials to our Allies; they brought the movement of shipping in enemy coastal waters almost to a standstill and seriously reduced the capacity of the ports and shipyards under German control.

17

PROSPECTS FOR THE FUTURE

BY 1945 THE countries bordering the North Sea had reached a state of complete exhaustion and economic disruption. Britain, for her part, after spending her overseas assets, had still increased her indebtedness to overseas countries by some £3,000 million. Our exports and invisible income by which we lived, were less than half what they had been in 1938, and our merchant navy was 30 per cent smaller than it had been at the beginning of the War. On the other hand, our expenditure abroad was five times as great as it had previously been.

The amount of destruction of installations and property varied considerably from one country to another, but although this was more obvious, it was possible to get ports open and factories working fairly quickly, and was less important than the dislocation of international trade and domestic economies.

On the whole, Belgium fared rather better than her neighbours. The War passed rapidly over the country, even though Antwerp—as the main port of entry for all British and American supplies—became the target for flying-bomb attacks. In the same way, the amount of hard currency which the Allied Forces brought into the country helped solve the immediate problems.

Elsewhere, the task of reconstruction presented superhuman

problems. Holland suffered from German occupation, from bombardment and from the resistance put up by the retreating Germans. The wartime tragedy of Rotterdam began in May 1940, when in a single day's bombing the whole city centre was levelled, and 100,000 made homeless. During the Occupation it was drained of shipping, equipment and manpower, and then it suffered the German scorched-earth tactics of 1944. In the ports a third of the quays were destroyed, as well as over half the warehouses, while nearly all the cranes were dismantled and taken to Germany. Denmark and Norway also suffered serious, if less dramatic, losses.

The damage inflicted upon the German ports was even heavier. At Hamburg, one of the worst-damaged cities in Germany, where 75 per cent of its buildings were totally or partially destroyed, and 55,000 of its inhabitants had been killed, the devastation seemed perhaps the more terrible because of the occasional building which escaped. The situation in these German ports seemed even more hopeless than elsewhere. The surrender was followed by the dismantling of shipyards and port installations as reparations. For some time there was disagreement among the Allies about the kind of future that Germany should be allowed to carve out for itself, and as late as 1947 the docks at Hamburg were dead.

The climb back was everywhere slow. Even at Rotterdam the harbour was not in full working order until 1951, and even then the authorities had still to attract back the traffic which had been driven elsewhere by the distortions of war, and by the stagnation of German trade and industry.

Recovery, when it came, came fairly quickly. Among the major factors were the adoption of the Marshal Plan, whereby the United States backed Europe's efforts to help itself; the devaluation of the German currency in 1948, and the decision of the United States to back German energy and business acumen in building Western Germany into a major force in Europe. More recently still, since 1958, Western Germany, Holland and Belgium, as members of the Common Market, have progressively integrated their economies with remarkable results.

One symbol of industry and faith in the future had been the Dutch Europoort, near Rotterdam, which even in the form in which it was planned some ten years ago sounded audacious. Today it is still far from finished, but it is already the largest port in the world in tonnage handled. With a turn-over of about 130 million tons a year it is a good deal busier than Marseilles, Nantes, St. Nazaire, Rouen, Le Havre and Dunkirk put together, nearly twice as busy as Hamburg, Bremen, Wilhelmshafen and Emden combined, and more than twice as busy as Antwerp.

The planners started with some important advantages. Rotterdam stands on the principal estuary of the Rhine, which will become, with the completion of the delta scheme, the only mouth of the Rhine. It has access to a maze of waterways by which goods can be transhipped to nearly every part of Europe. About 90 per cent of the cargoes entering Rotterdam are carried on to their destination by water, and, since water-carriage is so much cheaper, this attracts business. Much of the land required for the port was derelict, or had been levelled by bombing, so that the city was able to make a clean start, and labour has been co-operative.

Europoort is a chain of harbours stretching from the Hook of Holland to Rotterdam. Strictly, the name applies only to the western part, which stretches exactly twenty miles from the town bridges to the sea, for the inner harbours were all built before the War, although they are now being modernized. The whole enterprise is in the hands of the city. The managing director of the Harbour Authority is a city employee, and his plans and budget are under the control of the Rotterdam City Council. Money for the scheme is advanced to him without interest, and has to be repaid, although it will be a long time before all of it is recovered. So far the city has put over £100 million into the port, and its annual revenue is only now reaching £10 million. The Authority does not sell any of the sites, but leases them for 25 years at rents from 2s. to 7s. 6d. a square yard, according to the harbour facilities. Eventually, when the big reclamation scheme at the estuary has been carried out, the city will have 11,000 acres of leasable land.

The city has not only been ready to wait for a proper return on its outlay, it has been ready to turn away business to ensure the proper development of the port. Firms that did not need deep-water berths and could operate just as well elsewhere, have been turned away. Even so, the Harbour Authority has learned from experience. In the '50s, when the oil-terminal at Botlek was built, a forward-looking decision was taken to build berths for ships of 60,000 tons at a time when most tankers in service were of about 20,000 tons. After the Suez crisis, the oil companies began to use tankers of 85,000 tons, and Botlek was out of date. After that, the Authority made a survey of the North Sea to ensure that any ship that could cross the sea could find a berth at Europoort.

The giant terminals and refineries of the major oil companies and the I.C.I. site at Rozenberg, where a £12-million nylon-polymer plant began production in 1965, point the way to Europoort's dominance in chemicals and oils. Nor is there any lack of demand. Sites are being negotiated for that still lie under the water.

In spite of the money spent, there is still much to do. Between and behind the splendid wharves, the complex of pipes at the refineries and the new apartment blocks, and half-hidden by dykes, are the fields still waiting development. Beyond the B.P. refinery at the river mouth land has still to be reclaimed from the sea, and deep channels dredged. But the Authority is hoping that the work will be completed by 1972. When it is finished, shallow-draft ships will go straight up the Maas to the old port of Rotterdam, while bigger ships will enter by a separate channel without touching the river at all, and barges will be confined to canals having access to the upper reaches of the river. The scheme involves concentrating bulk storage of materials of all kinds in the Europoort area, and the Authority is already trying to persuade some of its tenants to move to more suitable sites. Looking to the future, the Authority sees the use of containers for quick handling of cargoes, and round-the-clock working as likely ways of increasing the productivity of the port.

The present position has not been achieved without considerable opposition from farmers and nature-lovers, or without stiff French and German competition. At the moment the struggle with French rivals to decide who shall provide the principal refining centre for Europe is particularly intense. And here, Rotterdam, in going ahead with the trial deep-water channel into the North Sea, is seeking to force the hand of the more cautious Government. A great deal depends upon the outcome. If the giant tankers of the future can reach Europoort, it is likely that in a few years five times as much as the present 10 million tons yearly will be piped inland through Rotterdam. And if that happens there are boundless possibilities for the development of the port.

The most ambitious scheme of reclamation—the draining of the Zuider Zee—is better known. This great undertaking, so long talked about, was begun as long ago as June 1918, and is still not complete. The decision to begin the work was taken when the need was seen for increasing food production and finding new jobs for agricultural workers at the end of the War. The plan was to build a dyke, 20 miles long, from the island of Wieringen to the coast of Friesland, behind which four polders would be reclaimed. This would add 550,000 acres of fertile land, equal to one-tenth of the cultivated land of the country. There would remain a body of water—the Ijsselmeer —into which the Yjssel and other rivers drain, and which was expected to become fresh in the course of time. Work began two years later in the north-western corner of the Zuider Zee. The area was drained in 1927–30, and work on making the 50,000 acres of polderland fit for cultivation began almost as soon as the difficult feat of building the enclosing dam was completed. Meanwhile, work on the dam across the inlet of the

Zuider Zee itself was in progress, and that was finished in 1932. A much bigger polder to the north-east was begun in 1937, and was completed in 1942 while Holland was under German occupation. This left the two biggest polders in the south-east and the south-west, with a total area of 380,000 acres, still to be tackled. In 1956 the 56 miles of dykes enclosing part of the south-eastern polder were completed, and, within a year, land that had lain beneath the water for centuries was exposed and is now bearing crops. Work on the fourth of the polders is now nearing completion. In 1968 the 50-mile-long dyke should be completed. It will then be drained, and soon two satellite towns of Amsterdam, each of 100,000 inhabitants, will arise on the polder. The draining of the Markerwaard, sometime between 1970 and 1980, will mark the end of the sixty-year plan.

In the meantime, the need for agricultural land, which prompted the scheme, had become less pressing as the Dutch have turned over increasingly from trading and farming to industry, and with it the percentage of agricultural workers among the population has dropped from 20.1 per cent to 10.7 per cent. This has affected the plans for the development of the Zuider Zee. Some of the earlier polders have been taken over for housing and industry, and some of the land elsewhere is being earmarked for purposes other than agriculture.

Where the great dyke was closed, stands a monument to a great achievement. The inscription is appropriate: "A Nation that lives, builds for the future."

But, already, before the scheme is finished, plans are far advanced for a further ambitious scheme, which will take 25 years to complete and cost between 2,000 and 3,000 million guilders. This is the so-called Delta Plan.

Two motives inspire the readiness of the Dutch to devote some 10 per cent of their national revenue to the fight against the sea: the growing shortage of fresh water, and the need to insure against disaster. In spite of its 1,900 miles of dykes, experts have long predicted that—perhaps once in three hundred years—conditions would arise in which the sea would invade.

Such a day came on February 1st, 1953, when the raging sea made more than five hundred breaches in the sea walls, ravaging one-tenth of the country and costing 1,800 lives. The damage was repaired within a year, but the Dutch had lost confidence in their dykes. The Delta plan was devised to safeguard the country's future.

In 25 years' time, five dykes will seal off a number of sea-arms running into south-west Holland and forming the delta area of the rivers Rhine, Maas and Scheldt. Most of the existing dykes will then be situated on still water, not immediately affected by the tides, and serving as a second-line of defence. The principal course of the Rhine will, itself, be barred by a dyke, whose seventeen locks will serve as an enormous stop-cock by which the level of the river can be regulated.

The Delta Plan will go a long way to meet Holland's pressing need for good-quality fresh water. The Dutch not only need water in the right amount and at the right time for their farms, but industry is demanding more. And, as elsewhere, the Dutch have been finding it increasingly difficult to meet these needs without reducing the level of the rivers to the point where they could not cope with industrial and urban waste. In Holland the position is complicated by the fact that approximately 40 per cent of the land reclaimed from the sea lies nearly 12 ft. below sea level and 60 per cent of the population of the country is concentrated within this low-lying area. A great deal of fresh water is, therefore, needed to repel the sea-water which seeps into the subsoil, and also the salt water which would otherwise penetrate the rivers.

The most sensational development on this side of the North Sea since the War has been the discovery of natural gas in large quantities off the coasts of East Anglia and Yorkshire. Even if the extravagant hopes that were once entertained about its contribution to the British economy are not realized, the finds are an important addition to the country's natural resources.

The event which alerted the oil companies to the possibility of reserves of gas and oil under the North Sea was the discovery of vast quantities of natural gas in the Groningen province of North Holland. Serious prospecting only began in 1935, and was then interrupted by the War. During the Occupation, the Germans in their need for oil resumed the search, and in 1943 the first two wells were brought into production in the Schoene-beek area, South of the present Groningen field. The Dutch, however, did everything possible to sabotage the work, and to such good effect that in 1944 the Germans managed to extract only 1,700 tons of crude oil.

After the War development was pushed ahead quickly, in spite of the fact that the Germans had removed much of the equipment. The oilfield that emerged was unlike anything seen anywhere before. There was no forest of derricks, no untidy shanty towns, no small-gauge railways criss-crossing muddy terrain. For the Dutch used portable derricks, which were removed as soon as the flow of oil allowed pumps to be installed. The necessary equipment has been designed to blend with the scenery. Local farm houses—some of them dating from the sixteenth century—were preserved, the pastures remained undisturbed, or were quickly reinstated, and the fat cattle of the district continued to graze among the wells. By 1950 the Dutch has raised output to roughly 700,000 tons, and were on the way to making it the largest single oilfield in Western Europe. Today, production approaches $2\frac{1}{2}$ million tons a year, and supplies a quarter of Holland's needs.

Meanwhile, the prospectors, in their search for new fields, had been attracted by the possibilities of the Slochteren area, where tests showed the upward bending of the underground strata to form peaks, or domes, which are often associated with the presence of gas or oil. Early drillings revealed, at 5,000 ft, a bed of salt big enough—were it ever exploited—to keep the Dutch supplied for 37,000 years! But it was not until 1959 that the Government had the first inkling of the bonanza in natural gas that lay beneath the soil. The reserves have proved to be of

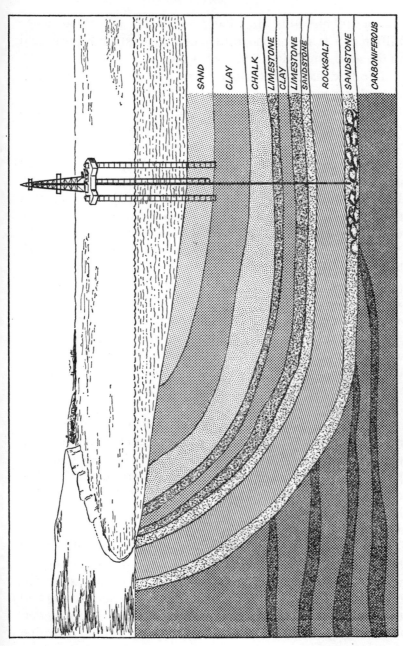

SAND

CLAY

CHALK

LIMESTONE

CLAY

LIMESTONE

SANDSTONE

ROCKSALT

SANDSTONE

CARBONIFEROUS

Imaginary diagram of an oil-rig in position in the North Sea, showing gas-bearing strata below impervious rock-salt

almost unbelievable size. Latest estimates put them at 39 billion cub. ft. (1,100,000 million cub. metres). Only a gas-field in the southern United States is bigger.

The find has meant a great deal to the Dutch. There is enough gas to meet Holland's needs for the next thirty years. Until recently, nearly 60 per cent of Holland's requirements had to be imported. The Dutch economy is bound to benefit whether the gas is used at home or exported.

Dutch law allows the Government to keep a firm hold on development. Anyone is free to apply for a permit to explore. But once minerals have been found, it is for the Government to decide who will get the concession to develop the find. The Groningen strike was followed by the establishment of the Netherlands Gas Union which has a monopoly to buy, distribute and sell all gas. The Government-owned State Mines (which besides the coal mines owns some petrochemical plant and pipelines) owns 40 per cent of Gas Union. Shell and Esso own 25 per cent each: the Government directly owns the remaining 10 per cent, and retains the right to regulate prices, and to decide upon the destination of the gas. In this way, through direct participation and company taxes, it is reckoned that the Netherlands Government takes at least 70 per cent of the profits from natural gas sold.

The news of the Slochteren find caused considerable excitement among the oil companies, and several of them moved in to begin drilling. Their interest was twofold. They naturally hoped to find gas or oil, but were also anxious to obtain information about the geological structure of the North Sea. Drilling over the sea itself awaited international agreements, and a clear statement of international law.

The conclusion of such agreements had been made urgent by the development of off-shore drilling in other parts of the world, and notably in the Gulf of Mexico. The law as it stood drew most of its authority from the laws of ancient Rome and the glosses of such writers as the jurist, Grotius. It was understood to give the finder the right to keep and exploit anything found beyond the limits of territorial waters. But the oil companies, who were proposing to invest millions of pounds in their searches, needed a more certain definition of their rights.

The United Nations Conference on the Law of the Sea met in Geneva in 1958, and produced a Convention which would give sovereign rights to the country concerned over the underwater "shelf", which extends round most land masses. The average shelf extends for about forty miles from the shore, but it may vary from a few miles to several hundred. For the purpose of the Convention, it was decided that the shelf should be considered to extend to the 200-metre contour line. Where an area of shallow water is bordered by several countries—as in the case of the North Sea—a median line is to separate each country's rights. The Convention was to come into force when ratified by twenty-two countries. Great Britain was slow to do so, and really passed the Continental Shelf Act in 1964 as a result of urgent promptings by the oil companies, which wanted to begin prospecting in the North Sea.

The Convention was probably the fairest possible. But, in the case of the North Sea, it was very favourable to Britain, with its long coastline. On the other hand, Western Germany, sandwiched between Holland and Denmark, got very little. A strict interpretation of the Convention would have led to bad feeling between Norway and Britain. For Norway's shelf is very narrow. A few miles off its coast a deep trench runs northwards from the Skaggerak. Strictly, therefore, Britain would have been within her rights in claiming rights of exploration almost to the coasts of Norway. But, in fact, an amicable agreement was reached in June 1965, by which each receives rights over one-half of the sea area which divides them.

There were a number of courses open to the British Ministry of Power, to whom fell the responsibility for regulating and licensing the search for oil and gas in the British sector. At the one extreme it could have set up a nationalized corporation to carry out the search, if the Conservative Government which was then in office had been willing to gamble millions of pounds on what might have been a fruitless search. It might, at the other extreme, have auctioned the rights to the highest bidders, with the possibility that the successful companies would have been left with insufficient capital to develop their concessions. The Ministry wisely allowed itself to be guided by the experience of other countries—notably the United States—which had faced similar problems.

The part of the British sector in which successful strikes were most likely to be made was about 100,000 square miles in area. It was decided to divide this up into blocks, each roughly 100 miles square. These blocks were big enough for the purposes of exploration, even if they were smaller than the oil companies would have liked. And, since there was bound to be keen competition for certain areas, it gave everyone a chance of some share in the most favoured areas.

The successful company was to have the right to its block for six years, with the option of retaining half of the area for a further forty years. The production licence cost £25 a square kilometre (or roughly £6,000 for a whole block) for each of the first six years. Then, in order to discourage companies from retaining sites which they did not intend to work upon, the rent was to go up to £40 a square kilometre in the seventh year, and so progressively to £290 a square kilometre. Companies that succeeded in finding gas or oil were to be able to offset the increased rental against the royalty of 12½ per cent which they would be obliged to pay on the minerals. The fees looked high, considering that the companies still had to face the heavy costs of drilling. The proof that the Ministry had calculated nicely lay in the large numbers of tenders which poured in.

The first allocation of sites was made in September 1964. There had been, on average, eight applicants for each of the most favoured sites in the area east of a line from Middlesbrough to Yarmouth. Probably no company got all it wanted, but the arrangement was fair. At the finish, twenty-four operators stood committed to gamble a minimum of £110 million over a six-year period. For a North Sea gas-strike to be profit-

Above, the tug, *Zwarte Zee*, towing one of the Dutch oil rigs; *below*, B.P.'s ill-fated drilling platform, *Sea Gem*

Another B.P. drilling platform, *Sea Quest*

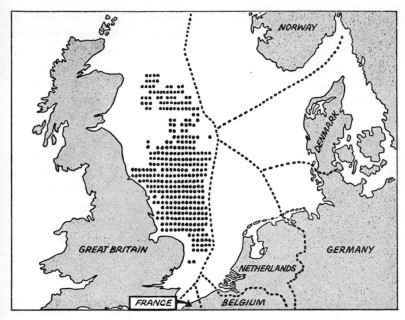

Sites taken up for gas exploration. The map shows how the geography of the area favours Britain

able, in view of the enormous cost of underwater exploration, it was considered necessary that a company would need to have at least three wells flowing at a minimum of 50 million cub. ft. a day, or, in the case of oil, to have found recoverable reserves of 175 million tons.

On the other side of the North Sea progress has been slower. Off Norway, companies to whom licences have been given have carried out survey work, but the shortage of drilling-rigs has delayed the programme. The country has benefited, however, by building rigs and providing equipment for work going on elsewhere. In the Netherlands, fresh companies have begun searches in the neighbourhood of Ameland and Terschelling, and around the Yssel Meer. But Holland, already the world's second largest supplier of natural gas, is probably more concerned with the orderly development of its astonishing resources. Progress in Germany was delayed by disputes over

I

the boundaries of her very small area for exploration, and by an internal dispute between the Federal Government and the individual provincial governments. As a result, Germany, which was quickly off the mark after the Slochteren discovery, has not achieved very much. A consortium of firms has been set up to undertake the work, each taking turns with the drilling. Originally it was intended that the consortium should be all-German, but now some foreign firms have been admitted. It was inevitable that they would be admitted, but foreign interests have made it more difficult for the consortium to reach decisions. In addition, some small off-shore concessions have been granted to various oil companies. So far, the most noteworthy German achievement has been the discovery by the rig *Mr. Louie* of a pocket of high-pressure, but commercially useless, nitrogen. The Belgian and French areas are generally considered to lie too far south to be of much promise. But Belgian and French firms are active elsewhere in the North Sea.

American oil-men have had a virtual monopoly of drilling over water. The earliest of such rigs, built in 1910 in the swamps of Louisiana, was no more than a wooden platform on piles upon which a derrick was erected. Since then the major oil companies have built up a considerable store of knowledge of off-shore drilling in different parts of the world. But the decision to explore the North Sea raised problems for which none of them had ready answers. There was, firstly, the size of the undertaking, which demanded more oil-rigs than were available. But, more important, was the nature of the North Sea itself. It is a much stormier sea than anything they had encountered before. Any rig used, therefore, had to be capable of lifting its drilling-platform clear of the highest waves that were likely to occur. It also had to be rigid in any conditions so that a reasonably straight and accurate bore could be made.

The companies had a number of floating platforms with retractable legs, which could be lowered to the sea-bed to raise the platform clear of the water, and other similar platforms of a makeshift kind were quickly fabricated. The early drilling in the North Sea was done from platforms of that kind. The difficulty in using them was that it was necessary to wait for a calm day before raising or lowering the platform. Otherwise the legs of the rig would have been pounded against the sea-bed when the rig was just afloat and would have been buckled. The risk in moving such a jacked-up rig was demonstrated by *Sea Gem*, which turned over and sank. The under-currents of the North Sea are another hazard, since they wash away the sand around the platform's legs.

It still remains to be seen whether the newer semi-submersible rigs fare better. They rest on floats that are set to remain buoyant at a depth unaffected by the surface movement of the waves. *Ocean Prince* and B.P.'s giant *Sea Quest* are the only rigs of this type working in the North Sea. But *Ocean Prince* has already been blown off its site during a bad storm, and at the end of March 1966 its crew had to be hurriedly removed when a severe gale was threatened. In the event, the rig stayed in position, although two of its eight anchors gave way. If these new rigs should prove unreliable in high winds, or their crews have to be evacuated frequently, their efficiency will be seriously reduced.

The oil-rig has come a long way since the days of the wooden platform used in the Deep South fifty years ago, and they are constantly being improved. A marine platform today is a self-contained unit providing comfortable quarters, ample food and everything else that the men may reasonably require when working, as well as machinery and materials for the drill itself. *Sea Quest*, which cost more than £2 million to build without the drilling equipment, stands on three pontoons, each the size of four pairs of semi-detached houses. Above them are the elephantine legs, rising another 140 ft. A network of tubular struts—some of them big enough to drive a lorry through—hold the giant pillars together. Each side of its triangular deck is over 100 yds. long, and the platform (in addition to the derrick and its associated machinery) also has room for air-conditioned living accommodation, a helicopter landing-deck, plant for making fresh water and a complex tele-communications and navigational warning system. It is large enough to store the drills, chemicals and other materials needed for drilling a 12,000-ft. hole.

Such a rig costs about £5,000 a day to operate. For the drilling there are three shifts of about a dozen men, two shifts working flat out for twelve hours each, so that the machinery can be kept going for twenty-four hours a day. The third shift is ashore on a week's leave. At any one time other staff, including super-visors, electricians, geologists, engineers and catering staff, will bring the number aboard the rig to about forty.

Hardly less important than the design of rigs capable of standing up to the harsh conditions of the North Sea has been the design of the workboats to supply the rigs. Drilling con-sumes enormous quantities of materials, and supplies must be maintained if work is to continue without interruption. Men and light equipment can be flown in and out by helicopter, but the heavier stuff must go by sea. It has been found necessary, therefore, to design boats capable of sailing up to 150 miles in the shortest possible time, and in all kinds of weather. They have to be capable of coming alongside in all conditions, and unload in any weather without damaging the rig, or losing the cargo.

With investments of such size at stake, the oil companies are careful to keep a close watch on the weather. A dozen com-panies now participate in providing a more elaborate weather service than the Meteorological Office can provide. The system works by using the rigs as observation posts and by feeding the data to a central office at Cleethorpes, where forecasts are pre-pared.

It is possible that at some future time drilling on the bed of the sea itself will prove both safer and cheaper than drilling from rigs. Such schemes, however, are unlikely to bear fruit during the present stage of the North Sea search, but the idea may be taken up by firms responsible for laying and maintain-ing the pipes that will take the gas ashore. The equipment, it has been suggested, could be taken to the bottom and placed in an atmospheric cocoon where operators and maintenance men could work at sea-level pressure.

The visitor to Yarmouth or Lowestoft cannot fail to notice the new atmosphere of activity which the arrival of the oil-men has brought to these towns, whether it is the noisy clatter of helicopters ferrying men and supplies to the rigs over the horizon, or the giant lorries loaded with drilling-tubes and equipment, or the ships of unusual shape that berth at places once crammed in the season by the herring fleet. In both towns large slices of the waterfront have been leased as marine service bases, and warehouses there are stacked with everything from drilling-bits to cardboard boxes for geological specimens. In the wake of the big contractors have come the specialist sub-contractors—names famous in the international oil business—who between them supply everything the enterprise requires, from echo-sounding devices to the highly sophisticated chemicals—the "mud" of the oil-men—used for floating to the surface the rubble which the drill cuts away.

If the wild hopes of Klondike prosperity, which some people entertained when drilling began, have not been realized, many East Coast towns from Scarborough to Lowestoft have benefited directly or indirectly. An influx of men earning high wages is bound to benefit many sections of a community, but it is obvious that the biggest immediate boom has been in rented accommodation. In Scarborough, a complete hotel was taken over for offices, and elsewhere hotels which had a seasonal trade now hope to stay open all through the year. At Yarmouth the river-front, which was almost derelict, became a thriving base in less than two years, and the corporation was able to find more than £1 million to rebuild part of the quay. Almost overnight, too, there was a demand for services of all kinds that had not previously existed, and anyone who could provide them was welcome to tender. Already a number of modest fortunes have been made by individuals in competition with big contracting firms. They were individuals with the courage to back their

[261]

own ability, with the energy to give a round-the-clock service and the readiness to learn quickly by their own mistakes. The effect of this new industrial activity has been most noticeable at West Hartlepool. This once-depressed town found work flowing in, and the Corporation launched a building programme, which among other things was intended to provide houses for key workers. Those who are anxious to see the development of industry along the coasts of East Anglia and Yorkshire are hoping that the discovery will be followed by the finding of oil.

Perhaps the most encouraging thing about the B.P. gas strike and others made since has been the speed with which they were made. American oil-men consider that one successful strike in ten is above average. And in Holland the immensely rich Slochteren gas-field was discovered only after a thirteen-year search during which two hundred holes were bored. Within a fortnight of their original announcement B.P. was able to announce that, after drilling the original bore-hole down to 10,000 ft., they had struck what promised to be a rich natural gas-field. Tests later showed that it was gas of very high quality, and that the well would yield between 50 and 100 million cub. ft. a day.

A statement from the Minister of Power in December 1965 made it clear that gas exists in sufficient quantity to justify bringing it ashore by underwater pipe-line. It should be possible, he thought, to deliver at least fifty million cub. ft. a day by 1968. B.P. had already said that their well, 42 miles east of Grimsby, was itself capable of producing 200 million cub ft. a day. At the time of the Minister's statement, B.P. were drilling further wells to discover the size of the field. The Company had to assure itself that there was gas enough for fifteen to twenty years to make it worth while to tap the supply. In June 1966 the Chairman of the Gas Council was able to hold out a hope that optimistic forecasts would be met. The North Sea, he said, was expected to supply at least as much gas as the Slochteren field, and to produce enough gas to supply four times Britain's present consumption for 35 years.

At the end of the 1950s Britain's gas industry was steadily being edged out of the fuel market. Making gas the old-fashioned way out of coal, and moreover obliged to use high-priced British coal, the Gas Council found that it was costing 1s. 7d. a therm from the works. Then quite suddenly the situation was transformed by the introduction of an I.C.I. process for the steam-reforming of naphtha (an oil refinery by-product, which till then had been virtually useless). This was essentially responsible for reducing the price to 10.34d. a therm in 1964. Almost simultaneously, methods were found of liquifying methane and carrying it at low temperature by ship. In that way it was possible to meet a tenth of Britain's gas needs at a price of 6¼d. a therm from the gas-fields of Algeria. At the time of the first North Sea gas strike, negotiations were in hand for importing Nigerian gas from Bonny Island at 5d. a therm. The Dutch, too, offered gas at 4½d. a therm, landed at Lowestoft provided that a pipeline were laid for getting it there.

It is against these facts that the Ministry has had to consider what price should be paid for North Sea gas. But, at the same time, this could not be a simple mathematical calculation. The interests of the community had to be weighed against the need to give the companies some incentive to carry on exploring. The Minister finally announced that a price of 5d. a therm would be paid to B.P. for up to 100 million cub. ft. a day for the first three years. This was 2½d. a therm more than the Gas Council was prepared to offer, and 1½d. a therm less than B.P. were asking. Any gas in excess of the agreed quantity, B.P. would be free to sell at any price that it could negotiate. The Ministry's views prevailed against the strongly expressed views of the Gas Council that the suppliers were being offered too good a bargain. But the arrangement seemed fair to commentators at the time, who noted that the agreement would enable B.P. to recover its capital outlay in the first three years before another agreement was negotiated. Since then the Gas Council

---

1 This was less of a bargain than it seemed, as the gas contains 14 per cent non-inflammable nitrogen.

and the oil companies have engaged in hard bargaining over the price to be paid. Quite small differences in the price per therm can turn handsome profits into disappointing returns. The price of 2½d. a therm which the Gas Council is offering has been indignantly rejected, and one major oil company is threatening to abandon exploration unless a higher price is offered. The final settlement, whatever it is, is likely to provoke a political storm.

After the first excitement, economists have become more cautious about expecting gas from the North Sea to perform miracles for industrial costs, or for Britain's balance of payments.

The discovery will certainly make gas, for the first time, really competitive in many industries with coal, oil and electricity. The bigger industrial users can obtain heat from coal at about 4d. to 4½d. a therm; fuel oil costs about the same, but would be cheaper without tax. If natural gas can be obtained at a landing price of 2d. or 2½d. a therm, it can be sold by the Board at about 4d. or 4½d. It would then be highly competitive because of its particular merits. But even if it were substantially cheaper than other fuels, it would not lead to drastic reductions in the costs of manufactured articles, since fuel accounts for only 20 per cent of the costs of the biggest industrial users. But even at a price of 3½d. a therm the Gas Council could quickly expand the 6 to 7 per cent share of the fuel market which it has at present.

Even if natural gas is not the threat that it once seemed to be the recent developments have been watched with some concern by the coal and electricity industries. The Coal Board profess to believe that it would be possible to sell 170–180 million tons in the 1970s, but the miners continue to express their frank disbelief in the future of the industry by leaving the pits. The electricity industry, in the middle of a £4,000 million expansion programme, has had its assumptions about growth rate upset by a competitor. Its response will almost certainly be to demand cheaper coal, or access to North Sea gas.

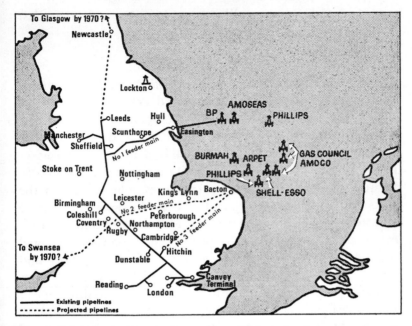

Natural gas from North Sea wells will be piped underwater to points along the East Coast and then into a national grid

It is, however, not unreasonable to expect that the demand for fuel will continue to rise in the coming years, even to the equivalent of 5,000 million cub. ft. of gas a day. This comfortably absorbs the 4,000 million cub. ft a day, which some experts think the North Sea will supply. It would clearly take the products of many North Seas to make the existing sources of heat, light and power totally obsolete and redundant.

The extent to which the East Coast is able to attract industry as a result of the supply of gas depends entirely upon the policy adopted by the Government. If the Gas Council were able to dispose of supplies cheaply at the point of landing, instead of piping it at great cost inland, it is likely that many industries would move to the East Coast to take advantage of the cheaper fuel. But it appears that the policy will be to supplement existing supplies over a wide area of Britain. If that

I* [265]

happens North Sea gas will not work the miracle that East Anglia at one time hoped for.

Further south, the small port of Felixstowe has produced its own success story. In 1951, when the docks were handed back to the Felixstowe Dock and Railway Company after war service, they were almost derelict, and only a dozen dockers worked there. Then came the East Coast floods of 1953, which cost 41 lives in the town, and caused extensive damage to the sea walls, the quays, railway tracks and warehouses. The future for the docks looked black. In 1955 the London dock strike gave Felixstowe its first opportunity. This strike, coming after several similar strikes, finally persuaded shipowners engaged in the Anglo-Scandinavian trade to look for another port, and they went to Felixstowe. Other firms, dealing with Dutch, German and Belgian markets, followed, and now Mediterranean traders are looking for berths. Even so, progress was at first slow. In 1962 the Rochdale Committee, investigating the future of Britain's ports, could only say: "... the ports of the rivers Stour and Orwell have been brought to our attention, including Ipswich, Harwich and Parkeston Quay, and Felixstowe. Undoubtedly, there is scope for building sheltered berths with reasonable depth of water, but while, as in similar cases elsewhere, the National Ports Authority should take care to see that the potential port value of such areas is preserved, we cannot accept the view expressed to us that development here is a matter of immediate national importance."

The statistics of cargo handled, in relation to men employed, at Felixstowe speak for themselves:

	Cargo (tons)	Employees
1957	81,584	100
1958	139,999	200
1962	364,951	221
1965	586,936	292
1966	over 1,000,000	381

The Company which prides itself on its modern, fast, damage-free handling of cargo, could equally pride itself on its record in labour relations, since it has not had a strike since it was incorporated in 1875. In theory the Dock should have reached the point of saturation by 1964, but business has grown and the Dock has expanded outside its original basin. A tanker terminal has been built off-shore, and a Continental ferry terminal was opened in the summer of 1966. Felixstowe has specialized in container-cargo, and when work at present in hand is completed a two-level bridge will connect with ships so that drive-on vessels can load and unload two decks at once. Felixstowe looks forward to handling more than 2 million tons of cargo in 1968, and together with developments at Harwich the progress at Felixstowe will make the Stour-Orwell Estuary into one of Britain's major ports in five years.

Britain's planners have not lacked vision, and two ideas, which may not go beyond the point of discussion for some years, are interesting to speculate upon. One concerns the future of the Wash: the other the development of a new metropolis on the Humber.

If our North Sea coasts have nothing as spectacular to show as the Dutch it would nonetheless be a mistake to underestimate British achievements. Our problems and opportunities in that area have been of a different kind. If any criticism is made in the light of history it may well be that successive Governments failed to take the opportunity to accept the leadership of Europe when the countries of western Europe would most willingly have accepted our lead.

The greatest problem of all has been the future of the Northeast. The problems of uneconomic coal-pits and redundant engineering plants are not new to the area, and the attempts in the post-war years to come to terms with the problem have often resulted temporarily in unemployment and social dislocation. In spite of that, tens of millions of pounds have been spent in re-organizing the shipyards (which are probably better equipped and more responsive to technological change than those of any other part of Britain), and in rationalizing the coal-fields and iron and steel industries. It is perhaps inevitable that the problems and difficulties of the older industries should have received more attention than their successes, and that the image of the older industries should have overshadowed the newer. Two developments in particular have done much to transform the economy of the North-east. The first has been the continuing expansion of Imperial Chemical Industries, and the second the Team Valley Trading Estate. Both date from before the War, but their progress since 1945 has been con-siderable. Today Tees-side has the biggest concentration of chemical manufacturing in the Commonwealth. The trading estate scheme has also grown far beyond its original plan, and has provided at least 68,000 jobs since early 1948. The English Industrial Corporation now operates in fifty places in the North-east. Its largest estates are at Team Valley, Tynemouth, Jarrow, South Shields, Sunderland, the Hartlepools, Tees-side, Aycliffe, West Auckland and Spennymoor. There has, of course, been much development also away from the trading estates.

The new structure of the North-east is best represented by the rough percentages of workers in various occupations: Agriculture, 2 per cent; Shipbuilding and Marine Engineer-ing, 4 per cent; Iron and Steel, $4\frac{1}{2}$ per cent; Chemical and Allied Industries, $4\frac{1}{2}$ per cent; Construction Industries, $7\frac{3}{4}$ per cent; Coalmining and other Extractive Industries, $8\frac{3}{4}$ per cent; other Manufacturing Industries, 23 per cent and Services and Non-Manufacturing activities, $45\frac{1}{2}$ per cent.

The developments had made considerable progress in the region when the credit restrictions of 1961–2 produced a crisis of confidence. The appointment of Lord Hailsham as Minister with special responsibilities, no less than the scale of expendi-ture on public works and the incentives offered to attract indus-try to the area, served to convince the region that the Government did not intend to allow it to slip backwards, and the momentum of progress in the region has been resumed.

An imaginative scheme, which is fanciful only with reference to Britain's financial problems, is a proposal to build a new metropolis somewhere in northern England. Since the suggestion was put forward, half in jest in the *Economist* a few years ago, the subject has had the serious attention of town planners and economists. In the summer of 1966, two proposals were put forward in the B.B.C's Third Programme.[1]

In essence, the argument of the protagonists is this. Population studies indicate that Britain will have to provide for twenty million more people living here by the turn of the century. This means not only more houses to live in, and more factories and offices, but a proportionate increase in all the other amenities of living. Moreover, as the Government's *South-East Study* has shown, unless the trend can be reversed, a large proportion will settle in the already over-crowded south-eastern corner of England. Nor, say the town-planners, will London continue to function properly if it is allowed to grow much bigger.

So far, Government studies have fallen into two categories. There have been wide-ranging studies of the problems of the South-east and the North-east, and there have been many small-scale studies of individual problems. Some experts now believe that the solution to many of Britain's economic and social problems lies in the creation of a second metropolis, which would counteract the magnetic attraction of London. "The strategy of the future," Leslie Lane, Director of the Civic Trust, has said, should be ". . . to create a second metropolitan city in a place where it can give a new dignity to the North. The Government now has powers to influence the movement of industry and office employment, but it needs to go further and take positive action to prevent the further growth of London. Investment in ports, railways, motorways and airports now being centred on London should be diverted northwards.

[1] *Listener*, LXXV (1966), pp. 751-3, 787-9.

"Most of history has taken place in the great metropolitan centres. Religion, learning, art, culture, politics, trade, commerce, and, until recently industry have always flourished in cities. There is every reason then for the creation of new metropolitan cities throughout the world. There is every reason to suppose that if such new cities are not consciously planned they will still appear in undesirable forms."

The siting of a northern metropolis were it ever built, would call for long and detailed studies. But, in the meantime, the claims for the development of Selby on the Humber, and for the building of an entirely new city on the Wash, have been put forward.

Of England's four great estuaries, the Humber is the least developed. Yet, as Mr. Lane points out, the Humber region, with its population of five million, offers promise of considerable development. Hull, Immingham, Goole and Grimsby are all ports of importance. The Goole-Knottingley area has the greatest concentration of electricity production in Europe. Important industrial developments, including docks and oil refineries, and to the wealth of natural resources which lie near at hand must now be added the natural gas which has been discovered off the mouth of the Humber. If, as experts confidently expect, Britain's foreign trade doubles in the near future, new port capacity will have to be created; there will have to be new techniques for cargo handling; and there will be urgent need for improved internal communications and regional planning. The Humber ports are among those most likely to benefit from such a development. Paradoxically, the miles of farmland which separate the Humber from the nearest industrial areas, and which have seemed to stress its isolation, are now seen as an asset. For the Humber is one of the few places left in England with plenty of undeveloped land around reasonably deep water, and within reasonable distance of large centres of population.

It was considerations such as these that have led Mr. Lane to suggest the ancient town of Selby as a suitable site for a new metropolis. Selby lies 30 miles west of Hull and 14 miles south of York, midway between the sea and the great industrial complex which includes Bradford, Leeds and Huddersfield. Standing at the point where the Vale of York opens out into the wide, flat expanses of Lincolnshire, it has great advantages as a communications centre. It is here that the Great North road and the East Coast railway-line from King's Cross to Edinburgh cross the railway and the proposed motorway from Hull to Liverpool.

To achieve its purpose Selby would need to be not just another New Town, but a carefully planned city with a population of a million, and with the industries, service and amenities of a capital city.

An alternative site for such a city has been put forward by the architect, Harry Teggin. He thinks that the under-developed and under-populated area of the Wash offers an ideal site. His plan would make rather more than half the Wash available for reclamation and the building of reservoirs, but he proposed that the two deep channels—the Boston Deep and the Lynn Deep—which make it difficult to dam off the whole of the Wash, should be turned to advantage as ship channels leading to a big new city and port with a population of 750,000. The port section of the city would be built in the shape of a horseshoe out over the Boston Deep, with the closed end towards the North Sea. Ships of up to 120,000 tons, bound for the port, would enter by the Lynn Deep before turning to enter harbour, which would thus be open to shipping even in severe Northeast gales.

A number of arguments have been advanced why such a development should take place on the Wash rather than on the Humber or lower Thames Estuary. Work to develop the communications by road and water in the area are too expensive and too complex to consider in relation to present needs, but would form an essential part of any big scheme. If, too, as some economists think, the finding of natural gas marks the beginning of an industrial revolution of prime significance for the East Coast, then it is necessary to plan on a big enough scale and far enough ahead. And if Rotterdam and its Europoort is to become the focal point of the Common Market, the Wash is well placed as a line of communication.

The detailed plans of this second proposal do not appear to have been worked out yet, and no doubt, these and other schemes will be long discussed before anything is done. Clearly, there is a practical limit to the amount of traffic which London can handle, and plans need to go beyond the limit of providing for overspill. The Dutch are showing what can be done.

Nor does this exhaust plans for the Wash. Already in Roman times many thousands of acres enriched by the silt brought down by the rivers had been won from the sea and turned into fertile agricultural land. The process of winning a few hundred acres here, and a few hundred there has continued until the present day. The gains, however, have been small and have not noticeably altered the outline of this part of the coast.

The idea of damming the Wash and pumping it dry was, however, not seriously entertained until modern times. It is possible that the idea may have been entertained by the Duke of Bedford and Sir Cornelius Vermuiden when they were engaged in draining the Fens in the mid-seventeenth century, but the first practical scheme was put forward by Sir John Rennie, who was called in, in 1840, to advise about improving the mouths of the rivers emptying into the Wash. His plan was to drain it and to create a new county—to be called Victoria County—out of the 150,000 reclaimed acres. The new county was never created, although the Norfolk Estuary Company was brought into being to provide money for the task. The Wash, with its deep channels, its high tides and rough seas presented a far more difficult problem than, for example, the shallow, land-locked Zuider Zee.

When the subject was revived after the Second World War, it was put forward as a contribution to existing world food shortages. By that time practical means of overcoming the great engineering difficulties probably existed. But the cost would have been enormous, and there were more urgent demands for money. No less important, it was realized that such a reclamation scheme would leave a vast sandy desert, unenriched for the most part by silt, which would add nothing to the world's food supply for many years to come.

The Norfolk Estuary Company did, however make the Marsh Cut and the Vinegar Middle Cut to discipline the meandering Ouse and bring it arrow-straight from the Wash to King's Lynn, and in so doing they added some thousands of valuable, fertile acres to the 75,000 acres which earlier generations had won in the same way by embanking and draining.

Now, a generation later, the problem of building a dam is being considered afresh against a different background. In spite of outcry whenever agricultural land is taken for an airfield, a motorway or housing, there is at present no shortage of agricultural land. The South-east of England is, however, using an ever-increasing amount of water for which new reservoirs will be required.

Recently a firm of consulting engineers put forward a scheme for converting part of the Wash into a vast reservoir. The scheme is simply to build a barrage across the Wash from a point near Skegness to a point near Hunstanton to keep out the sea and contain the waters of the Witham, Nene, Welland and Ouse. The fresh-water lake would be diverted into two reservoirs. To meet the needs of shipping, the barrage would have a lock and embanked channels would lead to the ports of King's Lynn, Wisbech and Boston. It is claimed that the reservoir could supply about 600 million gallons a day, enough for the 10 million people who are expected to live within a ninety-mile radius by the year 2000. The expected cost of £287 million is claimed to be reasonable when set against the £800 million spent on water supplies in the previous twenty years. It is reckoned that water could be supplied at a cost which would compare favourably with the price at present charged from other sources, and would cost much less than desalinated water. Advocates of the scheme claim that, in addition, it will make

50,000—150,000 acres available for reclamation: that a road crossing, following the line of the barrage, would relieve the traffic congestion in King's Lynn, and improve communications between Norfolk and Lincolnshire; and that if it is necessary to provide canals for the ships to reach ports, these might be the start of a suggested Midland Ship Canal.

The barrage, if it is built, will be a tremendous engineering feat. There are some people who even doubt the feasibility of building a barrage twelve miles long in water up to 100 ft. deep, and there have been others who feared the effect on Fenland drainage if the reservoir is maintained at high-water level. These are highly technical matters which will finally be solved only when the preliminary technical studies are undertaken.

In the meantime the situation in the South-east has reached the critical point where the summer flow of the Essex rivers is already inadequate to meet the demand for water and cope with growing sewage effluent. The same thing is beginning to happen to the Great Ouse and the Nene, so that before long these rivers will cease to be pleasant places for fishing and boating unless something is done to prevent flood waters from going to waste.

Economists have often spoken of the area that lies between the English Midlands and the North-east and the German Ruhr as the Golden Triangle. It encloses the greatest concentration of industrial power in Europe, and at its heart lies the North Sea. There is ample evidence of the growing rôle of the ports on both sides of the Sea. If, in due course, Britain becomes a partner in the world's second biggest economic bloc, the prospects for development are immense.

Bibliography

Admiralty, Naval Intelligence Div. *Belgium. Netherlands. Denmark.* (GEOGRAPHICAL HANDBOOK SERIES.) 1944.

Ashton, T. S. *Economic History of England: the Eighteenth Century.* METHUEN. 1955.

Behrens, C. B. A. *Merchant Shipping and the Demands of War.* (History of the Second World War). H.M.S.O. 1955.

Benham, Harvey. *Down Tops'l: the Story of the East Coast Sailing Barges.* HARRAP. 1951.

Benham, Harvey. *Once upon a Tide.* HARRAP. 1951.

Bindoff, S. T. *The Scheldt Question.* GEORGE ALLEN & UNWIN. 1945.

Blair, P. Hunter. *Introduction to Anglo-Saxon England.* C.U.P. 1956.

Cambridge Economic History. Vol. II Trade and Industry in the Middle Ages. C.U.P. 1952.

Churchill, Winston S. *World Crisis, 1911–1918.* THORNTON, BUTTERWORTH. 1923–7.

Cooper, B. & Gaskell, T. F. *North Sea Oil—the Great Gamble.* HEINEMANN [1966].

Cruttwell, C. R. M. F. *History of the Great War, 1914–18.* O.U.P. 1934.

Darby, H. G. ed. *Historical Geography of England before 1800.* C.U.P. 1936.

Defoe, Daniel. *Tour through England and Wales.* [1724–6]

Ellis, E. A. *The Broads.* COLLINS. 1965.

Ellis, K. *The Post Office in the 18th Century.* O.U.P. 1958.

Fiennes, Celia. *Journeys.* Ed. Christopher Morris. CRESSET PRESS. 1947.

Grant, I. F. *Social and Economic Development of Scotland before 1603.* 1930.

Guicciardini, L. *Descrittione di tutti i Paesi Bassi*. 1582.

Hamilton, H. *Economic History of Scotland in the 18th Century*. 1963.

Holmes, A. *Principles of Physical Geology*. NELSON. 1964.

Lambert, J. M. *ed. Making of the Broads*. (ROYAL GEOGRAPHICAL SOCIETY RESEARCH SERIES). 1960.

Lewis, M. *History of British Navy*. GEORGE ALLEN & UNWIN. 1957.

Lipson, E. *Economic History of England*. BLACK. 3 vol.

Marder, A. J. *British Naval Policy, 1880–1905*. PUTNAM [1941].

Marder, A. J. *From the Dreadnought to Scapa Flow*. O.U.P. 3 vol.

Mawer, A. *The Vikings*. C.U.P. 1913.

Mitchell, J. B. *ed. Great Britain: Geographical Essays*. C.U.P. 1962.

Nef, J. U. *Rise of the British Coal Industry*. ROUTLEDGE 1932. 2 vol.

Pimlott, J. A. R. *The Englishman's Holiday: a Social History*. FABER. 1947.

Power, E. *The Wool Trade*. O.U.P. 1941.

Power, E. & Postan, M. M. *Studies in English Trade in the Fifteenth Century*. ROUTLEDGE. 1933.

Robinson, H. *Carrying British Mail Overseas*. GEORGE ALLEN & UNWIN. 1964.

Roskill, S. W. *The War at Sea, 1939–45*. (History of the Second World War). H.M.S.O. 1954-61. 3 vol.

Samuel, A. M. *The Herring*. 1918.

Sawyer, P. H. *Age of the Vikings*. ARNOLD. [1962].

Scoresby, Rev. W. *My Father* [William Scoresby of Whitby]. 1851.

Smailes, A. E. *Northern England*. NELSON. 1960.

Stamp, Dudley "The geological evolution of the North Sea Basin". Conseil Internat. pour l'Exploration de la Mer, *Journal*, xi (1936).

Steers, J. A. *Coastline of England and Wales*. C.U.P. 1936.

Steers, J. A. *The Sea Coast*. COLLINS. 1953.

Taylor, E. G. R. *The Haven-Finding Art: a History of Navigation from Odysseus to Captain Cook*. 1956.

Unwin, G. *Studies in Economic History*. MACMILLAN. 1927.

Victoria County History of England. *Durham. Lincoln. Norfolk. Suffolk. Essex.*

Wilkes, L. & Dodds, G. *Tyneside Classical: the Newcastle of Grainger, Dobson and Clayton*. MURRAY. 1964.

Willan, T. S. *British Coasting Trade, 1600–1750*. 1938.

Willan, T. S. Studies in Elizabethan Foreign Trade. 1959.

Wilson, C. H. "The Economic Decline of the Netherlands". *Econ. Hist Review*, ix, 111–27.

Zimmern, H. *Hansa Towns*, T. FISHER, UNWIN. 1891.

Index

Index